Education and the Youth Labour Market

Education Policy Perspectives

General Editor: Professor Ivor Goodson, Faculty of Education, University of Western Ontario, London, Canada N6G 1G7

Education policy analysis has long been a neglected area in the United Kingdom and, to an extent, in the USA and Australia. The result has been a profound gap between the study of education and the formulation of education policy. For practitioners such a lack of analysis of the new policy initiatives has worrying implications particularly at such a time of policy flux and change. Education policy has, in recent years, been a matter for intense political debate — the political and public interest in the working of the system has come at the same time as the consensus on education policy has been broken by the advent of the 'New Right'. As never before the political parties and pressure groups differ in their articulated policies and prescriptions for the education sector. Critical thinking about these developments is clearly necessary.

All those working within the system also need information on policy making, policy implementation and effective day-to-day operation. Pressure on schools from government, education authorities and parents has generated an enormous need for knowledge amongst those on the receiving end of educational policies.

This series aims to fill the academic gap, to reflect the politicalization of education, and to provide the practitioners with the analysis for informed implementation of policies that they will need. It will offer studies in broad areas of policy studies. Beside the general section it will offer a particular focus in the following areas: School organization and improvement (David Reynolds, University College, Cardiff, UK); Critical social analysis (Professor Philip Wexler, University of Rochester, USA); Policy studies and evaluation (Professor Ernest House, University of Colorado-Boulder, USA).

Education and the Youth Labour Market:

Schooling and Scheming

Edited by

David Raffe

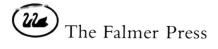 The Falmer Press

(A Member of the Taylor & Francis Group)

London • New York • Philadelphia

UK   The Falmer Press, Falmer House, Barcombe, Lewes,
            East Sussex. BN8 5DL

USA   The Falmer Press, Taylor & Francis Inc., 242 Cherry Street,
            Philadelphia, PA 19106–1906

First published 1988

British Library Cataloguing in Publication Data

Education and the youth labour market:
   schooling and scheming.
   1. Scotland. Adolescents. Education
   2. Scotland. Young persons. Unemployment
   I. Raffe, David
   370

   ISBN 1–85000–420–X
   ISBN 1–85000–421–8 Pbk

Jacket design by Caroline Archer

Typeset in Bembo by
David John Services Limited, Slough, Berks.
Printed and Bound in Great Britain by
Redwood Burn Limited, Wiltshire

Contents

Contents

To my parents

List of Tables and Figures

TABLES   **Page**

FIGURES

Acknowledgements

Work on this book has been supported by the UK Economic and Social Research Council (ESRC), through its funding of the Centre for Educational Sociology (CES) as a Designated Research Centre (ESRC grant no. C00280004).

The book draws on data collected in the Scottish Young Peoples Surveys, which now incorporate the Scottish School Leavers Surveys, from 1977 to 1987. Over this period the surveys have been supported by the Scottish Education Department (SED), the ESRC (formerly the Social Science Research Council), the Manpower Services Commission (MSC), the Industry Department for Scotland and the Department of Employment. Additional support has been received from Fife, Grampian and Tayside Regional Councils, and Western Isles Islands Council. The surveys are now conducted jointly by the CES and the SED; the CES is grateful to the SED officials and the staff members from all secondary schools in Scotland who have helped to construct the samples, and to careers officers across the country who have helped us to trace sample members whose addresses were out of date. And we thank the 100,000 or so young people who have filled in questionnaires, and hope that this book partly fulfils our promise to use their answers to help 'change things for the better'.

Large-scale survey research is a team effort. The authors of this book owe much to all past and present members of the CES who have helped to design, manage and administer the surveys, to code the responses, and to process and manage the data. Their work comprises the base of the iceberg, of which published products such as this are only the tip. The CES also acknowledges with gratitude the considerable support over the years of the University of Edinburgh Computing Services, and the more general support of the University.

I am grateful to Caroline Clark for the skill, patience and industry with which she has coordinated the production of the manuscript, seeing it through numerous drafts, preparing the tables and enforcing consistency across the chapters. In these tasks she has been ably assisted by Moira Burke and Margaret MacDougall. Joan Hughes proofed the final manuscript.

Other more specific contributions are acknowledged in respect of particular chapters. The authors are responsible for the opinions and judgments expressed in this book, which are not necessarily shared by the bodies or individuals named above.

Introduction: Surveying Education and the Youth Labour Market

INTRODUCTION

The Centre for Educational Sociology (CES) is about a year older than the Manpower Services Commission (MSC). Which of the two lasts longer remains to be seen. The coincidence is symbolic: the MSC (now renamed the Training Commission) has presided over, and in part been responsible for, some of the most radical changes in the youth labour market, in youth training and in the link between education and employment that Great Britain has ever seen. (Within Scotland, change has been further promoted by several policy initiatives of the Scottish Education Department (SED), but the SED has been around for rather longer than the CES.) Through the Scottish School Leavers Surveys, subsequently the Scottish Young Peoples Surveys, the CES has designed, conducted and helped to analyze a unique source of data that covers these changes from the mid-1970s through to the late 1980s and beyond. No other source for this period provides trend data with the national coverage and substantive range of the Scottish surveys. Although national surveys of young people have now been established in England and Wales (see chapter 1), the Scottish surveys remain unique by virtue of their design, of the amount and range of data they collect, and of their model of the organization and control of research. This model aims to integrate the functions of data-collection and data-analysis, and to give academic research the benefits of cooperation with government without compromising the legitimate interests of either.

This book is a product of this style of research. It summarizes the main findings from recent research based on the Scottish surveys. Each chapter uses survey data to address a topic of current importance concerning the education, training and labour-market experiences of 14–19-year-olds. The authors are all members or associates of the CES, although they come from a range of disciplines and backgrounds including education, sociology, economics, geography and psychology. Their perspectives and their approaches to the data are similarly varied. The CES has no party line, beyond a shared commitment to an open and public style of research. This embraces the pure and the applied, covers several social-science disciplines, often seeks to be policy-relevant but always tries to be independent, sometimes to the point of stubbornness.

There are now two main components of the Scottish Young Peoples Surveys: a series of school-leaver surveys extending back to 1977 (or 1971, for qualified leavers), and a newer series of longitudinal surveys of school year groups followed through to 19 years or beyond. The next two sections respectively describe the history and nature of the surveys and the model and philosophy of research based on them. The final section of this introduction reviews the chapters of the book and the themes that they raise.

THE SURVEYS

The CES was formally recognized by the University of Edinburgh in November 1972, but it had been in embryonic existence for a few years before this. In 1971 and 1973 it carried out postal sample surveys of the previous sessions' qualified school leavers. The surveys were funded by the SED which wanted an independent body to collect attitudinal data that it felt it could not legitimately collect in its own qualified leavers' survey. Those CES surveys covered only qualified leavers, then a minority of school leavers. In the spring of 1977 the CES conducted a further survey of the previous session's school leavers, funded by the SED and by the Social Science Research Council (SSRC) as part of a programme of collaborative research, described below. The 1977 survey covered a very large sample, of around 40 per cent. Initially planned for qualified leavers, it was extended to include the unqualified when pilot surveys showed that a high response could be secured. However in 1977 the unqualified leavers' survey remained geographically incomplete, and only loosely integrated with the qualified leavers' survey. In 1979 the SED funded a 10 per cent survey of qualified leavers, and the MSC, anxious for data on its new Youth Opportunities Programme (YOP), funded a 20 per cent survey of 'less qualified' leavers.

In 1981 the CES, this time with SSRC funding, conducted another large-scale leavers' survey with a sampling fraction of 37 per cent. The 1981 survey was distinctive for two further reasons. It was the first to integrate the unqualified leavers fully within the survey, on the basis of interlocking questionnaire types for different categories of school leaver and with randomized versions of each type; and from this date the survey formally became a joint exercise between the CES and the SED, with the latter responsible for the construction of each sample.

By 1981 a biennial sequence of school leavers' surveys had been established, and this has been maintained since. In the spring of every odd-numbered year a sample of the previous year's school leavers is surveyed. Since 1983 the sampling fraction has been stable at 10 per cent; in the mid 1980s about 85,000 young people left school in Scotland each year, so each target sample contained about 8500 leavers. However in 1985 the sample coverage was extended: in addition to the previous year's leavers, the sample also included all those who had been in the fourth year of secondary school in the previous year. (The fourth year is the last compulsory year for a majority of Scottish school students.) Since many of the leavers had left from fourth year the leaver and year-group samples overlapped, to become known within the CES as the 'L'-shaped sample. The change was made primarily to accommodate the MSC's Youth Training Scheme and the SED's 16-plus Action Plan (see chapters 7, 8 and 9). Both made it desirable to follow samples of whole year groups through the different post-16 options. The year-group sample first contacted in spring 1985 was therefore followed up in further surveys in spring 1986 and autumn 1987. A new biennial sequence has now been established: in the spring of every odd-numbered year an 'L'-shaped sample of the previous year's fourth year and leavers is contacted, and the year-group arm of the sample is followed up longitudinally in subsequent years. Nils Tomes provides further details of the design and conduct of the survey in appendix 1. Appendix 2 identifies the main survey data-sets used in each chapter of this book. Burnhill *et al.* (1987) provide a more analytical account of the development of the surveys, focusing on their methodological and political aspects.

THE RESEARCH PROCESS

The surveys provide the foundation on which the CES has built up a distinctive style of research, characterized at least in aspiration by diversity, openness and independence.

From 1975 the CES attempted, through a programme of 'collaborative research', to involve non-professional researchers in the survey process, especially 'practitioners' such as teachers, lecturers, administrators, advisers and careers officers (Gray *et al.*, 1983). This included giving them an opportunity to influence the survey design and questionnaire content, making data available and helping people with their analyses. Funding for collaborative research ceased after 1982. The data remain publicly available, subject to confidentiality restrictions, although resource constraints inevitably limit the practical effect of this. Collaborative research attempted to maintain and enhance a liberal model of research in the light of a recognition that governmental authority and resources were needed for the effective conduct of research. The rationale for this view and for the strategy of collaborative research was elaborated by McPherson *et al.* (1978) and by Gray *et al.* (1983, chapter 17). Even if the wider aims of collaborative research were not fully achieved, they have left their mark on the practice of CES research (McPherson, 1984; Burnhill *et al.*, 1987). Although the surveys are funded by a consortium of government departments, the CES has the final decision on matters of design and content, and the right to publish freely from the data. It has undoubtedly been helped by UGC funding (through the University of Edinburgh) and by recognition from the academic community, reflected in the decision of the UK Economic and Social Research Council (ESRC) to make it a Designated Research Centre in 1987.

It is for others to judge how far these principles reflect the practice, as opposed to the ideology, of CES research. Another, and more straight-forward, aspect of the research is that it mainly relates to Scotland. This, of course, can affect its reception by English-based audiences. Scotland is a long way north of Watford, and easily dismissed as 'different'. But the relative neglect of Scotland is due not only to English parochialism. Scotland's institutional differences can make it seem complex and difficult to understand, especially perhaps to overseas observers already baffled by the English system.

Yet in many ways Scotland offers valuable opportunities for research. It has a strong tradition of empirical social research, especially in education. Perhaps reflecting this, surveys have consistently achieved higher response rates in Scotland than south of the border. Its wide range of social, economic and geographical conditions provides enormous scope for internal comparisons, yet it is small enough for researchers to be familiar with the local settings that comprise this diversity (see chapter 10), and small enough for national studies to allow for reasonably detailed analysis of local conditions (see chapter 6). Policy changes are often swifter and more uniform than elsewhere in Britain; their evaluation can be more timely and often less equivocal (see chapters 8 and 9; and McPherson and Willms, 1987). Finally, the need for policy-related research in Scotland is stronger, and perhaps more keenly felt, than south of the border. Because Scotland is small, and media and political debates tend to be 'British' (English) in focus, it is even more important to maintain a climate for social research that sustains diversity of perspective and independent scrutiny of policy issues, and at least some sections of central government are mindful of this.

Some differences and similarities between Scotland and the rest of Britain are discussed in chapter 1. In many respects Scotland represents a passable 'microcosm' of Britain (see, for example, chapters 3 and 7); in other areas the experience of its distinctive institutions may provide both practical and theoretical lessons from which others can learn. This is true not only of pioneering policy initiatives such as the Action Plan, but also of more long-standing features of the Scottish system, such as its distinctive structure of post-compulsory schooling.

THE CHAPTERS

Some of these aspects of research in Scotland may be apparent in the chapters that follow. Yet these chapters are also notable for thei. diversity. They all use data from the same survey series to discuss a set of closely-related topics, but they approach the data in different ways, from different theoretical and practical perspectives, using different techniques of analysis. This makes it the more striking that the same themes recur in most of the chapters of the book. One of these themes is change: not only the longitudinal change involved in young people's transitions, but also the historical changes which have occurred in society, education and the labour market since the early 1970s. Another theme is policy: all chapters recognize the important role played by current policy initiatives in shaping and re-shaping education and the youth labour market. Perhaps most importantly, all chapters are concerned with the causes, the consequences or the processes of differen-tiation and inequality among young people, both in education and in the labour market.

In chapter 1 David Raffe and Gill Courtenay use data on the education and labour-market experiences of 16–18-year-olds to outline some key features of post-compulsory education and the youth labour market in Scotland. (Readers requiring further help with Scottish – and English – arrangements are referred to appendix 3, which contains a glossary of acronyms and brief descriptions of some of the main institutional terms used in the book.) Many readers may be more familiar with the system south of the border. Chapter 1 therefore describes the Scottish scene by comparing it with that of England and Wales, using data on comparable cohorts from the Scottish Young Peoples Survey and from the England and Wales Youth Cohort Study. In doing so, the chapter also serves a second purpose. Noting the current interest in comparisons with overseas countries, Raffe and Courtenay ask whether more might be learnt from comparisons within the UK, where 'confounding differences in each country's history, economy, culture and politics' are much smaller. They identify institutional differences between the education systems of Scotland and of England and Wales which, although small in international context, may have significant theoretical and practical implications. However these differences occur within similar social and especially labour-market contexts. Once the effects of educational differences and of a somewhat weaker labour market in Scotland are allowed for, the similarities between the two countries' youth labour markets are far more striking than their differences.

Chapter 2 provides an overview of earlier work based on the Scottish surveys on the youth labour market and its relation to education and training. While much of the chapter is given over to a summary of the main findings in each area, it concludes with a discussion of two themes that have recurred in much CES work. The first concerns the nature of recent changes in education and the labour market. Many of these, it argues, were 'shaped, mediated or accelerated' by the rise in unemployment, especially in the early 1980s. The second theme is the relation between differentiation in education and in the labour market. Education performs an important 'selective function' which in turn restricts the scope for educational change. Many analyses of the survey have reflected a 'dual perspective, with education influencing labour-market outcomes at the micro level, but constrained or shaped by the labour market at the macro level'.

The theme of social and educational change is continued in chapter 3. The role of higher education is often neglected in discussions of education and the youth labour market, but it is crucial. It affects the numbers of young people entering the labour market, and their composition; and it exerts a powerful downward influence on the school curriculum, often in conflict with attempts to increase its vocational relevance (see chapters 9 and 10). In chapter 3 Peter Burnhill, Catherine Garner and Andrew McPherson consider both of these influences. They show how changes in the family circumstances of pupils, and especially the rising educational levels of parents, have contributed to an increasing flow of school leavers qualified to enter higher education. But this increased flow has not been matched by an increased supply of higher education places, especially in universities. The authors suggest that despite the demographic decline up to the mid-1990s, rising levels of attainment mean that the flow of qualified school leavers will fall less than the current policies assume; moreover, governments can do more than is often admitted to increase this flow, notably by improving the articulation between arrangements for certification and the markets for certificates. In practice, however, 'the maximization of the rate of qualification for higher education has a lower priority for government...than its wish to restructure the type of higher education currently on offer. Perhaps, too, the government fears that its policies would be seriously compromised if the universities in their present form remained too full of students, and therefore too full of themselves'.

School leavers entering the labour market have also been better qualified in the 1980s than in earlier years, partly because some of the better qualified have been unable to enter higher education instead. But they have had to compete for a diminishing number of jobs. Not only did the total level of school-leaver employment fall by nearly a half between 1977 and 1983, but a larger share of what remained went to the better qualified. Consequently less qualified school leavers, despite becoming scarcer, experienced the greatest percentage-point rise in unemployment. In chapter 4 Michael Shelly outlines these changes and tests two rival explanations on the survey data. The 'structural' hypothesis attributes employers' increased demand for qualifications to occupational changes which have reduced the proportion of employment in occupations that recruit the less qualified. The 'labour-queue' hypothesis, by contrast, blames the declining level of employment rather than its changing composition. It argues that employers have 'traded up' in a slack market, recruiting better qualified school leavers to given jobs than they did when unemployment was lower. Shelly's shift-share analysis is complex but its results are relatively clear. With respect to females, both processes have been at work: there was a relative decline in jobs requiring less qualified labour, with a somewhat stronger tendency for employers to 'trade up' within occupations. With respect to males, 'trading up' accounts for nearly all the changes.

Shelly's analysis assumes that school-leaver unemployment was involuntary — that the unemployed wanted to work at current wage rates. In chapter 5 Andy Furlong explores this assumption on the basis of data on unemployed young people in 1986. He finds that young people were strongly committed to the employment ethic, with only small differences between the employed and the unemployed. There was a larger difference between those who had ever had a full-time job and those who had never had one, with the latter having lower employment commitment. Furlong suggests that it may be more plausible to view the employment ethic as something that is gained through employment, rather than lost through unemployment. However, young people's commitment to employment is not always reflected in a vigorous search for work. Those who had been continuously unemployed tended to have the most negative attitudes to looking for work, and to have made fewest job applications in recent months; they appeared to be discouraged by their prolonged unemployment and reluctant to invite further refusals. 'To suggest that high levels of youth unemployment are partly a consequence of the poor work attitudes of young people', Furlong argues, 'is to turn the problem on its head. For some young people it is the disillusionment which unemployment breeds which eventually leads to despondency and may result in reduced efforts in the search for work'.

Unemployment and its unequal distribution form the main theme of chapter 6. Inequalities in modern Britain are often described in spatial terms, such as the 'inner city' and the 'north/south divide'. But does this terminology merely obscure other more direct axes of inequality, which may be patterned spatially but which cannot be reduced to spatial differences? Catherine Garner, Brian Main and David Raffe compare the post-school destinations of school leavers in Aberdeen, Dundee, Edinburgh and Glasgow, cities with very different local labour markets. The employment prospects of young people with comparable levels of social and educational advantage varied widely across the four cities. Yet within each city there was little difference between the prospects of comparable young people from different parts of the city. Each city tended to function, in this respect, as a single labour market. The authors discuss the policy implications of their findings and warn against policies which 'merely hide the problem by gentrifying the inner city and decanting the disadvantaged to remote and less visible housing estates. Spatial terminology may provide a convenient label for the problems of inequality within cities, but it provides no guide to their solution'.

In discussing social change, labour-market change, unemployment and inequality the earlier chapters of the book draw attention to some of the problems to which policy-makers have felt obliged to respond. The following chapters focus more directly on three recent policy initiatives, all introduced in 1983 or 1984.

Brian Main and Michael Shelly note that the introduction of YTS in 1983 'marked an attempt to move away from the temporary counter-cyclical job-creation activities that had characterized YOP to a more constructive long-run manpower policy that would enhance the productivity of participants through the provision of both on-the-job and off-the-job training'. In chapter 7 they evaluate YTS as a manpower policy, on the criteria of the probability of participants finding a job and of the probability of their finding a good job, as measured either by pay or by occupation. Using longitudinal data on the second year group to pass through the scheme, they estimate that YTS increased young people's chances of employment, often lowered their wages in employment (although this could be attributed to higher average levels of training received by former YTS trainees), and gave access to a wide range of occupations. The authors conclude that, although the change to a two-year YTS may produce further benefits to trainees, for these benefits to be realized it will be necessary 'to maintain or improve the quantity, quality and marketability of the training received by participants'.

The MSC hopes to improve the quality and marketability of YTS training by giving all trainees the opportunity to obtain or work towards recognized qualifications. The reform of vocational qualifications has been proceeding in all parts of Britain, but has been swiftest and most radical in Scotland. The 16-plus Action Plan, published in 1983 and implemented from 1984, has replaced all non-advanced vocational courses by a system of modules, each of notional forty hours' duration, assessed by a single National

Certificate. The Action Plan has attracted considerable attention from the rest of Britain and (perhaps more so) from overseas, and chapters 8 and 9 present some of the first systematic research evidence of its impact.

In chapter 8 David Raffe analyzes the background and rationale of the Action Plan and argues that the key to its strategy is the concept of 'institutional versatility'. The Plan uses a single national modular framework to provide integration, coordination and established lines of progression across a wide range of types of education and training provided in a wide range of institutional contexts. Raffe analyzes data on the first year group to pass through the new modular system, and suggests that the strategy of institutional versatility may be particularly suited to the structure of Scottish education, and that it provides a key to understanding many of the Action Plan's successes and failures. The Plan has widened opportunities, it may have increased participation, and it has been successful in respect of the internal labour market – of employers' use of modules to train their own employees and trainees. The evidence is less encouraging with respect to the external labour market. The new modules appear to have had a limited impact on young people's chances of a job with employers other than those who have provided their training. But these are early data, and employers' awareness and recognition of the new modular certificate may increase with time.

The new modules have been used widely within schools, as well as in further education colleges and training centres. In chapter 9 Nils Tomes examines their use in the fifth year of secondary school, notionally the first post-compulsory year. (Scottish pupils start secondary school at 12, so fifth year is typically entered at 16.) Traditionally the preserve of high-attainers who study Higher courses to qualify for higher education, the Scottish fifth year now attracts a growing number of lower attainers who stay on at school because jobs are scarce. It also caters for a substantial (and growing) number of compulsory-age pupils, the 'conscripts' who are too young to leave after fourth year and must stay on for the first and longest term of fifth year. Tomes describes the varied uses of National Certificate modules among these different client groups, and discusses the impact of the new modules on the curriculum, certification opportunities, articulation with other courses and progression after school. She argues that traditional academic certification is likely to remain dominant for as long as the modules can offer only restricted or uncertain opportunities for progression to higher education or elsewhere.

Colin Bell and Cathy Howieson report students' reactions to another educational innovation, the Technical and Vocational Education Initiative (TVEI). They too raise questions concerning the status and marketability of vocational education. For while students mainly appreciate the newer approaches to teaching and learning and the relevance to work and adult life of TVEI courses, overall these courses 'are still less valued than traditional education because of problems about the status of vocational education, its perceived client group and its value in the market places of further and higher education'. However, Bell and Howieson point out that the 'association of new technology, a desirable and high-status area, with TVEI seems to temper the traditional attitudes to vocational courses as low ranking. Perhaps new technology will be the critical factor in changing attitudes to vocational education. At the same time the stranglehold of traditional certification is crucial. Until employers and further and higher education change their attitudes to and use of certification then the value of alternative courses and alternative certification will be questioned by pupils whatever their merits'. The authors also discuss the model of innovation pursued by TVEI, and suggest that it may have been responsible for some of the problems faced by the initiative.

For the most part this chapter draws, not on the quantitative data collected in the surveys, but on open-ended comments written by young people on the back pages of their questionnaires. As such it presents a less conventional form of survey analysis. In the final chapter Geoffrey Walford discusses this source of data and its potential uses in social research. He argues that despite their limitations the back-page comments are a particularly useful resource for the generation of grounded theory, similar to historical data or documents obtained from searching a library. He describes how they can be used to challenge assumptions, investigate key words and cliches and discover links with macro-sociological variables. In a book whose chapters all draw on the same survey series, it is fitting to conclude with a discussion of the potential if less conventional uses of the data. Walford stands back from the main substantive concerns of other chapters to discuss aspects of the methodology of survey research. Yet his chapter remains particularly close to the subject matter of this book. For in illustrating how 'the important thing is to consider the data in the context in which they were collected' he powerfully conveys the flavour and quality of young people's lives, expressed in their own 'shouts of joy' and 'cries of pain'.

REFERENCES

BURNHILL, P., McPHERSON, A.F., RAFFE, D. and TOMES, N. (1987) 'Constructing a public account of an education system' in WALFORD, G. (Ed.) *Doing Sociology of Education*, Lewes, Falmer Press.

GRAY, J., McPHERSON, A.F. and RAFFE, D. (1983) *Reconstructions of Secondary Education: Theory, Myth and Practice since the War*, Henley, Routledge and Kegan Paul.

MCPHERSON, A. (1984) 'An episode in the control of research' in DOCKRELL, W.B. (Ed.) *An Attitude of Mind: Twenty-five Years of Educational Research in Scotland*, Edinburgh, Scottish Council for Research in Education.

MCPHERSON, A.F., RAAB, C.D. and RAFFE, D. (1978) 'Social explanation and political accountability: Two related problems with a single solution', paper given at the Annual Conference of the British Educational Research Association, Leeds, September.

MCPHERSON, A.F. and WILLMS, J.D. (1987) 'Equalisation and improvement: Some effects of comprehensive reorganisation in Scotland', *Sociology*, 21, 4, pp. 509–39.

Chapter 1

16–18 on Both Sides of the Border
David Raffe and Gill Courtenay

INTRODUCTION

The following chapters examine aspects of education, training and the labour market, using data from surveys of young people in Scotland. They address themes and problems common to a large number of countries, but use data specific to one system, Scotland. One aim of this chapter is to provide a context for these studies by outlining some of the main features of post-compulsory education and the youth labour market in Scotland. Since many readers of this book may be more familiar with arrangements south of the border, we seek to explain the Scottish system by comparing it with that of England and Wales.

People in the rest of Britain, even educationists, tend to be poorly informed about the Scottish education system. Their ignorance is understandable given the centralized politics and media of Britain. Debates about 'British' education tend to be internal to, and specific to, the English system; when Scottish developements are noted they tend to be appraised for their relevance to England.[1] Not that devolved media coverage necessarily provides the answer. The *Times Educational Supplement* publishes a separate Scottish edition, in which several pages carry Scottish news not published south of the border. While it improves coverage of Scottish affairs within Scotland, this arrangement has the unfortunate side-effect that English readers 'learn a great deal more about education in China and the Republic of Ireland than they do about (the) Scottish system' (Roberts, 1984). Scotland is not a nation-state, and is often left out of comparative studies by representative international organizations as well as by independent academics. Writers comparing the British and other systems often treat England as representative of Britain or use the terms interchangeably.

Many of these studies seek to learn from foreign experience and draw conclusions that can be applied in Britain. Yet they often find that the lessons of other countries can only be applied very indirectly, because of confounding differences in each country's history, economy, culture and politics. Yet the irony is that fewer studies have sought to learn from comparisons *within* the UK, where these confounding differences may be much smaller. A second aim of this chapter, therefore, is to offer an assessment of the extent of the differences between Scotland and England and Wales, and to see if we can identify a point where, institutional differences having been discounted, the essential similarities prevail.

We use data from the Scottish Young Peoples Surveys of 1985 and 1986 and from the 1985 and 1986 surveys of the first cohort of the England and Wales Youth Cohort Study. The design of the England and Wales study was influenced by the Scottish experience (Clough and Gray, 1986) and there are several similarities between them. Both surveys were conducted by post, collected data on a wide range of educational, training and labour-market topics from a cross section of young people and have followed up their samples longitudinally over (at least) three data-sweeps. This chapter is based on the first two sweeps. The Scottish sample covered the year group who entered fourth year of secondary school in 1983, nearly all of whom were eligible to leave school by the end of 1984. Pupils normally transfer to secondary school at 12 in Scotland and at 11 in England and Wales; the Scottish fourth year is roughly equivalent to the English/Welsh fifth year, in that both mark the 'normal' end of compulsory schooling. The English and Welsh sample covered young people aged 16 on 31 August 1984, who were all eligible to leave school either at Easter or summer 1984.

Before we present data on the two samples, we note three differences between the studies that may affect the comparison.

First, there are differences in method. The conduct of the Scottish surveys is described in appendix 1; that of the English/Welsh surveys by Courtenay (1987 and 1988). Perhaps the most important difference is that the first-sweep survey in England and Wales was required to distribute many of its first-sweep questionnaires, together with reminders for non-respondents, through the schools. This produced a relatively low response rate, 69 per cent compared with 84 per cent for the Scottish first-sweep survey when the figures are calculated on the most nearly comparable basis. There were knock-on effects on response to the second sweep, since the survey team in England and Wales lacked addresses for some of their first-sweep respondents. As a result the proportion of first-sweep respondents who returned usable questionnaires at the second sweep was again somewhat lower in England and Wales (75 per cent) than in Scotland (82 per cent). The data in this chapter are based on young people who responded to both sweeps.[2] They

13

are weighted to compensate for differential non-response, using population figures for qualifications at 16, gender, staying-on at school, and (for English and Welsh leavers only) region and school type. Early data from the second cohort of the English and Welsh study, from which the response was much higher, suggest that the weighted estimates from the first cohort are not seriously affected by non-response.

Different questionnaires were used in the two studies - necessarily, since institutional differences made many of the questions asked in one study inappropriate to the other. In addition the Scottish questionnaire was differentiated into types, with randomized versions within each type, whereas the English and Welsh study used a single questionnaire. We have restricted our comparisons to items included in all Scottish questionnaire versions and to data which are, we believe, comparable between the studies.

The second difference between the surveys is that the Scottish sample includes young people from independent schools and the English and Welsh sample does not. Since one purpose of this chapter is to describe the Scottish system we have not excluded independent schools from the figures presented below. Excluding them from the Scottish figures would reduce the percentage staying on at school by about one percentage point for girls and two percentage points for boys. It would make no discernible difference to any estimates based on labour-market entrants. However the independent sector is smaller in Scotland where it accounts for less than 4 per cent of the age group, compared to England and Wales where it accounts for 7 per cent. Adding independent schools to the English and Welsh data might make much more difference than subtracting them from the Scottish data.

Third, the Scottish survey describes a school year group, all of whom were in the fourth year of secondary school in 1983/84, whereas the English and Welsh survey describes a birth cohort, all of whom were aged 16 on 31 August 1984 and became old enough to leave school either at Easter or in the summer of that year. In practice the English and Welsh sample roughly coincided with a school year group — most were in fifth year in 1983/84 — and most members of the Scottish year group were eligible to leave school by the end of 1984. However arrangements both for entry to primary school and for the end of compulsory schooling differ between the two countries. The Scottish year group was some four months younger, on average, than the English and Welsh birth cohort. One in seven were 16 years old by the end of February 1984 and had therefore been eligible to leave the previous Christmas (or in a few cases at the end of third year) although most in fact stayed on to complete the fourth year. (The two statutory leaving dates in Scotland are 31 May and at Christmas.) A majority of the Scottish year group became 16 between 1 March and 30 September 1984, and was eligible to leave school on 31 May. However nearly three in ten of the Scots were still only 15 at the end of September and had to remain at school until Christmas 1984 (or, in a very few cases, summer 1985). The proportion of these 'conscripts' in each year group has grown in recent years, a consequence of changes in primary entry arrangements a decade or so earlier (Burnhill, 1984). The autumn term in Scotland is by far the longest, starting in August, and most schools start the new session at the beginning of June, during the summer term. This means that a substantial minority of each age group must stay on at school for about half of what is notionally the first 'post-compulsory' school session. The curriculum and certification of the conscripts (or school-leaving age group 3 as they are more formally known) are discussed in chapter 9.

Table 1.1 shows the statuses of the two samples at four time points from October 1984 to April 1986. These time points cover the fifth and sixth years of Scottish secondary schooling and (for most sample members) the two years of the English Sixth form, together with their non-school alternatives. The Scottish data are based on questions asked in the 1985 and 1986 questionnaires, in each case asking respondents what they had been doing 'at the beginning of last October' and what they were doing 'now'. Since both Scottish surveys were despatched in the middle of March we shall interpret the 'now' figures as referring to the beginning of April (in fact they describe a spread of dates as some respondents replied earlier than others). The data for the first three time points for England and Wales are obtained from 'diary' items that asked what respondents were doing for all or most of each month from September 1984 to February 1986. The 'April 1986' figures refer to respondents' current status at the time of the England and Wales survey. Since the questionnaires were despatched at the end of February the median response referred to a date some two or three weeks earlier than the beginning of April; but for simplicity we shall refer to the current data from both 1986 surveys as describing April.

Our discussion focuses in turn on two main institutional locations of young people in each country: full-time education and the labour market.

FULL-TIME EDUCATION

Institutional Framework

At the first time point, in October 1984, twice as many of the Scottish sample as of the English and Welsh sample were still at school: 57 per cent compared with 28 per cent. However, half of these Scots were 'conscripts', still too young to leave. By April 1985, the second time point, virtually all members of both samples were eligible to have left school. There were still more Scots at school, but the differential had narrowed: 42 per cent

Table 1.1 Status at six-monthly intervals (percentages)

Date:	October 1984		April 1985		October 1985		April 1986	
Country:	Sc	E&W	Sc	E&W	Sc	E&W	Sc	E&W
Median age (approx):	16yr, 3m	16yr, 7m	16yr, 9m	17yr, 1m	17yr, 3m	17yr, 7m	17yr, 9m	18yr, 1m
School stage:	5th yr	Lower 6th	6th yr	Lower 6th	6th yr	Upper 6th	6th yr	Upper 6th
Full-time FE/HE	5	15	4	14	12	13	8	13
School	57	28	42	28	20	21	20	19
Full-time job	11	17	17	22	33	43	40	45
YTS	18	28	23	24	16	6	7	3
Unemployed	7	8	11	9	15	13	19	15
Others	2	1	2	1	4	3	5	4
NK	1	2	1	2	1	2	*	0
Total	101	99	100	100	101	101	99	99
n	(5292)	(6075)	(5292)	(6075)	(5292)	(6075)	(5292)	(6075)
Males								
Full-time FE/HE	3	10	2	9	9	9	6	29
School	54	27	38	26	19	20	19	50
Full-time job	12	21	19	26	35	47	43	3
YTS	21	30	26	27	17	5	8	15
Unemployed	7	8	12	9	17	14	21	3
Others	2	1	1	1		2	3	0
NK	1	2	2	2	3	2	*	
Total	100	98	100	100	101	99	100	100
n	(2598)	(2825)	(2598)	(2825)	(2598)	(2825)	(2598)	(2825)
Females								
Full-time FE/HE	7	20	6	18	14	16	11	36
School	59	30	46	29	22	21	22	41
Full-time job	11	13	16	19	30	39	38	4
YTS	15	26	20	21	14	6	7	14
Unemployed	6	8	9	8	13	12	16	6
Others	2	1	2	1	6	4	7	0
NK	1	2	1	2	1	2	*	
Total	101	100	100	98	100	100	101	101
n	(2694)	(3250)	(2694)	(3250)	(2694)	(3250)	(2694)	(3250)

Note. The England and Wales sample covered a birth cohort, not a school-year group, so the sample members may have been at different school stages.

* = <0.5

compared with 28 per cent. However, apart from the younger average age of the Scottish sample and the exclusion of the independent sector from the English and Welsh sample, this comparison must be further qualified by reference to institutional differences between the systems.

First, the institutional structure and balance of full-time post-compulsory education differs between the two countries. In Scotland most young people continuing in full-time education beyond 16 do so at school; except in some sparsely populated areas nearly all of these continue in the same school where they have spent their previous four years. The only other full-time education option is to study a vocational course in a college of further education. In England and Wales the range of options at 16 is wider, and is more likely to involve a move to a different institution. In addition to schools and colleges there are sixth form colleges (included with schools in our data) and tertiary colleges (included with colleges); the range of courses offered in college is considerably wider, and includes General Certificate of Education (GCE) courses, overlapping (and sometimes competing) with the options available at school. In some respects the transition beyond compulsory education is more clearly defined in England and Wales, whereas in Scotland it is more simply a matter of continuing or not continuing at school. This difference is reinforced by the statutory leaving regulations discussed above: for nearly half of Scots the end of compulsory education comes mid way through a school session.

So although in April 1985 more of the Scottish than of the English and Welsh sample were still at school, this was partly balanced by the smaller proportion entering full-time further education: 4 per cent in Scotland compared with 14 per cent in England and Wales. By October 1985 participation in further education appears to have evened out between the two systems: 12 per cent in Scotland compared with 13 per cent in England and Wales. However the 12 per cent in Scotland included 4 per cent, mostly on short courses, who had left by April 1986, and a further 2.5 per cent who were in full-time *higher* education. The opportunity to enter higher education at 17 years is a traditional feature of Scottish education, associated both with the 'myth' of wider educational opportunity and access and with the four-year structure of honours degree courses (Gray *et al.*, 1983). In practice, only a minority of higher-education students enter at 17. Despite the greater average age of English and Welsh sample members only a negligible proportion had entered higher education by spring 1986.

Transition patterns

This leads us to a further institutional difference between the two systems: their different transition patterns. In England and Wales there is a clearly defined transition point at 16 (summer 1984 for our sample members). Another will follow at 18, in summer 1986, although our present data do not extend this far. Some young people leave at 17 but for the majority post-compulsory education (below higher education) can be represented as a two-year stage with clearly defined start and end points, at 16 and 18 years respectively.

Scotland has the same two transition points, although we have suggested that the first of these is less clearly defined. However there are two additional transition points. The first occurs half way through the fifth year when the 'conscripts', who were too young to leave from fourth year, become eligible to leave school. The second occurs at the end of the fifth year, when half the voluntary school stayers leave school. This is not the result of dropping-out: most fifth-year students take one-year courses, and the sixth year usually comprises a discrete stage.

Not all fifth-year leavers end compulsory education at this point; about three in ten of those who left school at the end of fifth year in summer 1985 were in full-time further education in the following October, and a further one in ten were in higher education. More Scots entered full-time further education at 17 (from fifth year) than at 16 (from fourth year). Moreover, some two-thirds of the students who entered from fourth year left after a year, at 17. The 17-year-old transition point is therefore particularly significant for Scottish further education, which experiences a substantial turn-round of its full-time students at this point.

Some of these differences are summarized in table 1.2, which shows transitions between April 1985 and April 1986. The table only records *net* transitions: it does not, for example, show short full-time courses which young people entered and left between these dates. Of young people at school in England and Wales in 1985, nearly four in five were still in full-time education a year later, and more than two-thirds were still at school. By contrast, less than half (47 per cent) of the Scots who were at school in April 1985 were still there in April 1986. In England and Wales 11 per cent of those at school in April 1985 were in full-time further or higher education a year later. The comparable figure in Scotland was 14 per cent, and a further 5 per cent had already entered short courses and left (compared with almost none in England and Wales). Two-thirds of the full-time further education students in England and Wales in April 1985 were still there a year later, twice as many as in Scotland.

To summarize: in England and Wales we can identify two clear transition points at 16 and 18, with separate and largely alternative streams covering the intervening stage, and with relatively small movements between streams or out of full-time education at 17. In Scotland, by contrast, the 16-year-old transition is less likely to accompany an institutional break; it is

Table 1.2 Status in April 1986 by status in April 1985 (percentages)

Status in April 1985	Status in April 1986								
	FT FE/HE	School	Job	YTS	Unemployed	Others	NK	Total	n
Scotland									
Full-time FE	33	0	31	18	10	7	2	101	(182)
School	14	47	19	12	4	3	*	99	(2683)
Full-time job	1	0	84	1	11	2	0	99	(808)
YTS	2	0	56	2	36	4	*	100	(1022)
Unemployed	2	0	25	9	53	12	*	101	(448)
Others	3	0	25	3	29	39	1	101	(80)
NK	9	22	28	16	20	4	1	100	(69)
All	8	20	40	7	19	5	*	99	(5292)
England & Wales									
Full-time FE	65	3	20	7	4	2	0	101	(799)
School	11	68	13	5	2	2	0	101	(2741)
Full-time job	1	*	88	*	9	2	0	100	(1020)
YTS	2	*	65	1	24	7	0	99	(1049)
Unemployed	2	*	25	6	54	12	0	99	(325)
Others	8	1	36	9	19	26	0	99	(62)
NK	2	2	50	1	37	8	0	100	(79)
All	13	19	45	3	15	4	0	99	(6075)

Note. * = <0.5

more staggered, with a few young people leaving from the winter of fourth year and a significant exodus of 'winter leavers' in the middle of the fifth year; and there is a further and major transition at 17, when there is not only substantial movement out of full-time education but also significant movement between sectors, especially between school and further or higher education.

Courses in Post-compulsory Education

These institutional differences are reflected in the structure and content of post-compulsory courses in the two systems. This is evident if we consider the main school-based courses for post-compulsory students: in England and Wales the 'A' level of the GCE, in Scotland the Higher grade of the Scottish Certificate of Education (SCE). Both are subject-based and largely 'academic' courses; both provide the principal qualification for entry to higher education; both have proved relatively resistant to change. However they differ in length — 'A' levels are normally taken over two years, whereas Highers are normally taken over one year — and in content and level. The (very notional) qualifying level for higher education is two 'A' levels in England and Wales and three Highers in Scotland.

The traditional 'norm' for the curriculum for an academically successful student after 16 comprises three 'A' levels over two years in England and Wales and five Highers in one year in Scotland (Gray *et al.*, 1983). Five subjects were required for the pre-existing Scottish group certificate course. The possibility of completing them after five years of secondary school is of considerable symbolic importance: the Scottish system has seen itself as providing more scope for educational mobility than in England where seven years of secondary schooling are usually needed to qualify for university entrance. The larger number of subjects at Highers is the basis of the Scottish claim to offer greater breadth than the highly specialized English system.

However the Scottish system diverges considerably from this norm. In the first place, the structure of courses encourages many students to spread their Highers attempts over two years, although typically the decisions are taken incrementally and piecemeal (McPherson, 1984a and 1984b). Second and relatedly, the shorter length and lower level of Highers encourages many students to take one or a few subjects, usually in conjunction with resits or new subjects at 'O' grade. Thus, of the sample members in full-time education in spring 1985, 57 per cent of the English and Welsh were attempting at least one 'A' level, and more than three-quarters of these studied three or more (Clough *et al.*, 1988); many more of the Scots in full-time education attempted at least one Higher — about four in five — but only a quarter of these attempted five Highers in fifth year.

It follows that in the Scottish system the distinction between high-status 'academic' and other educational routes after 16 is both less sharp and less final: less sharp, because of the wide variation in numbers of Highers subjects studied in fifth year; and less final, because at least in principle the sixth year allows young people to upgrade their qualifications by taking further Highers or resitting old ones. In practice, many young people leave school after a predominantly academic fifth year to enter YTS or non-advanced vocational courses at college. The fifth year may keep young people's mobility chances alive, but it also performs an important 'cooling out' function.

The corollary is that the balance of the curriculum changes much more between the first and second post-compulsory years in Scotland than it does south of the border. In England and Wales, 19 per cent of those in full-time education in spring 1985, and more than half of those at college, were taking vocational courses only (*ibid*). These included courses offered by the Business and Technician Education Council (BTEC), the Royal Society of Arts (RSA) and the City and Guilds of London Institute (C&GLI). More than two-thirds said they were on two-year courses. A further 10 per cent – again, rather more of the college students – combined vocational with 'O' level or equivalent courses, and 14 per cent took 'O' level or equivalent courses only; a third or fewer of these students described their courses as lasting two years. Thus, between the first and second post-compulsory years in England and Wales the proportion of students following 'O' grade courses or combinations of 'O' grades with vocational courses might be expected to fall; but the broad balance between 'academic' 'A' level courses and the more traditional full-time vocational courses remained roughly constant.

By contrast, in Scotland in the first post-compulsory year very few school students and most of the college students were taking predominantly vocational courses; but college students comprised only 8 per cent of Scots in full-time education in spring 1985. A year later this proportion had risen to 23 per cent. This figure excludes higher education and takes no account of those who had already passed through short full-time vocational courses after the end of fifth year.

One final aspect of post-compulsory courses in Scotland must be noted. In January 1983 the Scottish Education Department published its 16-plus Action Plan (SED, 1983), which proposed to replace all non-advanced vocational courses by a system of modules, each of notional forty hours' duration. The modules were to be available at school or college, to full- or part-time students, and were to be accredited through a single certificate, the National Certificate of the Scottish Vocational Education Council (Scotvec). The proposals were implemented very swiftly, and our year group was the first to experience the new modular system after fourth year. Their experiences, and the strategy of the Action Plan, are discussed in more detail in chapter 8, and the impact on the school fifth-year curriculum is examined in chapter 9. In principle the new modular system keeps options open and provides mobility ladders in respect of vocational education: something which the structure of Highers courses, again in principle, may do for academic education.

Differentiation

Beneath the various institutional differences we have described there may be underlying sociological similarities. In saying this we do not deny that sociological processes are influenced by their institutional context; nor do our data allow us to compare sociological processes in the two systems as comprehensively as their institutional structures. We will simply point to two aspects of differentiation, by gender and by previous qualification level, which hint at sociological similarities. First, in both systems more girls than boys continued in full-time education, and among those who continued more girls entered college. Second, in both systems continued full-time education, especially at school, was strongly related to attainment at 16. Table 1.3 shows the proportions of 'higher-' and 'lower-qualified' young people in different statuses in April 1986. In England and Wales young people with at least one GCE 'O' level at grades A–C or at least one Certificate of Secondary Education (CSE) at grade 1 are counted as 'higher-qualified'; in Scotland young people with at least one SCE 'O' grade in bands A–C are so counted. The Scottish 'O' grade is roughly equivalent to the English 'O' level; in 1984 these were the main examinations taken at the end of compulsory schooling. However, most parts of Scotland lacked an equivalent to the English CSE; as a result 'O' grades were taken by a larger proportion of the age group than typically took 'O' levels in England and Wales. Consequently the benchmarks used to define qualification groups in the two countries are not fully comparable: 65 per cent of the Scots, compared with 57 per cent of the English and Welsh, count as higher-qualified in table 1.3. Comparisons should therefore be made between qualification groups within each country, rather than between countries within each qualification group. Within each country the proportion continuing in full-time education is much larger among the higher qualified; almost none of the lower qualified is still at school. Conversely the proportion in the labour market, and especially the proportion unemployed, is much larger among the lower qualified.

Later Transitions

When discussing transition points earlier in this section we were unable to present data on the transition at 18 years; this occurs in summer 1986 for our

Table 1.3   Status in April 1986, by qualifications at 16 (percentages)

	Scotland		England and Wales	
	Higher qualified	Lower qualified	Higher qualified	Lower qualified
Full-time FE/HE	11	3	18	6
School	30	1	33	1
Full-time job	38	45	37	57
YTS	8	7	3	4
Unemployed	9	36	6	26
Others	4	7	3	7
NK	*	*	0	0
Total	100	99	100	101
n	(3931)	(1349)	(4341)	(1734)

Notes.   Higher qualified: Scotland: any S4 'O' grade at A-C.
England and Wales: any ABC1 at 16.
Lower qualified: all others.

year groups, and we will only have data on it when the third sweeps of our respective samples have been completed. Earlier data for Scotland showed that some two-thirds of young people still at school in the sixth year continued in higher or other full-time education (SED/SEB, 1982; Raffe, 1984a). If these patterns have continued we infer that only a third of our sixth-year school students, equivalent to some 6 or 7 per cent of the age group, would enter the labour market at 18; they would probably be joined by a smaller number (but larger proportion) of college students. It is probable that rather more young people in England and Wales would enter the labour market at 18, since fewer of them had done so at 17. Nevertheless, it is clear that most of the young people in our two samples who were to enter the labour market as teenagers had already done so by April 1986. With this in mind, we turn to consider differences in the youth labour markets of Scotland and of England and Wales.

THE YOUTH LABOUR MARKET

Key Differences

Our surveys point to two key differences between the youth labour markets of Scotland and of England and Wales. Most other apparent differences, we shall argue, can be explained in terms of these two; beyond them, the similarities are far more striking.

The first key difference results directly from the institutional differences described above. This is that entry to the labour market among members of each cohort is more staggered in Scotland than in England and Wales. Of young people in the labour market in April 1986, 25 per cent in Scotland had been in full-time education a year earlier, compared with 15 per cent in England and Wales. This reflects the greater transition at 17 in Scotland. This difference is significant but not huge; many of the transitions at 17 in Scotland are between sectors of full-time education rather than out of them and into the labour market. The more striking contrast is in the proportion who were in full-time education eighteen months earlier, in October 1984: 48 per cent in Scotland compared with 18 per cent in England and Wales. This difference is due to the Scottish winter leavers, the 'conscripts' who had to stay on at school beyond summer 1984 but left when they were able to, in December.

The second key difference is that the Scottish labour market is weaker. However, because of the institutional differences we have just described it is impossible to summarize this relative weakness in a single pair of statistics. Table 1.4 shows the employment rates of the two year groups at each of the four time points shown in table 1.1. The first set of employment rates is based on all in the labour market, and includes YTS trainees with the non-employed. The second set of rates is based on young people who were either in full-time jobs or unemployment, and excludes YTS.

Among year-group members in the labour market in October 1984 the proportion in full-time jobs was 32 per cent in both countries. Excluding YTS trainees from the calculation considerably boosts the estimated employment rate but results in a slightly lower rate in Scotland (63 per cent)

Table 1.4 Employment rates

	All		Males		Females	
	Sc	E&W	Sc	E&W	Sc	E&W
Full-time jobs as % of labour market (incl YTS)						
October 1984	32	32	30	35	34	28
April 1985	34	41	33	42	36	39
October 1985	51	70	51	71	52	68
April 1986	61	72	59	73	62	69
Full-time jobs as % of employed and unemployed						
October 1984	63	68	62	72	65	62
April 1985	62	72	60	74	63	70
October 1985	68	77	67	77	69	76
April 1986	68	76	67	77	70	74

than in England and Wales (68 per cent). (This appears to reflect a slower rate of entry into YTS among unemployed young people in Scotland: see Raffe and Courtenay, 1987.) Employment rates were higher among girls in Scotland and among boys in England and Wales. However, comparisons based on October 1984 may be inappropriate, since more of the Scottish year group were still in full-time education. By October 1984 the Scottish labour market had had a little more than a third of the year group to absorb, compared with more than a half in England and Wales (see table 1.1). More Scots entered the labour market over the following winter and summer; by October 1985 there was a wide gap between the two countries' employment rates, which stood at 51 per cent of the labour market in Scotland compared with 70 per cent in England and Wales. However, this comparison is also inappropriate: at least it must be interpreted in the knowledge that more Scots had recently joined the labour market and had had less time to look for work, and that more Scots were still on their one-year YTS schemes. In April 1986 the gap had narrowed – employment rates stood at 61 per cent in Scotland and 72 per cent in England and Wales – but there were still more Scots on YTS. If the YTS trainees are excluded, the difference in employment rates is slightly narrower: 68 per cent compared with 76 per cent. These two figures may provide as good a summary as can be found of the relative strengths of the two countries' labour markets, given that no single set of statistics can adequately express the difference. This is because it is impossible to find data that are simultaneously comparable with respect to duration in the labour market, age and season without restricting the comparison to an unrepresentative subset of young people in one or other of the countries.

The relative disadvantage of Scottish males, however, is well established despite these problems of measurement. In April 1986 their employment rate (net of YTS) was 10 percentage points lower than in England and Wales: 67 per cent compared with 77 per cent. Among females the gap was narrower: 70 per cent compared with 74 per cent.

There are, therefore, two key differences between the youth labour markets of Scotland and of England and Wales. Institutional differences in full-time education result in different patterns of entry to the labour market; and the Scottish market is weaker, especially for males. Once these differences are allowed for, the similarities between the two systems are more remarkable than the differences.

Occupational Structure

The (all-age) labour market in Scotland is often perceived to be biased towards manual occupations relative to that of England and Wales. To some extent the perception is true: the share of the workforce taken by manual jobs is some 4 percentage points higher in Scotland than in England and Wales (Kendrick, 1986). But this difference is largely due to Scotland's smaller proportion of managers, especially in the private sector: many firms operating in Scotland have headquarters based elsewhere, for example in the south-east of England. The relative scarcity of managers in Scotland is unlikely to have a large effect on the teenage labour market.

Table 1.5 shows the occupations of sample members who were in full-time jobs in April 1986. There were fewer Scots in the first two (non-manual) occupational categories shown in the table, especially clerical occupations. But these two categories were distinctive in Scotland because they had recruited around half their current (April 1986) employees from young people leaving school at the end of fifth year (at age 17). (No other occupational category had recruited more than 21 per cent of its current employees from young people leaving at the end of fifth year.) Moreover, in both countries many clerical employees had been recruited from YTS. It is therefore probable that the number of non-manual employees in Scotland in April 1986 would subsequently be swelled by 17-year-old school leavers who were then still on YTS; in England and Wales many fewer YTS trainees were still on the scheme. (However, if we are correct in anticipating a larger influx of 18-year-olds to the labour market in England and Wales, they may in turn boost the relative share of non-manual employment south of the border.)

In other words, the main difference between the countries' occupational distributions shown in table 1.5 may be at least partly attributable to the more staggered pattern of labour-market entry in Scotland, rather than to 'underlying' differences in the labour markets. All other differences in table 1.5 are small. Scotland had more young people working in personal services, in farming, fishing and related occupations and in materials processing, making and related (excluding metal and electrical) occupations. The last difference affects females and may reflect the relative importance of the textile and clothing and food and drink industries in Scotland.

There were slightly greater industrial than occupational differences between the two countries (table not shown). Construction accounted for 14 per cent of Scottish employment compared with 8 per cent in England and Wales; 7 per cent of Scots were employed in the metal goods, engineering and vehicles industries compared with 10 per cent in England and Wales. In most other respects the industrial structures of the two countries were similar: for example, in both countries manufacturing only accounted for a small proportion of young people's employment (23 per cent in Scotland, 28 per cent in England and Wales).

One particular feature of the two countries deserves comment. The scale and character of gender differention in employment was very similar. In both

Table 1.5: Occupations of all in full-time employment in April 1986 (percentages)

	Males and females		Males		Females	
	Scotland	England & Wales	Scotland	England & Wales	Scotland	England & Wales
Professional, managerial and related	4	5	3	5	5	6
Clerical and related	20	26	7	10	35	46
Selling	8	8	6	6	11	11
Security and protective services	3	2	5	4	*	*
Catering, cleaning, hairdressing and other personal services	12	9	5	5	20	15
Farming, fishing and related	5	3	9	4	1	1
Materials processing, making and repairing (exc metal & electrical)	16	14	16	17	15	9
Processing, making, repairing and related (metal and electrical)	14	13	24	22	2	1
Painting, repetitive assembling, product inspecting, packaging and related	5	7	5	7	5	7
Construction, mining and related not identified elsewhere	4	4	8	6	0	0
Transport operating, materials moving and storing and related	3	4	6	7	*	*
Miscellaneous	1	1	2	2	*	*
NK/inadequately described	6	4	6	5	6	2
Total	101	100	102	100	100	98
n	(2007)	(2261)	(1046)	(1124)	(961)	(1137)

Note. * = <0.5

27

countries more than half of all girls worked in just two occupational categories (clerical and personal services), and two more categories (selling, and materials processing, etc., excluding metal and electrical) accounted for most of the remainder. Other categories (notably metal and electrical processing) were largely the preserve of boys. The table almost certainly underestimates the extent of this differentiation. Several of the categories shown in the table are broad and include a wide range of constituent occupations which are themselves gendered. To the gender differentiation between the categories shown in table 1.5 must therefore be added a further substantial amount of differentiation between occupations within each of these categories. In both countries fewer girls than boys reported receiving training in their current job, and, of those that did, girls reported considerably shorter average periods of training.

The Youth Training Scheme

YTS is a British-wide scheme, run by the Manpower Services Commission, and its framework and structure are essentially the same in Scotland as in England and Wales. It aims 'to provide a foundation of broad-based vocational education and training, and planned work experience' for young people leaving full-time education before 18 (MSC, 1986, p.2). When our year groups entered it, it was a one-year scheme; a minimum of thirteen weeks were spent off-the-job, and the balance largely consisted of work experience with one or more employers. All 16-year-old school leavers were eligible to enter, and 17-year-old leavers could enter if they were un-employed. YTS has since been extended to a two-year scheme, for 16-year-old leavers; it remains a one-year scheme for 17-year-olds but they no longer have to be unemployed to enter. The aims of YTS have been extended to give 'all trainees the opportunity to obtain a vocational qualification related to competence in the workplace, or to obtain a credit towards such a qualification' (*ibid.*, p.2).

In both countries YTS, despite its standard framework, is internally heterogeneous. It has been used by employers as a way of inducting, screening and training young workers; about a third of trainees find work with the employers responsible for their schemes (Gray and King, 1986). However, YTS also provides a safety net for unemployed young people. At the time our year-group members were 16, minimum-age school leavers who could not find jobs, training or further education places by the following Christmas were guaranteed the offer of a suitable place on the scheme. (The guarantee has since been extended to all leavers under 18.) YTS is therefore torn between its function as an unemployment-based scheme and its aims of developing and extending a new youth training framework: a conflict of purposes that has been diagnosed in both countries (Bevan and Varlaam, 1987; Mansell and Miller, 1987; Raffe, 1987).

The pressures on YTS to function primarily as an unemployment-based scheme are evident in our data. The relative scale of YTS in the two countries is in inverse relation to the relative strengths of their labour markets: 42 per cent of the Scottish year group had entered YTS by spring 1986, compared with 37 per cent of the English and Welsh.[3] More young people entered YTS in Scotland, we suggest, because fewer could find jobs instead. This interpretation is supported by the observation that the difference in participation rates was smaller for girls (39 per cent compared with 35 per cent) than for boys (46 per cent compared with 39 per cent); as we have seen, the relative weakness of the Scottish labour market was also less pronounced for girls. In both countries YTS tended to attract less-qualified members of each year group. Thirty per cent of the higher qualified in Scotland (see table 1.3) entered YTS compared with 66 per cent of the less qualified; in England and Wales the difference between higher and lower qualified, defined on a different basis, was broadly similar: 24 per cent compared with 54 per cent. This difference is largely due to the greater proportions of the better qualified continuing in full-time education, but it also reflects a tendency for better qualified leavers to enter jobs rather than YTS.

YTS trainees in Scotland had more difficulty finding jobs at the end of their schemes. In April 1986 56 per cent of former YTS trainees in Scotland were in full-time jobs compared with 67 per cent in England and Wales. Table 1.2, which shows transitions between April 1985 and April 1986, tells a similar story: among those on YTS in April 1985 the employment rate one year later was 56 per cent in Scotland compared with 65 per cent in England and Wales. The difference was slightly greater among males (57 per cent compared with 67 per cent) than among females (56 per cent compared with 63 per cent).

In each country the same proportion of full-time employees in April 1986 had been on YTS (49 per cent), with little difference between the male and female proportions (table 1.6). In Scotland this figure would probably grow further after April 1986, when those still on YTS entered employment. In both countries more young people could be expected to enter employment from full time education in summer 1986, without going on YTS, with a somewhat larger influx in England and Wales than in Scotland. In the longer term, therefore, the role of YTS as a route to employment may be slightly greater in Scotland than in England and Wales, reflecting the relative weakness of the Scottish labour market and the role of YTS as, in part, an unemployment-based scheme.

Table 1.6: Percentage ever on YTS, by occupation: all in full-time employment in April 1986

	Males and females		Males		Females	
	Scotland	England & Wales	Scotland	England & Wales	Scotland	England & Wales
Professional, managerial and related	24	37	(18)	39	31	37
Clerical and related	43	46	39	31	44	50
Selling	57	55	56	54	57	55
Security and protective services	18	24	18	(23)	*	*
Catering, cleaning, hairdressing and other personal services	51	55	(53)	(45)	51	60
Farming, fishing and related	55	(48)	54	(44)	*	*
Materials processing, making and repairing (exc metal and electrical)	56	48	57	51	56	44
Processing, making, repairing and related (metal and electrical)	43	56	43	57	*	*
Painting, repetitive assembling, product inspecting, packaging and related	56	46	(58)	51	(54)	40
Construction, mining and related not identified elsewhere	64	46	64	46	*	*
Transport operating, materials moving and storing and related	61	57	62	59	*	*
Miscellaneous	(68)	(60)	(71)	(61)	*	*
NK/inadequately described	44	45	49	50	39	32
All in full-time jobs	49	49	49	48	48	50

Note. Bracketed numbers indicate unweighted base n less than 50; asterisks denote base n less than 20.

In neither country, apparently, had YTS monopolized access to particular sectors of employment (see also chapter 7). YTS trainees were widely spread across the differential occupational categories shown in table 1.6. The only categories in either country in which fewer than 40 per cent of their employees had been on YTS were security and protective services (which largely comprises the Armed Forces) and professional, managerial and related occupations. However in Scotland, at least, the latter category, which recruits the largest proportion of 17-year-old school leavers, would probably increase its proportion of former YTS trainees when young people still on YTS in spring 1986 entered it. Conversely, in neither country did YTS trainees account for as many as two thirds of the employees in any occupational category. The highest proportion was 64 per cent, for the residual 'construction, mining and related (not identified elsewhere)' category in Scotland. More detailed occupational categories would probably reveal tighter associations between particular occupations and YTS; nevertheless it remains clear that YTS did not monopolize access to any broad areas or segments of employment.

There is one difference between the two countries which, although it results from the institutional differences discussed earlier, may have important consequences, both for YTS and for the education system. This is that in Scotland there is more overlap between YTS and full-time post-compulsory education, in terms of students attending both. We have seen that in England and Wales post-compulsory education and training can reasonably be represented as a two-year stage, with relatively little movement between institutions during that stage. The different options entered at 16 are, by and large, alternatives; few young people enter more than one. As a result few of those who opt for school or further education at 16 ever enter YTS: only 7 per cent of those in further education in spring 1985, and only 5 per cent of those at school, were on YTS a year later (table 1.3). In Scotland, by contrast, the comparable figures are 18 per cent and 12 per cent; decisions at 16 typically commit the student only for one further year; there is a further transition point at 17, when many young people leave full-time education for YTS. (Relatively few young people in either system move in the other direction, from YTS to full-time education). The conversion of YTS to a two-year scheme will not remove this national difference, and may even consolidate it; it will confirm the 16–18 period as a two-year stage in England and Wales, but 17-year-old school leavers will still be entitled to a one-year YTS.

The overlap between full-time post-compulsory education and YTS in Scotland becomes far greater if we include fifth-year winter leavers, some two-thirds of whom go on to enter YTS. Strictly these young people have not left 'post-compulsory' education: they have stayed at school compulsorily because they were not old enough to leave after fourth year. However they tend to follow 'post-compulsory' courses so their experience reinforces our general point. This is that the greater overlap between post-compulsory education and YTS in Scotland, as well as between different types of post-compulsory education, makes for greater problems of integration and articulation. Some of the implications of this are pursued in chapter 8.

Labour-market Dynamics

Table 1.7 summarizes much of our argument concerning differences and similarities in the two countries' labour markets. The table is restricted to

Table 1.7: Typology of labour-market experiences, by sex: all in labour market in October 1984

	All		Males		Females	
	Scotland	England & Wales	Scotland	England & Wales	Scotland	England & Wales
In full-time job in April 1986:						
no previous YTS	25	29	25	33	25	25
previously on YTS	35	39	35	38	33	40
On YTS in April 1986:						
no previous job	1	1	1	1	1	1
previously in a job	*	1	*	1	*	1
Unemployed in April 1986:						
no previous job or YTS	3	4	4	3	3	5
previously in a job, no YTS	4	5	4	5	5	5
previously on YTS, no job	14	9	16	9	12	8
previously in a job and on YTS	9	5	8	5	10	5
Not in labour market in April 1986	8	8	6	6	11	10
Total	99	101	99	101	100	100
n	(1576)	(2263)	(884)	(1151)	(692)	(1122)

Note. * = <0.5

early entrants, that is to young people in the labour market in October 1984. It therefore partly 'controls' for one of the two differences noted earlier, that is the different pattern of labour-market entry arising from institutional differences in full-time education. This 'control' is imperfect since the young people covered by the table are less representative of their year group in Scotland than in England and Wales. The table summarizes young people's 'careers' up to April 1986 by showing their April 1986 status and the other labour-market statuses they had experienced up to this point.

In both countries a majority of these young people were in jobs in April 1986, but more were in jobs in England and Wales (68 per cent) than in Scotland (60 per cent). The difference was smaller among girls than among boys. More than half of those in jobs had been on YTS; this proportion is larger than that shown in table 1.6, reflecting the fact that these early entrants to the labour market were particularly likely to go on YTS. Only a handful of these early entrants were still on the scheme in April 1986. In each country, 8 per cent of the early entrants had already left the full-time labour market; in each country, more girls than boys had done so. The remainder were unemployed: 30 per cent in Scotland compared with 23 per cent in England and Wales, with the differential again larger among boys than among girls. However the difference in unemployment rates is entirely accounted for by the larger proportion of Scots who had been on YTS and then returned to unemployment. The proportion of young people in Scotland who remained or became unemployed without ever having been on YTS was fractionally smaller in Scotland (although when the Scottish figures are adjusted to exclude very early leavers from YTS, not recorded in the data for England and Wales, this proportion becomes the same as for England and Wales). In other words the 'hard core' of young people who remained unemployed and did not go on YTS was about the same size in the two countries; Scottish youth unemployment was higher, not because the coverage of YTS was less effective, but because fewer young people found jobs after going on the scheme.

In both countries the 'lower-qualified' early entrants were more than twice as likely to be unemployed as the 'higher qualified', and several times more likely to have remained continuously unemployed without going on YTS.

Geographical Variation

The common perception of Scotland as a part of the 'depressed north' of Britain tends to imply that Scotland is itself internally homogeneous. In presenting aggregate data on the two systems we may ourselves have encouraged this impression. Yet Scotland is far from homogeneous. The 'north/south' divide within England has a rough parallel in a 'west/east' divide within Scotland.

This is illustrated if we disaggregate the Scottish data in table 1.7 to separate Strathclyde Region from the rest of Scotland. Nearly half the population of Scotland lives in Strathclyde, which includes Glasgow and the Clydeside conurbation. Of the early entrants to the labour market shown in table 1.7, only 15 per cent in Strathclyde were in full-time jobs in spring 1986 and had not been on YTS; the proportion in the rest of Scotland was more than twice as large, at 33 per cent. The most striking contrast was in the proportion who were currently unemployed, had been on YTS but had never had a job: 22 per cent in Strathclyde compared with 7 per cent in the rest of Scotland. (The 'hard core' of young people who had remained unemployed without going on YTS was the same size, at 3 per cent, in both parts of Scotland).

In spring 1986 employment rates (net of YTS) among our sample members stood at 68 per cent in Scotland and 76 per cent in England and Wales (table 1.4): unemployment rates were therefore 32 per cent and 24 per cent respectively. Within Scotland this rate differed between Strathclyde (39 per cent) and the rest of Scotland (25 per cent); at a more local level it ranged from 10 per cent (Grampian) and 15 per cent (Borders) to 44 per cent (Lanarkshire) and 48 per cent (Glasgow). (Orkney and Shetland had the lowest unemployment rates, but based on small sample numbers.) Similarly, the average unemployment rate of 24 per cent in England and Wales masks a wide variation ranging from 11 per cent (South-east) and 17 per cent (Greater London) to 32 per cent (North-west), 33 per cent (Yorkshire and Humberside) and 34 per cent (Northern England and Wales).

DISCUSSION

It is with respect to the 16–18 stage that the structure - and perhaps also the philosophy - of Scottish education differs most visibly from its southern counterpart. We have described these differences in terms of institutional structures, with less institutional variety in Scotland and a smaller further education sector; in terms of the greater number of transition points, and in particular a significant transition point at 17 years; in terms of the weaker definition of many of these transitions; and in terms of the weaker boundaries between the educational tracks followed beyond 16, with a larger number of students taking Highers and a wider range in the number of Highers taken. On the other hand the curricular boundaries between institutions, that is between vocational college courses and largely academic school courses, are stronger in Scotland than in England and Wales, although the Action Plan reforms and current proposals for institutional restructuring in some local authorities seek to weaken them. Alongside these differences are contrasting systems of qualifications, both academic and vocational, although vocational qualifications have recently been reformed in Scotland and are currently undergoing reform in England and Wales.

The 'myth' of Scottish education views the system as offering greater breadth and wider access than the English system, and many of the differences we have noted can be rationalized in these terms. The interplay of myth and practice is complex (Gray *et al.*,1983), but several aspects of this myth deserve further sociological scrutiny in a comparative context. For example, the Scottish system has been described as being closer to a 'contest' model of mobility through education than England, which was Turner's (1961) original example of 'sponsored' mobility (McPherson, 1973). In contest systems selection decisions are postponed, and the bases for selection are less clearly prescribed, whereas in systems of sponsored mobility future members of the elite are identified at an early stage and given separate educational preparation for their future roles. The weaker boundaries between educational tracks after 16 (at least within school), and the opportunities which the one-year Highers course provides for students to add further subjects in the sixth year, brings the Scottish system closer to the contest model than in England and Wales where the tracks entered at 16 appear to be more clear cut and more final. The Action Plan reform of vocational education, with its aim of providing ladders of progression that climb over institutional and status boundaries, can also be represented in 'contest' mobility terms (Raffe, 1985).

If the educational horizons of Scottish post-compulsory students remain broader for longer, it may follow that the 'cooling-out' function is also emphasized more in Scottish post-compulsory education (Clark, 1961). We have seen that several of the transitions among 17-year-olds in Scotland were 'downwards' in terms of conventional status distinctions: from academic school courses to non-advanced further education, from college to YTS, or from school to YTS. We do not know the educational and occupational ambitions of our sample members when they entered fifth year, but it is likely that for many of them the end of fifth year was the time when they had to lower their sights. We have already noted that the frequent transitions during the post-compulsory stage in Scotland make the need for coordination, integration and coherent lines of progression more urgent; our argument suggests that often these lines of progression can be seen as leading 'downwards' rather than 'upwards' as the term is more usually understood. Of course the notion of level is more complex than this, but our analysis points to a sociological view of progression that must be added to the educational and curricular one. The importance of the 'cooling-out' function is emphasized by evidence from earlier surveys suggesting that some of the

17-year-old leavers entering the labour market might have done better had they left at 16 (Raffe, 1984a).

We conclude that the institutional differences between the two countries' education systems may be theoretically, and practically, significant. On the other hand these differences occur within contexts, reflected in the two countries' labour markets and in patterns of differentiation among young people, which appear to be very similar. It follows that more focused comparisons between the two countries may offer considerable scope for teasing out the specific effects of institutional and policy differences. Earlier in this chapter we referred to 'confounding differences' which reduced the value of comparisons with overseas countries: many of these are indeed smaller within Britain. England and Wales could learn from Scotland, and *vice versa*.

The scope for such learning may be further increased by the fact that the institutional differences between the two countries are small in an international context. In comparison with most European countries, North America or Japan, both the Scottish and the English and Welsh systems have characteristics that mark them out as distinctively 'British': a relatively low level of participation beyond 16; a relatively small full-time technical or vocational sector; and a significant, if untidy, part-time vocational sector, now further complicated by the distinctively British YTS.

Several factors have prevented too great a divergence between the Scottish and the English and Welsh systems. One is the fact of centralized political control; another is the influence of the universities, which tend to promote uniformity across the UK. A third factor, which we have examined more closely in this chapter, is the influence of the labour market.

Whereas our discussion of the two education systems has focused on their differences – albeit slight, in international context – our discussion of the two countries' labour markets has focused on their similarities. Some educational differences have knock-on effects on labour markets, resulting for example in a more staggered pattern of entry in Scotland; and the Scottish youth labour market, particularly for boys, is weaker. Once these two factors are allowed for there are no substantial differences between the youth labour markets of Scotland and of England and Wales that we can discover. The occupational structure, the role of YTS, differentiation by gender and qualifications, patterns of movement in the labour market – all of these are broadly similar in Scotland and in England and Wales. Even the relative weakness of the Scottish labour market is small beside the geographical variation *within* each country.

This similarity helps us to point to the labour market, and the 'context' for education which it helps to provide, as a source of some of the common problems facing British education systems (Raffe, 1984b and 1987). For example, the relatively low participation in full-time education after 16, and in particular the lack of a developed technical or vocational sector, may largely reflect employers' preferences for recruiting at 16 and their stigmatization of young people who have followed lower-status 'non-academic' courses. It also follows that in areas where educational policy is closely tied to the labour market, such as the development of vocational courses and qualifications, Scotland's freedom of manoeuvre is restricted.

With respect to education we suggested that comparisons between Scotland and England and Wales might yield conclusions that are of both theoretical and practical value. With respect to the labour market, on the other hand, it is not wholly misleading to treat Scotland as a 'microcosm' of Great Britain. This is not to say that the Scottish labour market is precisely representative of Britain, rather that the Scottish market is internally varied and contains most of the ingredients contained in the wider British market, if not always in the same proportions, and that labour-market processes are very similar.

ACKNOWLEDGEMENTS

The Scottish Young Peoples Survey is carried out by the Centre for Educational Sociology (CES) at the University of Edinburgh in conjunction with the Scottish Education Department (SED). It is funded by the SED, the Manpower Services Commission (MSC), the Industry Department for Scotland and the Department of Employment (DE). The England and Wales Youth Cohort Study is carried out by Social and Community Planning Research in collaboration with the University of Sheffield. It is funded by the MSC, the DE and Department of Education and Science (DES). Work on this chapter was supported by the Economic and Social Research Council (grant number C00280004), of which the CES is a Designated Research Centre. The authors are responsible for the opinions expressed in this chapter.

NOTES

1   We refer to Britain rather than the UK because in certain respects Northern Ireland provides an exception to the centralized politics of the UK, although many of our other comments may apply at least as strongly to Northern Ireland as to Scotland. We apologize to Welsh readers that for simplicity of expression we occasionally refer to England and Wales as a single country.

2   Some estimates therefore differ very slightly from earlier papers (Raffe and Courtenay, 1986 and 1987) based on all first-sweep respondents.

3   The gap between the countries may be slightly exaggerated as the English and Welsh study does not record spells on YTS concluded before September 1984 and spells too short to appear in the month-by-month 'diary' data. The effect of the former exclusion, at least, is slight: excluding spells concluded before September 1984 from the Scottish data only reduces the proportion who had ever been on YTS by a single percentage point.

REFERENCES

BEVAN, S. and VARLAAM, C. (1987) 'Political pressures and strategic aspirations in the Youth Training Scheme' in HARRISON, A. and GRETTON, J. (Eds) *Education and Training UK 1987*, Newbury, Policy Journals.

BURNHILL, P. (1984) 'The ragged edge of compulsory schooling', in Raffe, D. (Ed) (1984) *Fourteen to Eighteen: The Changing Pattern of Schooling in Scotland*, Aberdeen, Aberdeen University Press.

CLARK, B. (1961) 'The "cooling-out" function in higher education' in HALSEY, A.H., FLOUD, J. and ANDERSON, C.A. (Eds) *Education, Economy and Society*, New York, Free Press.

CLOUGH, E. and GRAY, J. (1986) *Pathways 16–19: National Youth Cohort Study (England and Wales) 1985–1990*, Sheffield, University of Sheffield, Division of Education.

CLOUGH, E., GRAY, J. and JONES, B. (1988) 'Curricular patterns in post-compulsory provision: Findings from the National Youth Cohort Study', *Research Papers in Education*, 3.

COURTENAY, G. (1987) *England and Wales Youth Cohort Study: Report on Cohort 1 Sweep 1*, Sheffield, MSC.

COURTENAY, G. (1988) *England and Wales Youth Cohort Study: Report on Cohort 1 Sweep 2*, Sheffield, MSC.

GRAY, D. and KING, S. (1986) *The Youth Training Scheme: The First Three Years*, Research and Development Series No. 35, Sheffield, MSC.

GRAY, J., McPHERSON, A.F. and RAFFE, D. (1983) *Reconstructions of Secondary Education: Theory, Myth and Practice since the War*, Henley, Routledge and Kegan Paul.

KENDRICK, S. (1986) 'Occupational change in modern Scotland' in McCRONE, D. (Ed.) *Scottish Government Yearbook 1986*, Edinburgh, University of Edinburgh, Unit for the Study of Government in Scotland.

McPHERSON, A. (1973) 'Selection and survivals: A sociology of the ancient Scottish universities' in BROWN, R. (Ed.) *Knowledge, Education and Cultural Change*, London, Tavistock.

McPHERSON, A. (1984a) 'Post-compulsory schooling: The fifth year', in RAFFE, D. (Ed.) (1984). *Fourteen to Eighteen: The Changing Pattern of Schooling in Scotland*, Aberdeen, Aberdeen University Press.

McPHERSON, A. (1984b) 'Post-compulsory schooling: The sixth year' in RAFFE, D. (Ed.) (1984) *Fourteen to Eighteen: The Changing Pattern of Schooling in Scotland*, Aberdeen, Aberdeen University Press.

MANPOWER SERVICES COMMISSION (1986) *Guide to Content and Quality on YTS/ Approved Training Organisations*, Sheffield, MSC.

MANSELL, J. and MILLER, J. (1987) *The Organisation and Content of Studies at the Post-Compulsory Level: Country Study: England and Wales,* OECD Educational Monographs, Paris, OECD.

RAFFE, D. (1984a) 'The transition from school to work and the recession: Evidence from the Scottish School Leavers Surveys, 1977–1983', *British Journal of Sociology of Education,* 5, 3, pp. 247–65.

RAFFE, D. (Ed.) (1984b) *Fourteen to Eighteen: The Changing Pattern of Schooling in Scotland,* Aberdeen, Aberdeen University Press.

RAFFE, D. (1985) 'The extendable ladder: Scotland's 16+ Action Plan', *Youth and Policy,* 12, pp. 27–33.

RAFFE, D. (1987) 'The context of the Youth Training Scheme: An analysis of its strategy and development', *British Journal of Education and Work,* 1, 1, pp.1–31.

RAFFE, D. and COURTENAY, G. (1986) 'Post-16 transitions in Scotland and in England and Wales compared', Edinburgh, University of Edinburgh, Centre for Educational Sociology.

RAFFE, D. and COURTENAY, G. (1987) 'Wha's like us? Post-16 transitions in Scotland and England and Wales compared', *Scottish Educational Review,* 19, 1, pp. 28–38.

ROBERTS, A. (1984) 'The (not so) famous four', *Times Educational Supplement (Scotland),* 23 November, p. 22.

SCOTTISH EDUCATION DEPARTMENT (1983) *16–18s in Scotland: An Action Plan,* Edinburgh, SED.

SCOTTISH EDUCATION DEPARTMENT/SCOTTISH EXAMINATION BOARD (1982) *Full-time Education after S4: A Statistical Study,* Dalkeith, SEB.

TURNER, R.H. (1961) 'Modes of social ascent through education: Sponsored and contest mobility' in HALSEY, A.H., FLOUD, J. and ANDERSON, C.A. (Eds) *Education, Economy and Society,* New York, Free Press.

Chapter 2

The Story So Far: Research on Education, Training and the Labour Market from the Scottish Surveys
David Raffe

INTRODUCTION

Since 1971 some 100,000 young people have taken part in surveys conducted by the Centre for Educational Sociology (CES) at the University of Edinburgh. They have completed and returned questionnaires asking about their education at school, college or university, their training, employment and unemployment, and their family life. They have supplied 'objective' information on these experiences, and they have described their own attitudes, aspirations and expectations. They have ticked boxes and ringed numbers in response to 'closed' questions, and offered in their own words their answers to open-ended ones.

These young people are respondents to the Scottish Young Peoples Survey, formerly the Scottish School Leavers Survey. The information they have supplied has contributed to research on a wide range of educational, labour-market and related issues. Many of the published products of this research are listed in the annotated bibliography of CES work, which currently runs to 118 pages and lists more than 400 books, reports, articles and papers. These are written variously for the general reader or for the academic specialist in a variety of disciplines. Around a quarter deal with employment, unemployment, training or the relation of education to the labour market. This chapter summarizes the main conclusions from this work and assesses its practical and theoretical implications. Like the rest of the book, the chapter focuses on the youth labour market and its relation to education and training; other areas of CES research, which covers several aspects of secondary and post-secondary education, school effectiveness, educational policy-making and survey methodology, are not included. The chapter is also restricted to work based on the Scottish surveys and to writings which seek to interpret that work; and it focuses largely on studies published in the 1980s. Even with these restrictions the summary in this chapter must be highly selective, and my selection and interpretation are necessarily personal. Others who have worked on the CES data would not necessarily share all the priorities and judgments contained within this chapter, although I suspect that most of them would agree with most of what I write.

Each of the following sections of the chapter summarizes the main conclusions from research on a particular substantive topic. They cover, respectively: recent trends in the youth labour market; explanations for the decline in school-leaver employment; youth wages and wage expectations; young people's aspirations and preparedness for work, and vocational guidance; entry to the labour market, in relation to patterns of staying on in, and leaving, full-time education; young people's movements after they have entered the labour market, especially between jobs, schemes and unemployment; the factors associated with young people's success in finding jobs; and the effect of employment and training schemes on individuals' job chances. The two final sections of the chapter offer a more integrative discussion of general themes which recur in much of the work on the surveys.

Two features of the survey data underlie much of the work summarized in this chapter. The first is the wide range of topics covered, including detailed information on both 'sides' of the education-labour market transition. Second, the surveys cover a period, from the mid 1970s onwards, of major changes in the youth labour market and its relation to education. They provide a unique instrument for identifying areas of continuity, and areas of change, over this period.

LABOUR-MARKET TRENDS

Table 2.1 presents data from the biennial sequence of school leavers' surveys since 1977. Each survey covered leavers of all ages from the previous school session, and the table shows where they were at the time of the survey in the following spring. For a majority of leavers this was some nine or ten months after leaving school.

The period since 1979 has been dominated by a single trend: the decline in school-leaver employment. Since 1979 the proportion of school leavers in employment has fallen by more than a half. The table covers leavers of all ages; among 16-year-old leavers the proportionate decline in employment has

Table 2.1: Destinations of previous session's school leavers: Scotland, spring 1977–1987 (percentages)

	1977[1]	1979	1981	1983	1985	1987[2]
Full-time education	20	18	22	26	23	23
Full-time job[3]	62	64	51	38	36	30
Schemes/YOP/YTS	4	6	13	17	21	27
Unemployed	11	9	13	15	15	16
Others/not known[3]	3	3	1	4	5	4
Total	100	100	100	100	100	100

Notes: 1 The 1977 estimates are based on Fife, Lothian, Strathclyde and Tayside (unqualified leavers in other Regions were not surveyed in 1977). Together these four Regions contain abour three-quarters of the Scottish population. In 1979 the rounded percentage estimates for the four Regions were identical to those for the whole of Scotland.
2 1987 figures are provisional, based on an early data-set and provisional weights.
3 In 1981 the job category included young people in part-time jobs who were not in full-time education. In other years these are included with 'others'.

been even steeper. A second trend has largely mirrored the decline in employment: the growth of work experience and training schemes for young people. In 1977 a range of schemes, notably the Work Experience Programme and Job Creation Programme, accounted for only a handful (4 per cent) of the previous year's school leavers. In 1978 these were replaced by the Youth Opportunities Programme (YOP), also targeted on unemployed young people, and the number of participants grew as the labour market collapsed in the early 1980s. In 1983 YOP was replaced by the Youth Training Scheme (YTS). Unlike YOP, YTS is available to employed as well as unemployed young people; it has incorporated or displaced some of the jobs formerly available to school leavers, and consequently encouraged the decline in 'ordinary' employment.

The 'snapshot' data in table 2.1 underestimate the scale of these schemes, since many young people had already entered and left schemes by the time of their survey. For example nearly 45 per cent of all 1985/6 school leavers had at least started a YTS scheme, but only 27 per cent were still on it at the 1987 survey. The observed growth since 1983 in participation on schemes largely reflects their longer duration, as YOP schemes, typically of six months' duration, were replaced first by the one-year and then by the two-year YTS. As a result more trainees were still on their schemes at the time of the survey, which took place from nine to sixteen months after most respondents left school. The 'snapshot' data may also underestimate the decline in school-leaver employment; in the late 1970s a majority of the non-employed in the labour market had had at least one job since school, but by the early 1980s this was no longer the case (Raffe, 1984a).

School-leaver employment fell in nearly all industries after 1979, although the rate of decline varied (Shelly, 1987). Manufacturing industries tended to be hardest hit; in this as in many other respects the school-leaver labour market provides a magnified reflection of trends in the all-age market. The percentage of school-leaver employment in manufacturing fell from 38.9 in 1977 to 26.5 in 1981, recovering slightly to 29.0 in 1983.[1] This decline was considerably steeper among girls than among boys, partly because girls tended to be concentrated in a limited number of manufacturing industries (notably food, textiles and clothing) where employment fell by more than the average.

The occupational composition of boys' employment changed relatively little over the period 1977–1983. Among girls, there was a proportionate increase in clerical and other white-collar employment, and a decline in manual occupations such as textile workers and semi- and unskilled operatives (Shelly, 1987, and chapter 4 in this volume). This largely resulted from the decline in manufacturing; most of the occupational change over the period could be attributed to shifts in the relative shares of industries with different occupational distributions. There is little evidence of a secular shift in the occupational composition of school-leaver employment within industries.

These changes in the industrial and occupational composition of school-leaver employment occurred over a period when the total level of employment fell by nearly a half. For the most part the question is one of the relative rate of decline of different industries and occupations. Compared to the massive change in the level of employment the changes in its composition were relatively small. Analyses over a longer period would probably uncover larger industrial and occupational shifts, but it is significant that longer-term shifts of this kind were not more closely related to the short-term collapse of employment around 1980.

Inequalities in the school-leaver labour market tended to persist or even intensify during the recession. Qualified school leavers seeking employment were less likely to be successful in the 1980s than in the 1970s, but the gap between their chances and those of the unqualified remained at least as wide as before: the labour-market value of qualifications declined in absolute but not in relative terms (Raffe, 1984a; Shelly, 1987, and chapter 4 in this volume). School-leaver employment fell in nearly all parts of Scotland, but it fell more in the west-central belt and less in the more peripheral and less urbanized regions (Raffe, 1983a). In this respect too it mirrored trends in the general labour market (Fraser and Sinfield, 1987). The recession had a similar impact on the employment levels of male and female school leavers, but the occupational and industrial segregation of their employment tended to increase after 1979 (Shelly, 1987).

EXPLAINING THE DECLINE IN SCHOOL-LEAVER EMPLOYMENT

The Scottish surveys do not provide data for a full explanation of the decline in school-leaver employment after 1979. Nevertheless they contribute to such an explanation, and they provide sufficient evidence to test some of the specific explanations commonly put forward. They suggest that the decline in school-leaver employment was largely the result of trends affecting the general labour market, rather than of factors specific to young people.

Thus, on the one hand, the data confirm the close link between youth and adult labour markets. Underlying trends in school-leaver unemployment have closely followed trends in adult unemployment, albeit on an exaggerated scale (Raffe, 1984a; Shelly, 1987). This is seen more clearly from the surveys than from some official sources, notably the unemployment statistics, where underlying trends have been obscured by statistical, institutional and policy changes (Raffe, 1987a). Regional trends, and analyses across local labour markets described later in this chapter, also show a close connection between school-leaver and adult unemployment rates. Industrial and occupational trends in school-leaver employment, discussed above, similarly reflect adult trends.

On the other hand, the data enable us to test, and largely to discount, explanations specific to the youth labour market, notably demographic and structural explanations.

Demographic trends caused the annual flow of school leavers to increase from 75,000 in 1966/67 to over 93,000 in 1977/78. They doubtless contributed to the growing weakness of the youth labour market in the 1970s. However they do not explain its dramatic collapse around 1980. The second cohort of leavers in table 2.1, surveyed in 1979, left school in 1977/78. This was the year when the flow of school leavers in Scotland reached its peak; the massive decline in school-leaver employment since that date cannot be attributed to demographic trends (Main and Raffe, 1983a).

'Structural' explanations attribute youth unemployment to a growing mismatch between the supply and demand of young workers (Raffe, 1986a). For example, occupational changes are alleged to have left many school leavers insufficiently qualified for most of the jobs available. While it is true that unqualified school leavers have borne the brunt of unemployment, their plight is not mainly due to occupational change. Shelly's chapter in this book shows that unqualified school leavers have lost out because employers took advantage of a slack labour market and recruited better qualified school leavers to given jobs than a few years earlier. Unqualified school leavers have been the victims less of occupational shifts than of qualifications inflation, itself the result of the general scarcity of jobs.

In any case occupational changes in school-leaver employment were small, at least in relation to its absolute decline. More important for the present argument, occupational shifts were largely derivative of industrial shifts. The 'structural' explanation of youth unemployment claims that young people have been disproportionately represented in declining industries, and that their share of total employment has fallen in consequence. However analyses of employment changes over different periods, relating trends in school-leaver employment to all-age data for Scotland, show that school leavers were not significantly overrepresented in declining industries. Only a tiny fraction of the decline in school-leaver employment since the mid-1970s can be attributed to industrial shifts; the problem is rather that school leavers have lost their share of total employment *within* industries (Main and Raffe, 1983a; Shelly, 1987).

Other structural explanations locate the source of mismatch on the supply side of the labour market, alleging a decline in the quality of school leavers. As far as the more easily measurable aspects of 'quality' are concerned, the qualification levels of school leavers have risen substantially in recent years (Main and Raffe, 1983a; McPherson and Willms, 1987). Other aspects of school-leaver quality are harder to measure in surveys. However the data demonstrate that the desire for employment among the unemployed is strong (Gow and McPherson, 1980), as Furlong's chapter in this volume illustrates. Even among young people who reject YTS the wish for a 'real' job is widespread (Raffe, 1986c; Raffe and Smith, 1987). And young people's wage expectations, discussed in the following section, are generally realistic. Most youth unemployment is not voluntary in any meaningful sense of the term.

YOUTH WAGES

A widely expressed explanation for the increase in youth unemployment is that young people have 'priced themselves out of jobs'. However, relative wages cannot supply the sole explanation for recent trends: since 1979, while youth employment levels have fallen sharply, youth earnings have risen slower than adults. Nevertheless it is possible to argue that youth earnings have fallen too slowly to clear the market, and that the wage expectations of young people seeking work are too high. Main (1987b) used data from the 1985 survey to compare the actual earnings of current employees with the earnings which those not in jobs (the unemployed and YTS trainees) expected to receive when they found work. Among those in employment, earnings varied with age, qualifications and gender (males earning more than females). The analysis therefore had to control for these factors, making further adjustments for the fact that, even among young people of the same age, qualifications and gender, those in jobs were likely to be more 'employable' and to have higher earning power than those not in jobs. The analysis found that unqualified 16-year-olds who were unemployed or on YTS expected to earn about 11 per cent more, on average, than their employed peers, but the difference was not statistically significant. Other school leavers' expected earnings were significantly below actual earnings by as much as 15 per cent.

Most young people's wage expectations were therefore 'realistic' and more likely to err on the side of pessimism than of optimism. In a separate analysis Main and Shelly (forthcoming) examined non-employed school leavers' reservation wages, the lowest wages at which they would be prepared to accept employment. Their analysis suggested that reservation wages were generally 'reasonable' and would not lead to an exceptionally high rate of rejection of likely job offers. The level of reservation wages was influenced by benefit levels, but on the most likely assumptions about the distribution of job offers higher benefit levels would not result in substantially increased school-leaver unemployment.

In 1985 the survey sample was split randomly in two: one half was asked questions relating to gross earnings, the other half was asked about net (take-home) earnings. The two sets of questions yielded consistent responses from the employed, but among the non-employed expected earnings expressed in net terms were high relative to those expressed in gross terms. It appeared that sample members with no experience of employment underestimated the amount of deductions for tax and National Insurance (Main, forthcoming). This may seem a minor methodological point but it has important substantive implications. Job offers are usually expressed in terms of gross pay. Studies which ask young people for their reservation wages or expected earnings in terms of net pay are likely to yield exaggerated estimates and thus spuriously attribute youth unemployment to the excessive wage expectations of young people (Main, 1988).

ASPIRATIONS, GUIDANCE AND PREPAREDNESS FOR WORK

Comparisons of Highers-qualified leavers surveyed in 1971 and 1981 respectively revealed a convergence between male and female aspirations especially among entrants to higher education (Burnhill and McPherson, 1983 and 1984). A larger proportion of young women in 1981 than in 1971 were planning a full-time occupational career, and the qualities they sought in their ideal job more closely resembled those of young men. There was a similar convergence in the reasons given by university entrants for applying to higher education, with women offering more instrumental job-related reasons in 1981 than in 1971. Most significantly, perhaps, a growing proportion of young men were prepared to accept these prospective changes in the career patterns of women as legitimate. This trend towards equality had its limits. Kelly's (1981) analysis of 1977 data showed how the lower enrolment of girls in science subjects could be traced back to decisions relatively early in their secondary school careers, which tended to be irreversible. Among pupils dropping science at 14, girls were far less likely than boys to believe that science was useful for getting a job. Another analysis of the 1977 survey data, prepared for the Finniston Committee, found that only four of the 272 sample members in full-time engineering degree courses were female (Raffe, 1978). The same analysis examined degree students' views on jobs in manufacturing industry. The balance of opinion was that such jobs were well paid and offered good promotion prospects, but had low status, unpleasant working conditions and were insecure. In the light of more recent events we cannot say that they were wrong.

A retrospective school leavers' survey cannot expect to chart the development of occupational aspirations in school pupils; nor can it observe the process of vocational guidance. It can however record young people's retrospective views on their use of different sources of advice, and their relative helpfulness. A recurring theme in these judgments is the importance of informal sources of guidance, especially parents (Gray,1980; Raffe and Tomes,1986). Gray's analysis of 1977 data attempted to assess the impact of the new structure of guidance provision that had recently been introduced into Scottish schools. With respect to vocational guidance he concluded that its impact had been least among the least academic, 'non-certificate' pupils.

Yet non-certificate pupils also faced the highest unemployment rates. The 1977 data were used by a Working Party of Principal Careers Officers (1978) to examine the expressed needs of unemployed school leavers, and to help in the planning of the Youth Opportunities Programme which was then being launched. Several unemployed sample members reported difficulties with job-finding skills, and a concurrent analysis, not restricted to the unemployed, found a significant minority reporting literacy and numeracy problems (Freeman and Staite, 1978). However the unemployed youngsters clearly rejected conventional schooling; the Principal Careers Officers stressed that any measures to help them should be a fresh start, not a continuation of school. Such measures might learn from the experience of link courses (provided at college for school pupils) and work experience, generally popular with pupils. The analysis also showed that the incidence of work experience organized by the schools was substantially less than that of the informal work experience gained through part-time employment. A third of the non-certificate school leavers who had held part-time jobs thought these had helped them to get jobs on leaving school. Multivariate analyses of later surveys confirm that young people who had held part-time jobs during their school years were more likely to find jobs on leaving (Main and Raffe, 1983b). By contrast, neither school-organized work experience nor link courses appeared to have much effect on employment chances. Moreover, the pupils who attended them appeared to be selected on largely negative criteria, in particular the absence of examination commitments. Many link courses were attended by pupils least likely to benefit from them (Raffe, 1980).

More recent attempts to prepare young people more effectively for work include YTS and the Technical and Vocational Education Initiative (TVEI), both supervised by the Manpower Services Commission (MSC), and the 16-plus Action Plan of the Scottish Education Department (SED, 1983). YTS is discussed more fully later in this chapter, and in chapters 1, 5 and 7 of this book. TVEI and the Action Plan are newer initiatives, and the first major uses of the survey data to assess their impact are reported in chapters 8, 9 and 10 in this volume.

Unemployment may influence young people's orientations and motivation while they are still at school. Between the mid-1970s and the early 1980s self-reported truancy rates declined, even while unemployment levels increased; moreover in a given year truancy tended to be lower among otherwise comparable pupils in areas of higher unemployment (Raffe, 1986b). One should be wary of attributing causality to this association (among other things the trend may reflect the school system 'settling-down' after the raising of the school-leaving age) but it challenges the popular view that unemployment has had a demotivating and demoralizing influence on school pupils; more tentatively, it suggests that unemployment may act as an instrument of social control in schools, as in the labour market.

An attempt to review the more subjective aspects of the transition from school to work is hampered by the difficulty of generalization from one of the main sources of data. In each survey sample members have been invited to write open-endedly about their own experiences and opinions, in response to a set of general and often wide-ranging prompts (see chapters 10 and 11 in this volume). Their 'back-page comments' provide a rich source of qualitative data, and offer insight into how the structural processes revealed by some of the quantitative data impact on individual biographies. At the same time, only a few young people choose to comment on any one topic: it is difficult to generalize from their comments to the experiences or views of young people in general. The interested reader is referred to two published collections of their writings, edited by Gow and McPherson (1980) and by Hughes (1984).

ENTRY TO THE YOUTH LABOUR MARKET

One of the most important features of the full-time youth labour market is that the supply of youth labour is a residual; it excludes young people who continue in full-time education. Not only has educational expansion combined with more recent demographic trends to reduce the supply of youth labour, but those who are creamed-off tend to be the more academically successful and socially advantaged members of the age group.

Staying on at school in Scotland is not a one-off decision; there is a sequence of possible transition points, discussed in chapter 1. Unpublished analyses of survey data covering the period 1980–1984 show a steep increase in the proportion staying on for the first term of fifth year, a slight fall in the proportions of those entering fifth year staying on to complete fifth year, and an increase in the proportion of fifth-year completers staying on to sixth year. These trends partly reflect the effect of school-leaving regulations in Scotland. Although a majority of each year group is eligible to leave school at the end of fourth year, a minority is too young to leave then and must stay on to the Christmas of fifth year. Because of changes in primary school entry arrangements in the 1970s, the size of this group has been increasing and is now around a third of each year group. Once they have been forced to stay on for what amounts to the first half of fifth year, these 'conscripts' have, in the past, been more likely to complete fifth year than other members of their year group (Burnhill, 1984a; Dixon, 1984).

Apart from the conscripts, who are broadly representative of their year group, those staying on beyond fourth year have had much better fourth-year qualifications on average than early leavers. They have also tended to be middle-class and to have parents who have themselves stayed on beyond minimum age (Burnhill, 1984a; Shelly, 1987). Unpublished analyses show that the increase from 1980 to 1984 in the proportion of all pupils staying on to the end of fifth year can be entirely attributed to the increased proportion of conscripts, as discussed above, and to changes in the social-class composition and educational background of parents. The effects of educational expansion appear to be cumulative from generation to generation. As more parents have stayed on beyond minimum age, their higher participation rates are transmitted to their children (see chapter 3).

The decision to leave school at 16 reflects the influence of family, friends and school itself (Burnhill, 1984b). Young people's reasons for leaving early tend to combine 'push factors' associated with school and 'pull factors' associated with the labour-market or post-school opportunities. More than half of early leavers in summer 1983 said they left because they were 'fed up with school', and others left because they did not think they could improve their school qualifications; but early leavers were as likely to refer to the positive attractions of life at work or college, the need for money or the wish for financial independence (Bryant *et al.*, 1985). The wish to 'start a particular job while I had the chance' was given as the most important reason by 16 per cent of boys and 5 per cent of girls among the early leavers, and was a particularly important reason for leaving among the better qualified; however this appears to have been a less important reason for early leaving in 1983 than in 1980 (Burnhill, 1984b). In a weak labour market, the 'pull' factors may pull less hard.

Young people who have stayed on beyond 16 are in turn relatively likely to continue with some other form of full-time education when they leave school. Qualifications, gender and age on leaving school are all associated with entry to full-time education (Shelly, 1987). At least for some groups participation appears to be affected by local labour-market conditions; some school leavers opt for further education when suitable local employment opportunities are scarce. This may help to explain local and gender differences in participation and attainment (Willms and Kerr, 1987; chapter 6 in this volume) as well as the growing rate of entry, at least up to the early 1980s, to full-time post-school education.

TRANSITIONS IN THE LABOUR MARKET: JOBS, YOP AND YTS

Even in the 1970s, when unemployment was low at least by the standard of the 1980s, the transition from school to work was not always a simple one-stage process. More than half the school leavers who entered the labour market in summer 1976 experienced some unemployment over the following ten months, often for a brief spell between school and their first job (Gray *et al.*, 1983). Many young people, especially the less qualified, changed jobs early in their occupational careers. Among less qualified leavers in 1978 more than 40 per cent of those who had found jobs by the spring 1979 survey had already left their first job, and two-thirds of these had found another job. Although most of these job-quitters had left their jobs voluntarily, job-quitting appeared to be more closely related to occupational than to personal factors: it was more the product of unstable jobs than of unstable workers (Raffe, 1983c). Youth unemployment was still largely frictional, comprised mainly of relatively short spells between jobs. Two-thirds of the 1976 school leavers unemployed in spring 1977 had had a job since school (Gray *et al.*, 1983; Raffe, 1984a).

With the higher unemployment of the 1980s these patterns changed. The summer-term recruitment season became less important. Fewer young people changed jobs: the pattern of frequent movements in and out of jobs changed to a pattern of movements in and out of work experience and training schemes (Raffe, 1984a). Rather than being concentrated at the bottom end of the labour market, job-changers were now more likely to be relatively well qualified young people in areas of lower unemployment, who still had the market strength to change jobs (MacLeod *et al.*, 1983; Main and Raffe, 1983c). Few of the unemployed had held any full-time job since school (Raffe, 1984a and 1986c).

However, the biggest change in the transition process was the development of MSC schemes as an intermediate stage between school and work. From a scheme catering for a disadvantaged minority, YOP grew, by 1982/83, to a point where it catered for more than half of all school leavers entering the labour market. The introduction of one-year YTS in 1983 and two-year YTS in 1986 has not dramatically affected the numbers of young people involved, but it has substantially increased the average length of their involvement. Moreover the enhanced training content of YTS means that it is by far the most important source of vocational education and training for early leavers (Raffe, 1987c). However after YTS replaced YOP more school leavers, especially the less qualified, remained unemployed without going on any scheme (Bryant *et al.*, 1985; Raffe, 1987d).

The most important difference between YOP and YTS is in their declared aims. YOP was a temporary unemployment measure, restricted to the young unemployed. It aimed to mitigate the longer-term effects of unemployment by providing the experience and learning opportunities that ordinary jobs would have provided. YTS, far from being a job substitute, aims to transform the experience and learning opportunities of employed as well as unemployed young people. It is a permanent training measure, open to all school leavers under 18.

In practice, however, YTS tended to inherit YOP's 'image' and position in the labour market, as well as its function as a safety net for the unemployed. Instead of attracting well-qualified and employable school leavers away from jobs which did not carry YTS training, the scheme initially recruited trainees similar to the unemployed young people who formerly entered YOP. Young people's patterns of entering and leaving YTS, and their reasons for these decisions, provide further evidence that it functioned, in its early years, largely as an unemployment-based scheme like YOP (Raffe, 1987b and 1987d). It is likely that YTS will gradually enhance its status and acquire a more exalted (if very differentiated) place in the labour market. But its development will still depend on future levels and patterns of unemployment; and its scale and function will continue to vary locally according to the level and structure of local employment (Tomes, 1988). More generally, the surveys provide graphic evidence of the difficulties of innovating from the bottom up, and of reconciling the unemployment and training functions of YTS.

This continuity between YOP and YTS is also reflected in young people's attitudes to the two schemes. An analysis of 1981 survey data suggested that while most young people could find something positive to say about YOP, many had criticisms (Raffe, 1984c). These tended to focus on the level of the allowance, the alleged exploitation of trainees by employers, and the scheme's failure to help many trainees find jobs. Relatively few complained about the quality or amount of education and training. However when YTS replaced YOP the policy priority was to improve training rather than to redress any of the other defects of YOP. In this sense the new policy did not directly respond to young people's criticisms of YOP. Consequently young people's attitudes to YTS in the first two years of the scheme were very similar to earlier attitudes to YOP (Raffe and Smith, 1987; Raffe, 1987d). While young people express instrumental and often very positive views of particular schemes and of their benefits to the individual, they share a pervasive cynicism about the government's and employers' motives behind YTS.

Even under the one-year YTS many trainees did not complete their schemes. By spring 1985 three in ten of the second cohort of YTS trainees had quit the scheme, nearly all prematurely. Many left for employment — suggesting that they saw the scheme primarily as a temporary refuge from unemployment — but others, especially boys and the less qualified, became unemployed (Raffe, 1986c and 1987c). About six in ten of all young people leaving YTS found employment; the impact of YOP and YTS on young people's employment chances is discussed later in this chapter.

WHO GETS JOBS?

Each school leavers' survey provides one or more snapshots of young people at given intervals after leaving school, together with information on their family, educational and geographical characteristics. The data can therefore be used to analyze the separate effects of these different characteristics on the employment chances of school leavers who enter the labour market. Analyses of this kind have been conducted on every leavers' survey since 1977, usually to predict the probability of a school leaver being employed or not employed, but sometimes also to predict the type of employment obtained.

Girls and boys tend to enter different occupational areas, with girls concentrated in a much narrower range of occupations (Shelly, 1987). They also have different patterns of participation in education and of entry to the labour market (see chapter 1 in this volume). Apart from this their overall levels of employment have not differed greatly, and the factors influencing employment chances have been broadly similar for boys and girls (with the exception of age, discussed below). The following discussion draws mainly on analyses predicting employment, but parallel analyses predicting occupational level produce broadly similar results.

The ethnic minority population in Scotland is small, and only recently have the surveys included a question on ethnicity: even when these data are available the sample numbers will probably be too small to allow the employment chances of ethnic minorities to be properly examined. Apart from this, analyses based on several surveys identify five characteristics of school leavers which are consistently and independently associated with success in finding employment.

The first and most important is the level of qualifications gained at school, particularly 'O' grade qualifications attempted at the end of compulsory schooling (Gray *et al.*, 1983; Raffe, 1984b; Main, 1985, 1987a and 1987b; Main and Shelly, 1987; Shelly, 1987). In many analyses even D or E band awards at 'O' grade — widely if informally regarded as 'fail' grades — appear to contribute to employment success; this may reflect the extent to which employers recruit on the basis of examination attempts, before results are known, although it may also reflect the influence of unmeasured personal characteristics not included in the analysis.

The second and related factor in employment success is the curriculum or subject(s) in which qualifications have been obtained. Analyses of the 1977 survey show that qualifications in 'academic' subjects were most strongly correlated with employment; school qualifications in vocational subjects were poorly correlated with employment, although business studies subjects appeared quite important for girls. In general the academic status of a subject seemed to be more important than its intrinsic relevance to the job in question (Gray *et al.*, 1983; see also chapter 10 in this volume). A study using the 1981 data found only a slight connection between taking science subjects at 'O' grade and entry to science-based occupations or industries (Krol, 1984). Longitudinal analyses of 1985 and 1986 survey data suggest that vocational qualifications gained after school may also have limited value in the (external) labour market, at least for this age group and at a relatively low skill level. This finding tends to be stronger for boys; it may reflect employers' general distrust of broad-based vocational education and training, and the British pattern of training (if at all) for the internal labour market based on selection at 16 (Raffe, 1988, and chapter 8 in this volume).

The third factor is age. Other things being equal, boys who leave school at 16 and enter the labour market have a higher probability of employment, several months after leaving school, than those who left at 17 or 18 (Raffe,

1984b; Main, 1985 and 1987b). In practice, of course, other things are not equal: older leavers tend to be considerably better qualified and therefore have lower unemployment rates. The point is rather that boys who stay on at school may need to increase their qualifications very substantially if they are to improve their employment chances. This finding does not apply to girls — at least, the data are less consistent — and probably reflects age restrictions on entry to particular jobs, especially apprenticeships, which mainly recruit boys. The conclusion that staying on may adversely affect boys' employment chances should be qualified in two ways. First, the effect will be exaggerated in the data by any tendency for young people to stay on at school *because* they cannot find jobs. Second, older leavers tend to enter different kinds of jobs and to have higher earnings; benefits from staying-on may accrue over a much longer period than the nine or ten months typically covered by the leavers' survey (Payne, 1987).

The fourth factor is the school leaver's family background. All analyses find an influence on employment, although the precise family variables found to be significant vary between surveys and according to the specification of the model. Thus analyses have variously found an independent influence of parental education (Main, 1985) or of father's social class (Main and Raffe, 1983b; Raffe, 1984b; Main 1987b); most frequently, where relevant data have been available, they have found that young people whose fathers were unemployed were, other things being equal, significantly less likely to find employment themselves (Raffe, 1984b; Main, 1987a; Main and Shelly, 1987; Shelly, 1987; Garner *et al.*, 1987a and 1988).

The fifth and final factor is area. School leavers' chances of (un)employment vary with the all-age unemployment rate in the local labour market (Main and Raffe, 1983b; Raffe, 1984b; Main, 1985 and 1987a; Main and Shelly, 1987; Shelly, 1987; Tomes, 1988). Within local labour markets (more precisely, within cities) differences between areas in the employment chances of school leavers can be explained in terms of their family and educational characteristics (Garner *et al.*, 1987a, 1987b, and 1988, and chapter 6 in this volume).

This list of factors influencing employment is not exhaustive. It is generally limited to factors on which postal surveys can easily collect data. Other factors have been included in some analyses and shown to be significant. Young people who have held part-time jobs while at school have better prospects of subsequent employment, as discussed earlier. Former truants are rather more likely than other school leavers to be unemployed (Main and Raffe, 1983b). The effect of truancy increases over time; former truants are about as likely as otherwise comparable young people to find jobs, but are more likely to leave their first jobs for unemployment (Gray *et al.*, 1983; Raffe, 1983c).

A further factor which influences young people's employment prospects is their access to the informal networks through which they may come to hear about available jobs and perhaps receive more direct help in getting them. Analyses of the 1983 survey data suggested that about as many young people found jobs through 'informal' channels as through 'formal' channels such as the careers service or job centre. Informal channels were used to recruit to all kinds of occupations, but were used most often for farm, sales and manual jobs. Young people recruited informally appeared to need fewer qualifications than those recruited to the same occupations through more formal channels. The corollary is that young people who had neither qualifications nor access to informal networks were particularly disadvantaged in the labour market. A comparison of data from the 1977 and 1983 surveys suggests that informal methods of recruitment became more important as employment levels fell, but only because YOP provided additional channels through which such recruitment could take place (Raffe, 1985a).

The importance of informal networks may partly explain the influence of family background on school leavers' employment chances, and in particular the correlation between parents' and children's unemployment. Unemployed parents are unlikely to be able to help their children gain access to job-finding networks. It may also help to explain why school leavers who have had part-time jobs at school are more successful in looking for full-time jobs later on.

Most of the analyses reviewed in this section used multivariate techniques to test the separate effects of different predictor variables on young people's employment. They are, in effect, sophisticated ways of reporting associations, but are not proof of causation. This is a particularly important consideration with respect to the role of qualifications in occupational selection. The strong correlation between qualifications and employment, even after controlling for such factors as age, social background and the local unemployment rate, may still partly be attributable to other variables not included in the analysis. For example Jones (1985) has suggested that the association between qualifications and occupation can partly be explained by the different aspirations, expectations and job-seeking behaviours of the better qualified. (On the other hand these aspirations, expectations and behaviours may largely anticipate the opportunities avail able to young people with different levels of qualifications.) There is an apparent conflict of evidence between surveys of employers, which tend to stress the relative importance of non-academic criteria in selection (for example, Hunt and Small, 1981; Ashton *et al.*, 1982) and surveys of young people (including several English studies, such as Roberts *et al.*, 1981 and 1987, and the Youth Cohort Study — see chapter 1 in this volume) which consistently find large and apparently independent 'effects' of qualifications on employment. There is also evidence from the Scottish surveys that young people themselves feel that qualifications are not the most important selection criterion (Gray *et al.*, 1983; Raffe, 1984b). However, these apparent discrepancies can be attributed to differences of method and to the nature of the recruitment process and the way that qualifications are used within it. The recruitment process tends to display the following features: qualifications tend to be used flexibly as selection criteria, rather than as fixed requirements; they are used as proxy measures of ability and other personal and social qualities; they are used most in the earlier screening processes of selection; perceptions of an individual's qualifications are consistent across employers whereas judgments of non-academic qualities are not; young people applying for jobs must concentrate on self-presentation and attitudes because their qualifications are, in the short term, fixed. Once these points are recognized it becomes possible to reconcile the analyses of 'objective' data which suggest that qualifications are important, with the perceptions of participants in the process who appear to underestimate their importance (Raffe, 1983b and 1984b).

THE IMPACT OF YOP AND YTS ON EMPLOYMENT CHANCES

Another potential influence on employment chances, not discussed in the previous section, is participation on YOP or YTS. Several analyses of the survey data have sought to measure the effectiveness of YOP in helping young people find jobs. They have compared young people on YOP at a given time point with those who were currently unemployed; these two groups' relative employment rates at a later time point are an indication of the contribution of YOP. The analyses control for different characteristics of YOP trainees and others, but their interpretation is nevertheless problematic, partly because many of the unemployed might expect to enter YOP sooner or later if they did not first find jobs. The analyses have been conducted in respect of the first, third and fifth (final) years of YOP. Being on YOP rather than unemployed in October 1978 improved a less qualified school leaver's chances of employment the following spring by 6 percentage points for males and 14 percentage points for females (Main and Raffe, 1983b). An analysis for 1980/81, not restricted to the less qualified, shows a YOP effect of 4 percentage points for males and 8 for females (Main, 1985). In 1982/83 the estimated effect was 5 percentage points for males and 18 for females (Main, 1987a). The relative consistency of the YOP effect is the more remarkable in view of the substantial decline in employment rates among young people leaving YOP over this period. It suggests that this decline was entirely due to the worsening labour market to which YOP trainees returned, and not to any diminution of the 'effectiveness' of YOP. Of course the analyses only estimate the effect of YOP on the employment prospects of individual trainees; they do not necessarily indicate a positive effect on the total level of employment. YOP may have done little more than reshuffle the employment chances of young people, and its effect on employment totals, allowing for substitution and displacement, may well have been negative (Raffe, 1983d and 1984d).

Main and Shelly have investigated the effects of YTS on employment and other outcomes, following a similar approach to the studies of YOP described above. Their conclusions are summarized in chapter 7 in this volume.

Another issue explored in several studies is whether YOP or YTS have influenced the distribution of employment, as distinct from its level. The 1979 and 1981 surveys produced tentative evidence that the correlation between qualifications and subsequent employment among YOP trainees was weaker than would have been expected among other young people (Raffe, 1981 and 1984c). It appeared that employers using YOP schemes to screen potential employees had less need of indirect educational measures of qualities that could be observed on the job. Main and Shelly (1987) suggest that the determinants of employment may differ between former YTS trainees and other young people, but that the differences are likely to be small. In assessing any redistributive effect of YTS it must be remembered that the scheme is internally heterogeneous. YTS schemes vary widely in the probability that they will lead to employment, and in the type of employment to which they will lead, and this informal hierarchy is correlated with qualifications at 16, on entry to YTS (Raffe, 1987b). In other words, many of the key selection decisions are still taken at 16. One aspect of differentiation on which YTS has had little discernible impact is gender: the differences between males' and females' occupations have been much the same within YTS as in ordinary employment (Raffe, 1987c and 1987d).

RECURRING THEMES: CHANGES AND CONTINUITIES

Not all the work reviewed in this chapter has a specifically historical focus. Nevertheless much of it contributes to an overview of changes that have taken place since the early or mid-1970s. In particular, it helps us to distinguish the elements of change over this period from the elements of continuity. The changes it identifies include rising qualification levels of school leavers, lower rates of employment, especially among early leavers;

new patterns of mobility and job-changing in the labour market; the introduction of the Youth Training Scheme as an intermediate stage between school and employment for a majority of early leavers; developments in vocational education. A further change has occurred in the occupational and industrial structure of youth employment, but in the short term at least these qualitative changes have been dwarfed by the quantitative ones. An important implication of these changes is that attempts to learn from research into the youth labour market and training must be sensitive to the historical context. For example it may be misleading to generalize from the experience of youth unemployment in the 1970s to that in the 1980s.

The CES work has repeatedly drawn attention to the role of unemployment as a major cause or catalyst of the changes which have taken place. This is not to deny the importance of other longer-term changes in the labour market, in education and training, and in other aspects of society. But even their influence was often shaped, mediated or accelerated by the rise in unemployment, particularly in the early 1980s. A corollary is that at least some of the changes that have taken place might be reversed — or might be under pressure — if unemployment fell substantially. A further corollary is that there have been major elements of continuity which the surveys have sometimes helped to illuminate.

For example, the relationship between the youth and adult labour markets has, in many respects, changed very little. The survey data challenge the view that the recent rise in youth unemployment results mainly from a structural shift in this relationship. The fact that youth unemployment rose faster than adult unemployment is a reflection of this relationship, not of a change in it. Youth unemployment rates have always been more volatile than adult rates, and may be expected to fall faster as general employment levels recover. YTS may have some lasting impact on the relationship between youth and adult labour markets, but here again the surveys have demonstrated the persistence of labour-market structures and the difficulty of YTS in breaking out of the role it inherited from the Youth Opportunities Programme. Several analyses of survey data on the early YTS have drawn attention to the dominance of its unemployment-based functions, inherited from YOP, and to the constraints this has placed on its training function.

A second element of continuity is in the education system itself, whose structures, values and hierarchies are resistant to rapid change. This is illustrated by chapter 8, which reminds us that established institutional patterns are not easily changed even by radical policies such as the SED's Action Plan.

Third, the basic orientations of young people have changed relatively little. They continue to be committed to the employment ethic, to have generally realistic expectations and to have a broadly vocational and instrumental approach to choices in education and training.

Fourth, patterns of differentiation within education and the labour market remain strong. Far from being a homogeneous social group, 'youth' finds its experiences and chances differentiated by gender, geography, social and ethnic background and educational attainment.

This leads us to a final aspect of continuity which, in one form or another, has provided a theme of much CES work. This is the close link between differentiation in education and in the labour market. To adopt a different terminology, the selective function of education and of related structures such as youth training remains strong; this may be significant for the labour market, but the implications for education and training are even more powerful.

RECURRING THEMES: DIFFERENTIATION IN EDUCATION AND THE LABOUR MARKET

Several analyses of the survey data have examined the micro-level effects of education on labour-market outcomes. They have estimated the influence of qualifications, curriculum and other 'educational' experiences such as YOP or YTS on the subsequent employment, occupation or income of individuals. Typically this research has found a strong and apparently direct effect associated with education, and particularly of qualifications.

Further analysis of this effect suggests that it largely reflects, not the direct contribution of education to individuals' productivity and hence employability, but rather employers' solutions to the problem of information. Employers recruiting young people tend not to value specific vocational skills very highly; they tend to want people with ability and social and personal qualities which make them potentially good workers able to learn and develop on the job. These qualities are seen as closely related; there is, in effect, a single main dimension underlying most employers' preferences. The problem of information is simply that employers lack reliable measures of individual applicants' position on this dimension. Qualifications — and the position in the academic hierarchy which they tend to reflect — are used as proxy measures. Hence the preference for high-status over 'useful' subjects. Hence the flexibility of employers' preferences, and their willingness to trade up in a slack market. Hence the reduced importance of qualifications in situations (YOP, informal recruitment channels) where employers have alternative sources of information.

This account is consistent with Thurow's (1975) model of job-competition. In this model skills, and productivity, exist only in relation to jobs, and workers acquire most of their skills on the job. Wages are therefore also determined in relation to jobs, rather than through the interaction of supply and demand. The main task of the labour market is to match jobs requiring greater or lesser amounts of on-the-job training; workers are notionally ranked in a labour queue according to their trainability, as denoted by qualifications and other available indicators such as age and experience. Employers fill each job from as near to the front of the queue as possible; when jobs become scarce those towards the back of the queue remain unemployed.

Work based on the surveys has given qualified support to the model of job-competition, with respect to wages (Main, 1987b) and to the distribution of employment across qualification groups, over time and over labour markets (Raffe, 1984a; Shelly, 1987 and chapter 4 in this volume; Garner *et al.*, 1987a). There are limits to the model; for example, age and gender define breaks in the concept of a single queue. At the same time the above discussion suggests that analysis of the youth labour market in terms of labour-market segmentation (for example, Ashton *et al.*, 1987) is at best incomplete, since it fails to explain the shifting criteria by which young people are first allocated to segments. More generally, by focusing on micro or individual-level barriers to competition in the labour market, it overlooks the substantial macro or group-level competition that persists. Analyses of the survey data confirm the extent of competition both within the youth labour market and between youth and adult labour markets; segmentation may change the form of the competition rather than its extent.

Several implications follow from the view of the labour market being advocated here. One is that relative attainment matters more than absolute attainment. Improving the qualifications of school leavers will not necessarily ease the present problem whereby well qualified leavers are often in strong demand whereas low-qualified leavers face high unemployment rates. Educational expansion of this kind would merely change the level of qualifications needed to gain a given ranking in the labour queue and thus a given probability of employment. A second implication, if the queue is understood to embrace both adults and young people, is that it is inappropriate to specify a demand function for youth labour which does not take account of the availability of adults who might be ahead of young workers in the queue. Yet this is precisely what influential studies have tried to do (Wells, 1983).[2]

With job-competition the discussion has moved from the micro to the macro. Another theme of CES writing is the extent to which the selective function imposes constraints, or at least forces choices, on the education system (for example, McPherson, 1982; Gray *et al.*, 1983). This argument has been expressed in terms of the distinction between 'content' and 'context'. The success of new initiatives such as YTS, TVEI or the Action Plan depends less on the quality or relevance of their content than on their context, which is defined primarily in terms of their relation to differentiation and selection in education and the labour market (Raffe, 1984e, 1985b, 1987b, 1987d and

1988). The different tactics employers adopt in response to the problem of information, discussed above, result in distorted market signals being transmitted to young people making choices in education or training (Raffe, 1987b). They are distorted in the sense that they will not encourage decisions that are optimal either on educational or on labour-market criteria. The policy implication is that market forces alone will not secure the 'right' mix of types of education and training, and that the deficiencies are on the demand side as well as on the supply side. The more theoretical implication is that whereas at a micro level education is a major determinant of individuals' labour-market outcomes, at a macro level the labour market exerts a powerful, albeit unintended and distorting, influence on education. A further implication is that education is more affected by changes in the labour market than by changes in the labour process, since the demands of the latter are not effectively signalled in the market.

This dual perspective, with education influencing labour-market outcomes at the micro level, but constrained or shaped by the labour market at the macro level, has been a distinctive feature of much work on the Scottish surveys, and is likely to inform future work as well. On the one hand analysis of the surveys can reveal the implications of young people's experiences in compulsory schooling and the routes they follow thereafter for their subsequent prospects in the labour market and elsewhere. As the longitudinal series develops, this work is likely to look more closely at movements after entry to employment, at the role of age and experience in the labour market, and at the connection between young people's routes and their interests, activities and relationships outside education and the labour market.

But the surveys can do more than reveal the micro-level consequences of education and training routes for individual life-chances. They can also reveal the influences of this labour-market 'context' on education, by examining the effects of variations in context over time and across local labour markets. They can monitor the development of initiatives such as YTS, TVEI and the Action Plan, and record changes in their status and their position in relation to educational and labour-market differentiation. More speculatively, they can point to labour-market explanations for some of the chronic weaknesses of Scottish (and British) education, such as its academic bias, its low level of post-compulsory participation and the small scale of full-time technical education.

ACKNOWLEDGEMENTS

I am grateful to Peter Cuttance, Andy Furlong and Andrew McPherson for helpful comments on earlier drafts of this chapter.

NOTES

1   Based on Fife, Lothian, Strathclyde and Tayside. Trends in the composition of
     employment since 1983 are harder to interpret, since occupations and industries
     vary in the extent to which jobs have been 'taken over' by YTS.
2   Specifically, attempts to derive a youth employment function have not allowed
     for the adult unemployment rate as an influence. When adult labour — ahead of
     young people in the labour queue — is readily available, many employers
     switch recruitment away from young people. If it becomes scarce again,
     employers will switch back.

REFERENCES

ASHTON, D., MAGUIRE, M. and GARLAND, V. (1982) *Youth in the Labour Market*,
    Research Paper No.34, London, Department of Employment.
ASHTON, D., MAGUIRE, M. and SPILSBURY, M. (1987) 'Labour market segmentation
    and the structure of the youth labour market' in BROWN, P. and ASHTON, D.
    (Eds) *Education, Unemployment and Labour Markets*, Lewes, Falmer Press.
BRYANT, I., BURNHILL, P., LAMB, J. and RAFFE, D. (1985) *Report on the 1984 Pilot of
    the Scottish Young Peoples Survey*, Edinburgh, University of Edinburgh, Centre
    for Educational Sociology.
BURNHILL, P. (1984a) 'The ragged edge of compulsory schooling' in RAFFE, D.,
    (Ed.)*Fourteen to Eighteen*, Aberdeen, Aberdeen University Press.
BURNHILL, P. (1984b) 'Young people's reflections on staying or leaving' in RAFFE, D.,
    (Ed.) *Fourteen to Eighteen*, Aberdeen, Aberdeen University Press.
BURNHILL, P. and MCPHERSON, A. (1983) 'The Scottish university and undergraduate
    expectations', *Universities Quarterly*, 37, 3, pp. 253–70.
BURNHILL, P. and MCPHERSON, A. (1984) 'Careers and gender: The expectations of
    able Scottish school leavers in 1971 and 1981' in ACKER, S. and WARREN PIPER,
    D., (Eds) *Is Higher Education Fair to Women?* London, Society for Research in
    Higher Education.
DIXON, F. (1984) *Staying-On Rates and Pupil Projection Methods*, unpublished MSc
    dissertation and Report for Scottish Education Department, Department of
    Statistics, University of Edinburgh.
FRASER, N. and SINFIELD, A. (1987) 'The Scottish labour force in recession' in
    MCCRONE, D. (Ed.) *Scottish Government Yearbook 1987*, Edinburgh, University
    of Edinburgh, Unit for the Study of Government in Scotland.
FREEMAN, J. and STAITE, R. (1978) 'Basic skills and pupil motivation', *Collaborative
    Research Newsletter*, 3, pp. 3–10.
GARNER, C., MAIN, B. and RAFFE, D. (1987a) *Local Variations in School-Leaver
    Employment and Unemployment within Large Cities*, Edinburgh, University of
    Edinburgh, Centre for Educational Sociology.
GARNER, C., MAIN, B. and RAFFE, D. (1987b) 'Local variations in school-leaver
    unemployment within a large city', *British Journal of Education and Work*, 1, 2,
    pp. 67–78.

GARNER, C., MAIN, B. and RAFFE, D. (1988) 'The distribution of school-leaver unemployment within Scottish cities', *Urban Studies*, 25, 2.

GOW, L. and McPHERSON, A. (Eds) (1980) *Tell Them From Me: Scottish School Leavers Write about School and Life Afterwards*, Aberdeen, Aberdeen University Press.

GRAY, J. (1980) 'Guidance in Scottish secondary schools: A client evaluation', *British Journal of Guidance and Counselling*, 8, 2, pp. 129–45.

GRAY, J., McPHERSON, A. and RAFFE, D. (1983) *Reconstructions of Secondary Education: Theory, Myth and Practice since the War*, Henley, Routledge and Kegan Paul.

HUGHES, J. (Ed.) (1984) *The Best Years? Reflections of School Leavers in the 1980s*, Aberdeen, Aberdeen University Press.

HUNT, J. and SMALL, P. (1981) *Employing Young People: A Study of Employers' Attitudes, Policies and Practice*, Edinburgh, Scottish Council for Research in Education.

JONES, P. (1985) 'Qualifications and labour-market outcomes among 16-year-old school-leavers', *British Journal of Guidance and Counselling*, 13, 3, pp. 275–91.

KELLY, A. (1981) 'Choosing or channelling?' in KELLY, A. (Ed.) *The Missing Half*, Manchester, Manchester University Press.

KROL, W. (1984) *An Investigation of the Influence of Presentations for SCE O-grades in Science Subjects on the Employment of Sixteen Year Old School Leavers*, unpublished MEd dissertation, University of Edinburgh.

MACLEOD, A., MAIN, B. and RAFFE, D. (1983) 'The labour market for young people in Scotland', *Employment Gazette*, 91, 3, pp. 96–101.

McPHERSON, A. (1982) 'The pupils' voice' in SLATER, C. (Ed.) *In and Out of School: Options for 16–19 Year Olds*, Glasgow, Scottish Television.

McPHERSON, A. and WILLMS, D. (1987) 'Equalisation and improvement: Some effects of comprehensive reorganisation in Scotland', *Sociology*, 21, 4, pp. 509–39.

MAIN, B. (1985) 'School-leaver unemployment and the Youth Opportunities Programme in Scotland', *Oxford Economic Papers*, 37, pp. 426–47.

MAIN, B. (1987a) 'Earnings, expected earnings, and unemployment among school leavers', in JUNANKAR, P. (Ed.) *From School to Unemployment: The Labour Market for Young People*, Basingstoke, Macmillan.

MAIN, B. (1987b) 'The wage expectations and unemployment experience of school leavers', *Scottish Journal of Political Economy*, 34, 4, pp. 349–67.

MAIN, B. (1988) 'The youth labour market: Intelligence, analysis and policy' in DAVIDSON, R. and WHYTE, P. (Eds) *Information and Government*, Edinburgh, Edinburgh University Press.

MAIN, B. (forthcoming) 'The reporting of gross and net earnings in a postal survey: Evidence from the Scottish School Leavers Survey', *Quality and Quantity*.

MAIN, B. and RAFFE, D. (1983a) 'The industrial destinations of Scottish school leavers, 1977–1981', *Fraser of Allander Institute Quarterly Economic Commentary*, 8, 3, pp. 37–49.

MAIN, B. and RAFFE, D. (1983b) 'The determinants of employment and unemployment among school leavers: Evidence from the 1979 survey of Scottish school leavers', *Scottish Journal of Political Economy*, 30, 1, pp. 1–17.

MAIN, B. and RAFFE, D. (1983c) 'The transition from school to work in 1980/81: A dynamic account', *British Educational Research Journal*, 9, 1, pp. 57–70.

MAIN, B. and SHELLY, M. (1987) 'The effectiveness of YTS as a manpower policy', Edinburgh, University of Edinburgh, Centre for Educational Sociology, (mimeo).

MAIN, B. and SHELLY, M. (forthcoming) 'School leavers and the search for employment', *Oxford Economic Papers*.

PAYNE, J. (1987) 'Unemployment, apprenticeships and training — does it pay to stay on at school?', *British Journal of Sociology of Education*, 8.

RAFFE, D. (1978) 'The recruitment of Scottish school leavers to engineering degree courses', paper prepared for Committee of Inquiry into the Engineering Profession (Finniston Committee), University of Edinburgh, Centre for Educational Sociology (mimeo).

RAFFE, D. (1980) 'Link courses in Scotland', *Educational Research*, 22, 3, pp. 203–11.

RAFFE, D. (1981) 'Special programmes in Scotland: The first year of YOP', *Policy and Politics*, 9, 4, pp. 471–87.

RAFFE, D. (1983a) 'Some recent trends in youth unemployment in Scotland', *Scottish Educational Review*, 15, 1, pp. 16–27.

RAFFE, D. (1983b) 'Education and unemployment: Does YOP make a difference (and will YTS)?' in GLEESON, D. (Ed.) *Youth Training and the Search for Work*, Henley, Routledge and Kegan Paul.

RAFFE, D. (1983c) 'Employment instability among less qualified young workers', *British Journal of Guidance and Counselling*, 11, 1, pp. 21–34.

RAFFE, D. (1983d) 'Can there be an effective youth unemployment policy?' in FIDDY, R. (Ed.) *In Place of Work: Policy and Provision for the Young Unemployed*, Lewes, Falmer Press.

RAFFE, D. (1984a) 'The transition from school to work and the recession: Evidence from the Scottish School Leavers Surveys, 1977–1983', *British Journal of Sociology of Education*, 5, 3, pp. 247–65.

RAFFE, D. (1984b) 'School attainment and the labour market' in RAFFE, D. (Ed.) *Fourteen to Eighteen*, Aberdeen, Aberdeen University Press.

RAFFE, D. (1984c) 'YOP and the future of YTS' in RAFFE, D. (Ed.) *Fourteen to Eighteen*, Aberdeen, Aberdeen University Press.

RAFFE, D. (1984d) 'Youth unemployment and the MSC: 1977–1983' in McCRONE, D. (Ed.) *Scottish Government Yearbook 1984*, Edinburgh, University of Edinburgh, Unit for the Study of Government in Scotland.

RAFFE, D. (1984e) 'The content and context of educational reform' in RAFFE, D. (Ed.) *Fourteen to Eighteen*, Aberdeen, Aberdeen University Press.

RAFFE, D. (1985a) 'Degrees of informality: Methods of job placement among Scottish school leavers', *British Journal of Guidance and Counselling*, 13, 3, pp. 292–307.

RAFFE, D. (1985b) 'Education and training initiatives for 14–18s: Content and Context', in WATTS, A.G. (Ed.) *Education and Training 14–18: Policy and Practice*, Cambridge, CRAC/Hobsons.

RAFFE, D. (1986a) 'Change and continuity in the youth labour market: A critical review of structural explanations of youth unemployment' in ALLEN, S., WATON, A., PURCELL, K. and WOOD, S. (Eds) *The Experience of Unemployment*, Basingstoke, Macmillan.

RAFFE, D. (1986b) 'Unemployment and school motivation: The case of truancy', *Educational Review*, 38, 1, pp. 11–19.

RAFFE, D. (1986c) 'Unemployment among 16 and 17-year-old school leavers in Scotland', *Employment Gazette*, 94, 6, pp. 274–80.

RAFFE, D. (1987a) 'Youth unemployment in the UK 1979–1984' in BROWN, P. and ASHTON, D. (Eds) *Education, Unemployment and Labour Markets*, Lewes, Falmer Press.

RAFFE, D. (1987b) 'The context of the Youth Training Scheme: An analysis of its strategy and development', *British Journal of Education and Work*, 1, 1, pp. 1–31.

RAFFE, D. (1987c) 'YTS and Scottish school leavers' in HARRISON, A. and GRETTON, J. (Eds) *Education and Training UK 1987*, Newbury, Policy Journals.

RAFFE, D. (1987d) 'Small expectations: The first year of the YTS' in JUNANKAR, P. (Ed.) *From School to Unemployment: The Labour Market for Young People*, Basingstoke, Macmillan.

RAFFE, D. (1988) 'The status of vocational education and training: 2: The case of YTS', paper presented to ESRC/DE workshop on Research on Employment and Unemployment, Edinburgh, University of Edinburgh, Centre for Educational Sociology (mimeo).

RAFFE, D. and SMITH, P. (1987) 'Young people's attitudes to YTS: The first two years', *British Educational Research Journal*, 13, 3, pp. 241–60.

RAFFE, D. and TOMES, N. (1986) 'The experience of Scotvec modules in 1984–86: A preliminary analysis of the Scottish Young Peoples Survey', Edinburgh, University of Edinburgh, Centre for Educational Sociology, (mimeo).

ROBERTS, K., DENCH, S. and RICHARDSON, D. (1987) *The Changing Structure of Youth Labour Markets*, Research Paper No. 59, London, Department of Employment.

ROBERTS, K., DUGGAN, J. and NOBLE, M. (1981) *Unregistered Youth Unemployment and Outreach Careers Work: Final Report Part One: Non-Registration*, Research Paper No. 31, London, Department of Employment.

SCOTTISH EDUCATION DEPARTMENT (1983) *16–18s in Scotland: An Action Plan*, Edinburgh, SED.

SHELLY, M. (1987) *Scottish Young People's Post-School Destinations; 1977–1983*, unpublished PhD thesis, University of Edinburgh

THUROW, L. (1975) *Generating Inequality*, New York, Basic Books.

TOMES, N. (1988) 'Regional participation in the Youth Training Scheme', *Scottish Economic Bulletin*.

WELLS, W. (1983) *The Relative Pay and Employment of Young People*, Research Paper No. 42, London, Department of Employment.

WILLMS, J.D. and KERR, P. (1987) 'Changes in sex differences in Scottish examination results since 1975', University of Edinburgh, Centre for Educational Sociology (published in *Journal of Early Adolescence*, June 1987, with an authors' correction in a subsequent issue).

WORKING PARTY OF PRINCIPAL CAREERS OFFICERS (1978) 'Unemployed school leavers: The Holland challenge to education and the careers service', *Collaborative Research Newsletter*, 3, pp. 32–42.

Chapter 3:

Social Change, School Attainment and Entry to Higher Education 1976–1986

Peter Burnhill, Catherine Garner and Andrew McPherson

In this chapter we focus on two outcomes of schooling, namely the entry of young people to higher education, and their acquisition of the necessary qualifications. In particular, we examine what has been happening to these outcomes since the mid-1970s when the Scottish School Leavers Survey (SSLS) series assumed its present form. The series enables us to identify the net effects on qualifications and entry of a number of social changes that have occurred in the past decade, and even to disentangle some of these effects. The series also provides one basis for judging the changing quality of educational provision. It allows us to compare current levels of attainment and opportunity with the levels of earlier years. The three broad questions we ask in this chapter are whether opportunities for higher education have changed, whether any such changes have kept pace with the flow of qualified leavers from the schools, and whether this flow has in turn been affected by recent social changes. We also discuss some of the implications of our answers for current policies for the secondary and tertiary sectors.

We use the term 'social change' loosely here to refer to four main areas: to change in the size of pupil cohorts; to compositional changes in pupils' family backgrounds; to reforms of the school system since 1965; and to changes in the structure of post-school opportunity since the mid-1970s. This usage begs a number of questions, in particular about the ways in which these and other pertinent changes should be conceptualized, and about the ways they have acted on each other. In this chapter, however, we are less concerned with these wider questions of validity and causation than we are with establishing an empirical account of how the levels and associations of some important social indicators have varied since the mid-1970s.

The change in the size of birth cohorts stems partly from the birth cycles of earlier generations, and partly from more recent changes in patterns of marriage and reproduction. It began to affect the number of 17-year-olds only towards the end of our period. In Scotland, this number remained around the 90,000 mark from 1976–1985, peaking in 1982. But it will fall by 38 per cent of its 1982 level to a trough of just below 60,000 by 1995. The phasing of the fall elsewhere in Britain is similar, though its magnitude is smaller than in Scotland.[1] For present purposes, the significance of the fall relates mainly to current policies that anticipate the demographic decline, especially policies for the funding and control of higher education.

As well as affecting the size of pupil cohorts, the changing patterns of marriage and reproduction have also affected the social composition of the pupil body. But they are not the only factors that have led to compositional change. A further factor has been a change in the types of employment available to parents and pursued by them. Another has been the educational changes of the 1940s and 1950s that are currently feeding through in the form of a rising level of parental education. Overall these compositional shifts imply a major change in the educability of the young.

Recent changes in the school system constitute the third area of change. What we have in mind here are not the school reforms introduced by the Government earlier in the 1980s; their impact on school leavers was first to become apparent only in the mid-1980s. We are thinking rather of the continuing effects of an earlier phase of reform that began in the 1960s. This phase includes comprehensive reorganization, initiated in 1965 and fully implemented only in the mid-1970s. It also includes the raising of the school-leaving age (ROSLA) to 16 years, decided in 1964 and finally implemented in 1973. In the second half of the 1970s the schools were still adjusting to these changes, though the implementation of the major national reforms of curriculum and examinations that were intended to facilitate this adjustment began to reach the classroom only in the mid-1980s. Even so, the reforms of the 1960s and 1970s were having discernible effects from the late 1970s onwards. Standards of school examination attainment rose, especially among low-attainers, and among females and socially disadvantaged pupils. Some of this change is directly attributable to comprehensive reorganization and ROSLA (McPherson and Willms, 1987). We do not incorporate separate measures of these reforms into the design of the research reported in this chapter. But the general context of school reform must be borne in mind in any assessment of schooling outcomes over the past decade.

Our fourth area of change concerns the structure of opportunity available to school leavers consequent upon recession. It took several forms. Unemployment among school leavers rose steadily from 1974 onwards, and increased sharply in 1981. Employers 'traded up' in the qualifications they asked of young school leavers (see chapter 4 in this volume), and a succession of government schemes was provided. These culminated in the Youth

Training Scheme (YTS), introduced in 1983 and extended from one year to two years in 1986 (chapter 7 in this volume). In purely numeric terms, the change in opportunity structure had a greater effect on school leavers who held few or no examination qualifications. But recession also had an impact on the opportunities available to better qualified school leavers. Allied to the prospect of demographic decline, it led the government to impose severe financial constraints on university spending from 1981 onwards, thus requiring the universities to cut back on the places they would otherwise have offered to new entrants.

Subsequently, what had begun as a public-spending expedient then developed into an emergent government policy for the wholesale restructuring of higher education, with more emphasis on applied courses, on science and technology, and on public-sector institutions. Demographic decline appeared to offer considerable scope for such restructuring by means of the selective application of contraction. What was and is disputed, however, was the extent of the prospective decline. It was incontestable that the size of the age group of 17-year-olds would fall by 38 per cent in Scotland by the mid-1990s. But official projections of entry to higher education also recognized that the social composition of leaver groups was changing too, and that these changes alone could well raise future rates of entry (DES, 1984a and 1984b, chapter 6; SED, 1983 and 1985a). The official projections drew attention in particular to changes in the occupational structure that were increasing the relative size of the groups of occupations that constituted social classes I and II of the Registrar General's scheme. Rates of entry to higher education from these two social classes were historically high. If these rates maintained their historic levels as the two social classes themselves expanded, then the fall in the rate of entry to higher education might be considerably less than 38 per cent. An official projection in 1985 estimated that by 1995–96 the number of under-21 entrants to full-time higher education in Scotland would fall by 20–28 per cent of the figures for 1983–84 (SED, 1985b, p. 140). Our own evidence on social change leads us to conclude, however, that there is no reason why the fall in the numbers qualifying should not be substantially lower than the falls currently projected for Scotland and for Britain (see DES, 1986, table 4).

Two further introductory comments should be made. First, although the outcomes we analyze concern only terminal school qualifications and entry to higher education, the results of the analysis have wider implications for education from about the age of 14 onwards. This is because of the interdependence of the secondary and tertiary sectors whereby changes in the one often affect the other. Second, virtually all of the foregoing considerations apply throughout the United Kingdom. Their particular implications for Scotland, therefore, are mainly a function of the distinctive features of the

Scottish education system and its governance. The Secretary of State for Scotland, working through the Scottish Education Department (SED), has ultimate responsibility for most of Scottish education. But the Scottish universities are largely the responsibility of the Secretary of State for Education in England and Wales who works through the Department of Education and Science (DES). Because of the interdependence of the secondary and tertiary sectors, this arrangement complicates the problem of control. In our concluding discussion we comment on some of the ways in which current social changes are likely to activate this problem in all parts of the UK.

The rest of the chapter falls into five parts. First we describe trends in school leavers' qualifications and family backgrounds, and changes in the association between them. Second, we statistically model the effects of family background on qualifications. Third, we model the effects of family background and qualifications on entry to higher education. We then summarize our results and conclude with a discussion of some of their implications. All of the main analyses pay attention to stability and change over the period 1976 to 1984. Where results for 1986 are available we use these too, but their status is provisional. This is because our survey data for 1986 (collected in 1987) had not been fully validated at the time of writing (January 1988). In order to reduce bias in the estimates arising from survey non-response, all estimates have been weighted in the light of known population parameters of sex and school attainment. A fuller description of the data is available in appendixes 1 and 2. Leavers from schools in both the private and the public sectors are included in all analyses. Most of the analyses of trends are restricted to four regions in central Scotland that contain about 75 per cent of the Scottish population (see appendix 1). We are confident, however, that, with some allowance for the urban 'bias' of these four regions, all of our main empirical conclusions can be generalized to Scotland as a whole. We also think that our main conclusions on the changes in pupils' family circumstances and on the associated trends in school attainment can be generalized to the whole of the United Kingdom with few, if any, modifications.

TRENDS IN SCHOOL QUALIFICATIONS AND FAMILY BACKGROUND

The vast majority of entrants to higher education from Scottish schools fulfil entry requirements that are framed in terms of the Higher grade of the Scottish Certificate of Education (SCE 'H' grade, or 'Highers'). Accordingly, it is appropriate to base our discussion of qualifications on Highers.[2] The proportions of school leavers passing Highers rose steadily in the 1960s to a peak of 29 per cent in the early 1970s. It then fell by 2 or 3 percentage points, and remained at that lower level until the end of the 1970s when it started to rise again (SED, 1983 and 1986a). There has been a similar movement, though naturally at a lower level, in the percentages passing three or more Highers (*ibid.*; SED, 1985b, p. 142). This level of attainment is commonly taken as a proxy for qualification for entry to higher education, where 'higher education' is understood as all courses at an 'advanced' level (see appendix 3). We use the term 'qualify' below simply to denote this level of school attainment i.e., three or more Highers passes.[3] It is usually regarded as the functional equivalent of two or more passes in the GCE 'A' level.

The beginning of the SSLS series in 1976 coincided with a period of stable Highers attainment. This is reflected in table 3.1 which shows trends in attainment 1976–86. The percentages qualifying (i.e., with at least three Highers) rose from 17 per cent in 1976 to 18 per cent in 1978 and 1980, and then to 21 per cent in 1982 and 1984, remaining at that level in 1986 (provisional). These rises might seem small when expressed, as they are here, on the base of all school leavers. But their size is a function of the fact that the Higher is a qualification that is gained only by a minority of leavers. When expressed on the base of the percentage of leavers who attained three or more Highers in 1976 (i.e., on base 17), the rise constitutes an increase of around a quarter. From the point of view of those selectors in higher education and the labour market who select *among* applicants with Highers (or their functional equivalents), an increase of a quarter over an eight-year period is of considerable significance, especially when it relates to school populations that were at or near their demographic peak.

The rise in attainment has been steeper for females than for males. In 1976 similar percentages of males and females attained at least one Higher, and attained at least three Highers. But, by 1980, the females were moving ahead, and there they have since stayed.

Associated with the rise in attainment are two major compositional changes. The first concerns the education of the school leavers' parents. Table 3.2 is divided into two parts. Part (a) shows the trend in the percentages of leavers having parents who were schooled to various ages. The percentage from homes where there was only a minimum level of schooling fell from 69 per cent in 1976 to 57 per cent in 1984, and to 49 per cent in 1986. Part of this fall may be attributable to the rise of 6 percentage points (from 12 to 18 per cent) in missing information.[4] But much of the fall is to be explained by the level 'one or both parents to 16 years', where the percentage of leavers rose from 9 to 17 per cent, and then to 19 per cent in 1986. In the interpretation of all of the compositional changes discussed in this chapter it must be remembered that the SSLS series samples adults through their pupil

Table 3.1:   SCE awards by sex and year: Four regions only (weighted percentages)[1]

	1976	1978	1980	1982	1984	1986[2]
Males						
6+ Highers passes	4	3	3	3	4	4
5 Highers passes	6	6	6	7	7	6
4 Highers passes	4	5	5	5	5	5
3 Highers passes	4	4	4	4	5	4
1 or 2 Highers passes	9	8	8	10	9	10
'O' grades (A–C), no Higher	29	32	32	33	33	34
Other and none	45	42	42	38	38	37
Total	101	100	100	100	101	100
3+ Highers passes	18	18	18	20	20	20
Females						
6+ Highers passes	3	3	3	4	4	5
5 Highers passes	5	5	5	6	6	6
4 Highers passes	5	5	6	7	6	6
3 Highers passes	5	5	5	6	6	6
1 or 2 Highers passes	10	10	10	13	13	14
'O' grades (A–C), no Higher	29	31	31	31	31	32
Other and none	44	42	40	34	34	31
Total	101	101	100	101	100	100
3+ Highers passes	17	17	19	22	22	23
All						
6+ Highers passes	3	3	3	3	4	4
5 Highers passes	5	5	6	7	7	6
4 Highers passes	5	5	5	6	5	5
3 Highers passes	4	5	4	5	5	5
1 or 2 Highers passes	9	9	9	11	11	12
'O' grades (A–C), no Higher	29	31	31	32	32	33
Other and none	45	42	41	36	36	34
Total	100	100	100	100	100	101
3+ Highers passes	17	18	18	21	21	21
Unweighted n (all)	3850	4607	4203	5152	4683	4361

Notes: 1. Totals in tables 3.1 to 3.3 and in 3.6 are subject to rounding error.
2. Provisional estimates.

Table 3.2: *(a) Level of parents' schooling by year; and (b) percentages of leavers passing at least three Highers by level of parents' schooling and by year: Four regions only (weighted percentages)*

	(a) Percentage of leavers at each level						(b) Percentage in each cell passing 3+ Highers					
	1976	1978	1980	1982	1984	1986[1]	1976	1978	1980	1982	1984	1986[1]
Both parents to 15 years or less	69	65	65	61	57	49	12	11	11	13	13	13
One or both parents to 16 years	9	12	13	17	17	19	28	24	23	24	25	23
One parent to 17 years or more	7	8	8	9	8	9	46	46	46	46	50	55
Both parents to 17 years or more	4	5	4	5	5	5	56	61	60	64	64	62
Missing	12	11	10	8	13	18	11	10	17	20	17	15
Total	101	101	100	100	100	101						
Unweighted n (all)	3850	4607	4203	5152	4683	4361						

Note: 1 Provisional estimates.

offspring. Thus fertility, age and no doubt other factors, will influence the extent to which the SSLS data on parents are representative of the adult population in general. Nevertheless, we can safely say that the rise in the level of parental schooling reflects in part the increase in staying-on rates in the 1940s and 1950s when many of the parents were themselves at school. Because staying-on rates increased even more in the 1960s, we can predict with some confidence that the proportion of school pupils having parents with some experience of post-compulsory schooling will continue to rise.

Will this trend help to raise the attainment of school leavers in the 1990s? It almost certainly will if the rates of filial attainment associated with the various levels of parental schooling maintain their historic levels. Part (b) of table 3.2 presents the evidence to date. It shows by year, and for each level of parental education, the percentages of leavers who qualified with three or more Highers passes. Thus, among leavers from homes where only one parent had been schooled to 17 years or more, the percentage of leavers qualifying was maintained at 46 per cent until 1982, after which it rose to 50 per cent and then to 55 per cent. Where both parents were schooled to 17 years or more, the percentages qualifying were more than maintained, increasing from 56 per cent in 1976 to 64 per cent in 1984. Also apparent in the table is a large and relatively stable differential in filial attainment associated with the various levels of parental schooling. This differential may even have increased slightly, because, at the lowest level of parental schooling ('both parents to 15 years or less'), the percentage of young people who qualified remained obstinately stuck at around 11 to 13 per cent. Similarly, the percentage at the adjacent level ('one or both parents to 16 years') remained stuck at 23 to 25 per cent (the estimate of 28 per cent for 1976 is not significantly higher, in a statistical sense, than the estimates for subsequent years). The fact that the rise in the filial qualification rate has occurred only in families where there was parental experience of education to 17 years or more clearly has wider implications for the role of education in the inter-generational transmission of inequality.

The relative stability of the filial qualification rate for the level 'one or both parents to 16 years' is especially important for the argument about future qualification rates. This is because it is this level that so far has seen most of the increase in the incidence of parental schooling. From the concurrence of this increase with stable filial attainment one might infer that at least some of the general rise in school-leaver attainment recorded in table 3.1 is owing to the general rise in the level of parental schooling. Later in the chapter we ask whether such compositional changes constitute the *whole* explanation for the rising levels of attainment after 1976.

The second compositional change of note relates to social class. The structure of table 3.3 is identical to that of table 3.2, except that the social class of the father replaces parental education in the rows of the table. Social class is based on the father's occupation, and it is classified in terms of the Registrar General's scheme (OPCS, 1970; OPCS, 1980). The Registrar General claims that the scheme measures 'social standing in the community' (Marsh, 1986). Although it is the most commonly used measure of social class, it is widely criticized (*ibid.*). We refer to it as 'RG social class', the prefix of RG being intended to emphasize that we are talking about an indicator, and one of problematic validity.

There is a further difficulty in interpreting the results we get by applying the RG scheme to the data. In part (a) of table 3.3 we see that the residual 'unclassified' category rises in two stages, from 14 per cent in 1976 first to around 17 per cent, and then sharply to 24 per cent. This category contains all respondents for whom it was not possible to derive an RG social-class classification, whether for reasons concerning their personal circumstances or for reasons concerning the way they answered, or failed to answer, the relevant questions. Because it is not always possible to distinguish between these types of reason, the rise in the proportions of the unclassified throws the interpretation of part (a) of table 3.3 into some doubt. This is because we cannot assume that each of the RG social classes I to V has contributed in equal proportion to the rise in the unclassified. We must therefore treat the changing relative sizes of these social classes with some caution.

Two questions first asked of the 1980 leavers throw further light on this problem and on other aspects of economic and familial change that affect the interpretation of RG social class. The proportion of leavers who had lived in the same household as their father during their fourth year at secondary school fell from 84 per cent in 1980 to 78 per cent in 1984, and then to 77 per cent (provisional) in 1986 (table not shown). And over the same period, the percentage of fathers reported to be in full-time employment fell from 76 to 70 per cent, and then to 66 per cent. Both these circumstances will have made it more difficult for the leavers concerned to report their father's occupation (even though information on the father's last occupation was requested if he were currently unemployed). Nevertheless, we think that changes in our own survey practice, including more complete coverage and more stringent coding, were responsible for at least some of the rise in the unclassified category between 1982 and 1984.[5]

Bearing these considerations in mind, we see that table 3.3(a) records a decline in the percentages of leavers from skilled manual (IIIm) and semi-skilled manual (IV) backgrounds. The estimate of the direction of this change can almost certainly be trusted. This is because the magnitude of the decline up to 1984 (11 percentage points, i.e., 56 minus 45) is larger than the increase of 10 percentage points in the size of the unclassified group, part of which

Table 3.3: (a) Parents' RG social class by year; and (b) percentages of leavers passing at least three Highers by RG social class and by year: Four regions only (weighted percentages)

	(a) Percentage of leavers at each level						(b) Percentage in each cell passing 3+ Highers					
	1976	1978	1980	1982	1984	1986[1]	1976	1978	1980	1982	1984	1986[1]
I Professional	5	5	4	4	5	5	56	53	61	60	66	63
II Intermediate	14	16	16	18	16	18	38	39	40	44	44	45
IIIn Skilled non-manual	8	6	7	8	7	7	31	30	28	29	30	35
IIIm Skilled manual	41	38	37	38	33	32	11	10	11	12	14	12
IV Semi-skilled	15	14	15	12	12	11	10	9	9	10	14	13
V Unskilled	4	4	5	3	4	4	6	3	4	6	9	8
Unclassified	14	17	16	17	24	24	6	10	9	15	9	10
Total	101	100	100	100	101	101						
Unweighted n (all)	3850	4607	4203	5152	4683	4361						

Note: 1 Provisional estimates.

increase, we can in any case assume, is contributed by the non-manual groups (I, II and IIIn). Also, other sources have shown that there has been a substantial decline since 1961 in the proportion of employed adult males who work in manual jobs (Rudd, 1987a, table VII).

Another trend that we might expect on the basis of known changes in the occupational structure is an increase in the size of the intermediate RG social class (II) which consists of managers and employers. Between 1961 and 1981, the percentage of British men aged 35 to 59 in RG social class II increased from 16 to 25 per cent (*ibid.*). Table 3.3(a) does show an increase, though it is somewhat smaller, and at a lower level, than the figures for British males. There is a rise from 14 per cent in 1976, to 16 per cent in 1984 and 18 per cent in 1986.

Part (b) of table 3.3 shows by year the percentages of leavers who qualified with three or more Highers. Two conclusions stand out. First, in all five years, there is a steep downward gradient from RG social class I to RG social class V. Second, in each of the RG social classes (except IIIn), there is an increase over the eight-year period up to 1984 in the percentages who qualify. The increases are larger, however, for the professional and intermediate RG social classes than they are for the three manual RG social classes (IIIm, IV, V), or for the unclassified. The provisional figures for 1986 show a small downturn in qualification rates for the three manual classes. This may be explicable in terms of sampling error, or it may indicate the end of the trend since the mid 1970s towards the equalization of differences in school attainment associated with socioeconomic status.

Table 3.3(b) illustrates that RG social class continues to have considerable explanatory potential in the sense of statistical prediction. But our data on social change also highlight several impediments to the ready transformation of the statistical associations of RG social class into causal explanations that are well grounded in theory. One difficulty concerns the assumption, implicit in the use of RG social class, that the father is central. But in a growing minority of families, as we have seen, there is no father who might act as a mechanism of cultural transmission (though the absence of a father may of course influence life-chances in other ways). Also, we cannot rule out the possibility that the changing relative size of the RG social classes indicates a change in the significance of the membership of each. The relative decline or expansion of an RG social class increases the possibility that its current members have not been 'recruited' in the same way as earlier. It also means that their advantage relative to members of other RG social classes might have changed. Thus changes in size might well be accompanied by changes in the correlates of RG social class. Third, there might well be other reasons why the correlates of RG social class should change, for example as a result of policies that were socially progressive or regressive. The assumption that

RG social class has stable validity as an indicator is therefore one that should be tested where possible, and we do this in the two sections that follow.

Here the association between RG social class and parental education is germane. The level of parental education has risen in all the RG social classes, including the unclassified. But the rise has been greater in RG social class I than in any of the others. Between 1976 and 1984, the percentage of RG social-class I parents having some post-compulsory schooling rose by 19 percentage points (from 69 to 88 per cent). The rises for the other RG social classes were 15 percentage points (social class II), 4 points (IIIn), 12 points (IIIm), 9 points (IV), 9 points (V), and 10 points (unclassified) (full results not displayed).

Thus we see two potentially countervailing trends at work. To the extent that children's school attainment benefits from their having parents who themselves stayed on at school, then there has been an increase in the advantage accruing especially to children from RG social classes I and II. On the other hand, the size of these two RG social classes has also increased. This means that their average members are not so near the top of a percentile hierarchy of relative advantage, howsoever constituted, as were their counterparts of earlier years. Conversely, the members of a declining manual group are nearer the bottom of such a hierarchy.

NET EFFECTS ON SCHOOL QUALIFICATIONS

A useful way of statistically disentangling the effects of the various changes so far discussed is a method known as logit analysis (Baker and Nelder, 1978; Fienberg, 1980; Wrigley, 1985). This method attempts to separate the statistical contribution to the prediction of an outcome variable that is made by each of the predictor variables. Table 3.4 summarizes some results from a logit analysis of attainment.[6] The outcome variable in table 3.4 is the proportion of leavers who are qualified (with three or more Highers) among all leavers in the cells of a table formed by the cross-classification of the predictor variables. These predictors are the main variables discussed in the preceding section: RG social class, parental education, sex and year (1976–84, but not including the provisional observations for 1986). The levels of these categorical variables form the rows of the table. The five columns of the table carry information about the effects of the predictor variables on the outcome variable. The first column (deviance explained) indicates the size of the effect of each predictor variable on the probability of qualifying, net of the other variables. The larger the value the greater the effect, for any given change in the number of the degrees of freedom (d.f.) shown in the second column. The statistical significance of the effect of each predictor variable is indicated in the third column (pr).

Table 3.4: Effects of family background, sex and year on attaining three or more Highers: Four regions only (weighted estimates)[1]

	Deviance explained	d.f	pr	Relative odds	pr
RG social class	931	3	<.001		
IIIm, IV, V				1.00	
IIIn				2.76	<.001
II				3.88	<.001
I				5.85	<.001
Parental education	521	3	<.001		
Both to 15 years or less				1.00	
One or both to 16 years				1.69	<.001
One to 17 years or more				2.97	<.001
Both to 17 years or more				4.56	<.001
Sex	7	1	<.01		
Male				1.00	
Female				1.11	<.01
Year	20	4	<.001		
1976				1.00	
1978				0.89	n.s.
1980				0.93	n.s.
1982				1.03	n.s.
1984				1.17	<.05

Constant −2.30
Total deviance 3001.1
% explained by fitted model 93.8
Unweighted n 22380
Notes: 1. See footnote 6

The fourth column, relative odds, indicates the relative advantage of being in each level of each predictor variable. The relative odds may need some explanation if met here for the first time. We earlier discussed how the percentages of school leavers qualifying for higher education varied with such factors as parental education and RG social class. These percentages may be expressed as proportions (pi). In the logit analysis reported in table 3.4 we analyze the variation in the log of the odds ratio, (pi/1 − pi). The odds ratio, or odds, may be defined as the ratio of the probability of qualifying to the probability of not qualifying. (Strictly speaking, we compute the proportions in (pi/1 − pi) in order to estimate probabilities in (πi/1 − πi).) The analysis of the odds ratio is preferred to that of proportions (or percentages) in part because an increase, of say 0.05, in the proportions at one point in the scale, say around 0.5, is not regarded as equivalent in importance to an increase of 0.05 at another point (say at 0.1 or 0.9).

The logit analysis enables us to estimate the odds for individuals in each category of the various factors in the model, net of the influence of the other factors. It does this by first taking out a general term (the 'constant' in table 3.4) analogous to the constant in ordinary regression analysis. Thus, when the odds for each level of a given factor are multiplied together they give a product of one. Relative odds are the ratio of these odds: the odds for members of one category relative to the odds in another category which has been chosen as a reference category. For example, table 3.4 indicates that the relative odds for females are 1.1 times those of males. Again, the relative odds for a school leaver whose parents both left school aged 17 years old or more are more than four times (4.56) those of a school leaver whose parents both left before their sixteenth birthdays.

We learn from table 3.4 that each of the predictor variables has a separate and statistically significant effect on qualifying, but that the size of the effect varies considerably. The effect of sex is smallest (deviance explained = 7 for one degree of freedom, female relative odds = 1.11), whilst the largest effect is that of RG social class (deviance explained = 931 for three degrees of freedom). This effect is associated with large relative odds. The relative odds increase from 1.0 for leavers whose fathers are in the manual category to 2.76 for those whose father is in RG social class IIIn, to 3.88 for RG social class II, and to 5.85 for RG social class I.

Parental education also has a large effect on qualifying, over and above the effect of RG social class, and one may assess the size of this effect in a similar way. An alternative way of expressing the importance of parental education is in terms of its effect on the percentage qualifying from among a group having specified characteristics (this effect cannot be read directly from the table). For example, we may specify male school leavers in 1984 with fathers in manual occupations (RG social classes IIIm, IV and V, grouped). They had an 11 per cent qualification rate if neither of their parents had any post-compulsory schooling. But if one or both of their parents had stayed on at school to 16 years, their qualification rate was 17 per cent. For the counterpart leavers in RG social class II, the qualification rate was raised from 25 to 36 per cent by having one or both parents schooled to 16 years.

Rates of qualification have also been influenced by other factors that are associated with the passage of time. We do not measure these factors directly, but their net effect is indicated by the significant contribution to the explained deviance associated with the period variable 'year'. The relative odds for year fell slightly between 1976 and 1978, but then rose over each of the following three intervals up to 1984. When the years are considered individually, only the year 1984 has a qualification rate that differs from the reference year of 1976 at the 5 per cent level of statistical probability. However, a further test showed a statistically significant trend over the period.

In interpreting this trend, we should remember that none of our statistical models can safely be assumed to capture all of the changes in family circumstances that influence qualifying. For example, the percentage of school leavers from single-parent families and the percentage with unemployed fathers have both risen in recent years. We have not been able to include these factors in our models because they were first measured only in 1980. Both factors, however, are associated with a lower probability of qualifying. To the extent that these and other pertinent but unmeasured family circumstances are changing over time (i.e., correlated with year), we would mis-estimate the extent of any period change in qualification rates that might be attributed to unspecified factors other than family circumstance. Among these unspecified factors are included all of the third and fourth types of social change identified earlier, that is, changes associated with school reform and with recession. The most, therefore, that can be said of the period rise in qualifying, net of the other factors that are measured in table 3.4, is that the rise is consistent with the view that the school system itself has become more productive, either because of school reform, or because of recession, or because of other causal factors that we do not specify. Another way of putting this, with an eye on criticisms of comprehensive schooling, is that the data give no support to the view that comprehensive reorganization has adversely affected qualification rates. But to make a stronger, causal, statement about the effects on qualifying of reform and recession, we ideally require direct measures of the factors involved.

Finally in relation to table 3.4, it is interesting to note that further analysis (see note 6) indicated that there had been no change over time in the effect on qualifying of parental education or of RG social class.[7]

NET EFFECTS ON ENTRY TO HIGHER EDUCATION

There is plentiful evidence on trends in entry to Scottish higher education in the 1985 report of the Scottish Tertiary Education Advisory Council (STEAC) (SED, 1985b). The STEAC figures most comparable to ours relate to 'young Scots'. They cover indirect entry to higher education up to and including the age of 20, as well as entry direct from school. Our own figures relate only to direct entry, but direct entry is by far the largest single component of all entry. The STEAC picture is broadly one of rising levels of participation in all sectors up to 1980 (SED, 1985b, annex F, table 6). After 1980, however, the percentage of young Scots entering the Scottish university sector fell, from 8.9 per cent in 1980–81 to 7.7 per cent in 1983–84. Over the same period, by contrast, the percentage of young Scots entering public-sector higher education in Scotland (degree or non-degree) rose from 7.8 per cent of the age group to 9.6 per cent (*ibid*, table 16). The percentage of young Scots entering all forms of higher education outwith Scotland remained more or less constant from 1980–81 to 1983–84, at 1.3 per cent.

In one respect, these and similar figures indicate little change: the percentage of young Scots entering all forms of higher education has fluctuated between 17 and 19 per cent over the eight years up to 1984 (see also SED, 1985b, annex H, table 2). Within higher education, however, there has been some redistribution: public-sector courses increased their intake by more than 2 per cent of the age group, whilst university courses reduced their intake by more than 1 per cent of the age group. In 1976 the universities took 55 per cent of all new entrants (Scottish and non-Scottish) to higher education in Scotland. By 1983 the university share had fallen to 47 per cent (calculated from SED, 1985b, annex F, table 6). By contrast, public-sector degree courses increased their share from 13 per cent of all new higher-education entrants in 1976 to 20 per cent in 1983 (*ibid.*).

We conducted three logit analyses of entry. In the first analysis, the outcome variable was whether or not the leaver entered any form of higher education. In the second, the outcome was whether or not the leaver entered degree-level higher education. In the third, it was whether or not the leaver entered university degree-level higher education. These three outcomes are of interest in their own right. They also represent successively homogeneous levels of qualification. The three analyses were conducted with the same set of school leavers, but were restricted to those leavers who had qualified for higher education by passing at least three Highers. Identical predictor variables were used in all three analyses. The predictor variables of year, sex and parental education were exactly as in table 3.4. RG social class was also included, but in reduced form: non-manual (I, II, IIIn) against manual (IIIm, IV, V). Two further predictor variables were also included, both designed to measure the level of Highers qualification. One was a simple count of the number of Highers passes (excluding second passes in a subject gained as a result of a repeated attempt at that subject). The other was a count of the number of Highers awards at the 'A' grade. To avoid problems with small numbers, this was treated as a covariate in the analysis. This means that any difference in the mean number of 'A'-grade awards at Highers between each of the cells of the cross-classified table were statistically allowed for before the relative odds were estimated.

In table 3.5 we summarize the analyses by showing, for each of the three outcomes, five columns that contain the same summary statistics that were used in the previous table.[8] As one might expect, the number of Highers passes is by far the strongest predictor of all three outcomes. (Note that the reference category for this variable i.e., the category with relative odds of 1.0 is three Highers passes.) It is strongest in relation to entry to university degrees, probably reflecting the fact that universities have 'traded up' in the qualifications required of entrants rather more than have the public-sector institutions (see table 3.6 below). Though statistically significant, the covariate

Table 3.5: Effects of qualifications, family background, sex and year on three levels of entry to higher education: Among those attaining three or more Highers in the four regions (weighted estimates)

	All higher education					All degree level					University degree				
	Deviance explained	d.f.	pr	Relative odds	pr	Deviance explained	d.f.	pr	Relative odds	pr	Deviance explained	d.f.	pr	Relative odds	pr
Highers at 'A' grade	9	1	<.01			14	1	<0.001			29	1	<.001		
Highers passes	141	3	<.001			237	3	<.001			242	3	<.001		
6+				7.69	<.001				15.18	<.001				20.29	<.001
5				5.26	<.001				9.39	<.001				12.68	<.001
4				2.44	<.001				3.25	<.001				4.48	<.001
3				1.00	<.001				1.00					1.00	
Sex	3	1	n.s.			17	1	<.001			14	1	<.001		
Male				1.00					1.00					1.00	
Female				0.88	n.s.				0.72	<.001				0.73	<.001
Year	15	4	<.01			19	4	<.001			60	4	<.001		
1976				1.00					1.00					1.00	
1978				0.80	n.s.				0.97	n.s.				0.95	n.s.
1980				0.93	n.s.				1.16	n.s.				1.09	n.s.
1982				0.83	n.s.				0.95	n.s.				0.62	<.001
1984				0.64	<.001				0.69	<.01				0.47	<.001
RG social class	0	1	n.s.			2	1	n.s.			2	1	n.s.		
IIIm, IV, V				1.00					1.00					1.00	
I, II, IIIn				1.04	n.s.				1.14	n.s.				1.14	n.s.
Parental education	2	3	n.s.			3	3	n.s.			5	3	n.s.		
Both to 15 years or less				1.00					1.00					1.00	
One or both to 16 years				1.02	n.s.				0.95	n.s.				1.07	n.s.
One to 17 years or more				1.17	n.s.				1.15	n.s.				1.16	n.s.
Both to 17 years or more				1.01	n.s.				1.14	n.s.				1.34	<.05

Constant −0.32
Total deviance 1010.2
% explained by fitted model 67.8
Unweighted n 4299

Constant −1.47
Total deviance 1467.4
% explained by fitted model 80.6
Unweighted n 4299

Constant −2.50
Total deviance 1629.8
% explained by fitted model 83.3
Unweighted n 4299

(See note 8.)

control for the number of 'A'-grade passes at Highers adds little to the prediction.

Neither RG social class nor parental education are important predictors of entry. Their effects were mediated almost entirely through the acquisition of Highers qualifications (see note 8). Provided a leaver had the necessary Highers qualifications, RG social class and parental education did not influence the propensity to enter any of the three levels of higher education. It may be, however, that an earlier intention to enter higher education itself influences the propensity to qualify.

Females were less likely to enter higher education than males with comparable qualifications and family backgrounds. This sex effect is larger in respect of degree- and university-level courses than in respect of entry to all higher education. This is presumably a reflection of the fact that more than half the entrants to non-degree courses in the public sector were females.

What table 3.5 brings out very clearly is the effect of period change on entry. Entry to university degree courses was most affected. Here the relative odds for year remained more or less unchanged up to 1980. But in 1982 they fell to 0.62 of the 1976 odds, and in 1984 they fell again to 0.47. Some of this second fall may have resulted from the increase in the population of entrants to Scottish universities who had been educated outwith Scotland. But there can be little doubt that the financial cutbacks on university spending imposed in 1981 contributed substantially to the decline in the opportunities available to school leavers after 1980.[9] Had the rates of entry to university for qualified school leavers remained at their 1980 level between 1981 and 1986 an average of a further 1,800 Scottish school leavers *per annum* would have entered university, or over 10,000 in all.

The relative and absolute contraction of university entry after 1981 coincided with the expansion of entry to public-sector higher education. One presumes that many leavers who might previously have entered university were constrained to enter either degree- or non-degree advanced courses in the public sector, where the entry requirements in general were lower. Clearly, however, the expansion of such courses was not sufficient to compensate numerically for the university cuts. As regards degree-level courses (i.e., including both university and public-sector degree courses), the relative odds had increased slightly by 1980, but they fell back in 1982 roughly to their 1976 level (i.e., 0.95 compared with 1.0), and then fell again in 1984 to only 0.69 of their 1976 level. Thus the expansion of public-sector degree provision did not fully compensate for the places that were lost to the university sector. Nor did non-degree provision in public-sector higher education make up for this loss. Overall, the relative odds were about a third lower in 1984 (0.64) than they had been in 1976 (1.00).

Table 3.6: Percentage entering (a) university degree-level courses; (b) all degree-level courses; and (c) all higher-education courses: Four regions only (weighted)

	1976	1978	1980	1982	1984	1986[1]
(a) University degree						
6+ Highers passes	85	84	82	76	73	64
5 Highers passes	67	65	66	60	55	51
4 Highers passes	30	28	37	23	19	12
3 Highers passes	5	9	10	5	2	2
Among all leavers	8	8	9	9	8	7
Among qualified[2] leavers	45	44	47	39	36	32
(b) All degree level						
6+ Highers passes	88	90	90	86	86	81
5 Highers passes	76	78	80	79	73	67
4 Highers passes	44	41	51	47	40	33
3 Highers passes	16	20	21	20	12	10
Among all leavers	10	10	11	13	11	11
Among qualified[2] leavers	55	55	59	57	52	48
(c) All higher education						
6+ Highers passes	93	93	92	88	88	83
5 Highers passes	84	84	86	86	80	74
4 Highers passes	65	61	67	64	61	50
3 Highers passes	41	38	41	43	31	28
Among all leavers	13	13	14	17	15	14
Among qualified[2] leavers	70	68	71	70	64	59
Unweighted n (all)	3850	4607	4203	5152	4683	4361

Notes: 1. Provisional estimates.
2. A 'qualified' leaver is defined as a leaver with 3+ Highers passes.

Table 3.6 (a) describes our sample members' destinations in the academic session following that in which they left school. It shows very clearly one effect of the cuts in the university sector. Among leavers with four Highers, for example, the percentage entering university rose slightly from 1976 to 1980, and then fell from 37 per cent to 19 per cent in 1984. There were similar, if slightly smaller, falls for leavers with other numbers of Highers passes. Overall, the percentage of qualified leavers entering university fell from 45 per cent in 1976 to 36 per cent in 1984. The phasing and magnitude of this fall is comparable to that reported by STEAC for all university entrants, direct and indirect (SED, 1985b, table 15). It is therefore improbable that the fall shown in table 3.6(a) has been accentuated by any trend for school leavers to take a year (or two) off before matriculating.

University entrants comprise the majority of all degree-level entrants, so the post-1980 falls in the percentages of qualified leavers entering degree-level courses (table 3.6(b)) mainly reflect the university position. The falls are smaller, however, as they also are when all of higher education is considered (table 3.6(c)). It is interesting that the 1970s cuts in the number of places in colleges of education, which bore mainly on females, are not reflected in any reduction in the overall opportunity to enter higher education up to 1980 (table 3.6(c)). Table 3.6 also shows the percentages of all leavers, qualified and unqualified, who entered the three levels of higher education. At each level, the percentages remain fairly stable over time. The reason for this is that the decline in provision for qualified leavers was offset by the rise in the proportions of leavers who qualified (table 3.1). The percentages of qualified leavers entering the three levels are lower than the figures in the STEAC report (SED, 1985b), because table 3.6 describes only the direct entry of school leavers, whereas the STEAC figures relate to indirect entry as well.

As mentioned, all of the estimates for 1986 are provisional. (This is mainly because provisional weights have been used, pending the final determination of the weighting values.) We believe, however, that the final estimates will not differ greatly from those shown in the table. This being so, one is struck by the continuing decline in participation among qualified school leavers, not only at university level, but also in the degree-level sector as a whole, and indeed over the whole of higher education.

Table 3.6 can also be used to estimate the qualification levels of entrants to the three sectors of higher education separately considered. For example, in 1984 only 2 per cent of leavers with three Highers passes entered university. But a further 10 per cent entered non-university degree-level courses (i.e., 12 minus 2), and a further 19 per cent entered non-degree higher education (i.e., 31 minus 12). Reading the table this way we can infer that the average level of SCE attainment of university entrants was substantially higher than that of entrants to degree courses in the public sector, whose attainment in turn was substantially higher than that of entrants to non-degree courses in higher education. In fact 86 per cent of university entrants direct from Scottish schools in 1984 had passed at least five Highers, compared with 51 per cent of entrants to non-university degree-level courses, and 21 per cent of entrants to non-degree advanced courses (not shown directly in table 3.6). This ordering of attainment levels is perhaps not surprising. Less evident, however, are the implications of the attainment differentials for the restructuring of higher education that is now under way. We discuss these and other implications of our analysis after the summary of our results.

SUMMARY

We are now in a position to answer the three questions posed at the beginning of this chapter. We asked, first, whether opportunities for higher education have changed since the mid-1970s. In one rather limited sense opportunities have not changed substantially. The percentage of young Scots (aged under 21 years) entering higher education has fluctuated between 17 and 19 per cent. But to conclude from this that any change in opportunity has been minor is to answer a question that has been posed in an essentially trivial form.

The answer to our second question makes clear why this is so. The second question asked whether changes in opportunity had kept pace with the flow of qualified leavers from the schools. They clearly have not. Over the eight years up to 1984, the percentage of school leavers that qualified with at least three Highers passes increased by 4 percentage points. This constitutes an increase of around a quarter of the 1976 base of qualified school leavers. But the percentage of all school leavers entering higher education showed a smaller increase, whilst the percentages entering degree-level and university education barely changed at all. Once account is taken of the increase in the proportions of qualified leavers, it is clear that there has been a decline in the opportunity for higher education. The provisional figures for 1986 indicate no reversal of this decline. The decline affected the universities most, and the contraction there was so large that it was not numerically compensated for by the modest expansion of public-sector provision up to 1984. Moreover, the displacement onto public-sector courses of students who would otherwise have entered university courses, had they not been cut, probably meant that other potential students were in turn displaced from advanced public-sector courses. In this sense the decline in opportunity affected all sectors of higher education separately, as well as all higher education considered as a totality. It may also have contributed indirectly to the rise in the level of qualifications among labour-market entrants (chapter 4 in this volume).

Our third question asked about social change and its effect on the flow of qualified leavers from the schools. In answering this we distinguished between several types of social change. Two of our main measures were related to pupils' family circumstances. The level of parental schooling has risen, but the rise has been steeper for parents in the Registrar General's professional and intermediate social classes (I and II) than in the other RG social classes. There has also been a change in the RG social-class composition of the school population. Proportionately fewer pupils come from families where the father works in a manual occupation or, if unemployed, had last worked in one. We cannot, however, give precise estimates of this decline, nor of what is almost certainly an increase in the proportion of pupils from non-manual backgrounds. This is because there has also been an increase in the percentage of pupils whose paternal social class must remain unclassified, because they either cannot tell us about their father, or choose not to do so. It is virtually certain that at least some of this increase reflects a real-world change, a decline in the currency of the conventional two-parent family, and a decline too in the proportions of fathers either in employment, or so recently employed as to allow their child to report their job.

Our evidence, is that RG social class and parental education both had large effects on entry to higher education. But they did so almost entirely through their effect on the attainment of the qualifications needed for entry. Once pupils had the requisite numbers and grades of Highers, their chances of entry were a function partly of their sex — females were less likely to enter than were males, given their qualifications — but more especially of the calendar year in which they happened to have left school. Both parental education and RG social class had a substantial effect on the achievement of the qualifications required for higher education. We noted also that the level of filial educational attainment associated with each level of parental schooling has held up during a period in which the proportion of parents with post-compulsory schooling has expanded.

DISCUSSION

The current fall in the numbers of 17- and 18-year-olds is thought to face Government with the prospect of an emptying public sector in UK higher education in the first half of the 1990s. The three main types of courses — university, public-sector degree, and public-sector non-degree — are ordered in a hierarchy of qualifications and prestige, headed by the universities. Since 1981, curtailment of the supply of university places relative to the supply of qualified school leavers has probably redirected many potential university students into the public sector where they may in turn have displaced some potential public-sector entrants. If, by 1995, the flow of qualified young people were to fall by anything like the 20 to 28 per cent officially projected for Scotland, a reversal of this displacement process could be expected. *Ceteris paribus*, the universities could restore their *de facto* entry requirements to their lower historic levels anticipating that the greater prestige of the university sector would attract many marginally qualified school leavers whose school attainment would not have been sufficient to secure a university place in the mid 1980s (when cohort sizes were large and places were cut). In these circumstances it would not be unrealistic to anticipate that school-leaver entry to public-sector higher education would fall substantially by 1995, as the Government's advisers have recognized (SED, 1985b, para. 5.18). Such an eventuality would be general to the United Kingdom, and it would make the envisaged restructuring of higher education much more difficult. It helps explain the Government's plans to extend its control of university finance throughout the UK, and to acquire fuller control of funding for higher education in the public sector in England and Wales.

Even though central government already controls the funding of public-sector higher education in Scotland, the potential consequences of demographic decline are particularly acute north of the border. This is partly because the fall in birth-cohort size is larger in Scotland, but mainly because, relative to the rest of the UK, a greater proportion of higher education in Scotland has to date been provided by the universities. Also, Scotland provides much more than its *per capita* share of all UK university education (SED, 1985b, para.2.6). If these features of university education in Scotland were to continue into the 1990s, it would probably prove even harder to fill public-sector places in Scottish higher education. It thus becomes a matter of some priority for the SED, under its ministers, to gain more control of financial decisions affecting the volume of future Scottish university provision. It is in this light that one may interpret the STEAC majority recommendation that a single planning and funding council eventually be established for the whole of higher education in Scotland, including the universities (SED 1985b, paras 8.29–8.32). Although the Government has not to date acted on this recommendation, the representation that the Secretary of State for Scotland will have on the Scottish Sub-committee of the new Universities Funding Council indicates a greater potential for the unitary planning of Scottish higher education by the Scottish Office. Indeed, history may eventually come to recognize this representation as the first step towards the full implementation of the STEAC recommendation.

In several respects, therefore, the prospect of a decline in the absolute numbers of qualified school leavers might not be wholly unwelcome to the Government in London and Edinburgh. It provides a further argument and opportunity for the restructuring of higher-education provision that the Government wishes to achieve on other grounds (broadly of utility and cost); and it is an opportunity for the Scottish Office to extend its control over a vital element of the total educational provision in Scotland.

Our evidence suggests, however, that any decline in the numbers of qualified school leavers need not be as large as current policies assume. The current (as at January 1988) SED and DES projections of future qualification rates both allow for an increase in the proportions of pupils from RG social classes I and II. Neither set of projections, however, allows for the rising level of parental education, though the ministers responsible for the four national education systems of the UK have since acknowledged it as a factor of importance (Cm.114, 1987, para.2.6; see also Redpath and Harvey, 1987; Rudd, 1987a and 1987b). Our research shows that, even where parents have had only modest experience of post-compulsory schooling, such experience is associated with a substantial boost to the probability that the child will qualify for higher education. Moreover, the size of this boost has not changed over an eight- or ten-year period in which the level of parental schooling has risen substantially. We are confident that the level of parental schooling will continue to rise for the foreseeable future, and probably at a faster rate. On the basis of simple extrapolation, therefore, we would expect a continuing rise in the rate of qualification for higher education. Because official projections have not so far incorporated the changing level of parental education, it is probable *ceteris paribus* that the rise in the rate of qualification will be higher than that currently projected by the government. If so, the demand for university courses is likely to be more buoyant than is currently envisaged, and the public sector of higher education somewhat less empty.[10]

This conjecture, we emphasize, is based on simple extrapolation, not on a causal model of social change. Nor does it take any account of probable policy changes in levels and types of higher-education provision. In these respects, however, its logical status is no worse than that of the official projections to which current policy appeals, though the official projections are, of course, much more detailed both in their assumptions and in their conclusions. We emphasize that future projections should incorporate allowances *both* for the rising level of parental education, and for the continuing shift in the occupational structure away from manual occupations. This is because our analysis shows that both these factors separately influence qualification rates, and these effects are unchanged since 1976. Despite Moser and Layard's (1964) recommendation that parental education was one of a number of factors that should be explicitly built into future projections, DES lacks an adequate series for this purpose. However, it has used the Scottish Young Peoples Survey in the past to supply gaps in its own series (DES, 1984b, table 4.4 and para.6.7), so there is no obvious reason why it should not do so again, if only to supplement the nascent data available to it from the England and Wales Youth Cohort Studies (see chapter 1 in this volume).

Important though these issues are, there is more at stake here than the future volume and type of UK higher education, and who provides and controls it. The solution to the problems of the tertiary sector will also have a bearing both on other types of post-16 education, and on the 14–19 stage of secondary schooling in the UK. What is crucial here is the influence of higher education on the standing of the various types of national certification now available for 16–19-year-olds. National examinations provide a structure of incentives for pupils, parents and schools, and they put a potent mechanism of control into the hands of those who can shape their purposes. The historic function of school examinations for university matriculation has left the universities with considerable influence over them, and this influence extends into the secondary schools, upwards from the age of 14 when crucial decisions are made about the courses for the 14–16 years stage. For as long as the majority of the age group left school at 16 years or earlier, the university influence posed no particular problem for central government. Indeed government was happy to harness this influence to the development of its own policies for secondary education, and the universities were happy to comply. The logic of this situation begins to change, however, as an increasing proportion of the age group comes to present itself for certification at 16–19 years. Certification now must serve a variety of purposes. If these purposes are dominated by a flourishing university sector that is attractive to pupils and influential in the schools, then central government may find it more difficult to effect its other priorities for secondary schooling.

The contours of this problem are clearer in Scotland than elsewhere in the UK, partly because of the greater role that the universities have in the overall provision of higher education in Scotland, and partly because the policy response is further advanced in Scotland in both the compulsory and the post-compulsory sectors. Beginning in 1984, all vocational non-advanced further education (NAFE) in Scotland has been modularized under the Action Plan, and it is now certified by the National Certificate of the Scottish Vocational Education Council (Scotvec), a wholly Scottish body. This development has maintained Scottish control of NAFE in Scotland, and has thereby moderated the influence in this sector of the Manpower Services Comm ssion (MSC), a Britain-wide body (see chapter 8 in this volume). Scotvec modules are also used in schools, both before and after 16 years. But the success of the policy depends critically upon the status of the National Certificate, and this in turn will be determined largely by the credence that selectors give it. By the end of 1987, National Certificate modules had been accorded some recognition by selectors for public-sector higher education but virtually none by selectors for university.[11] Following university misgivings in the early 1980s, the SED had retreated from its earlier plan for a rapid extension of the principles embodied in National Certificate modularization to the whole of the post-16 curriculum, including SCE Highers courses. If the universities continue to enjoy a higher prestige than the other sectors of higher education, any reluctance on their part to recognize National Certificate courses will reduce the attraction of these courses to pupils and teachers. This in turn will limit the ability of the SED to deliver the type of school-based vocational education and training that is currently sought by the Government and the MSC (see chapters 9 and 10 in this volume).

Much the same type of argument applies to the Scottish Standard grade examination that has been developed for the 14–16 stage with the intention that it replace the SCE 'O' grade. The success of the Standard grade depends in part on the contribution it may make to an orderly pupil progression towards qualification for higher education, with a fourth-year presentation at the Credit level (the highest of the three presentation levels for the Standard grade) leading on to SCE Higher-grade presentations in the fifth year. Public-sector higher education has generally recognized the Credit level of the Standard grade. However, the measure of recognition so far given by the universities has been cautious. Nor are some people in the universities happy at the not-too-distant prospect of an extension of the Standard grade reform to Highers if this were to involve modularization along the lines of Scotvec National Certificate modules (SUCE, 1986, pp.5–8 and 1987, pp.12–18).[12]

Another reason why the problem of control is more apparent in Scotland is that it is focused in the first post-compulsory year. Elsewhere in the UK, it is spread over the first two post-compulsory years which themselves are provided in a variety of institutional settings, including sixth-form colleges, schools for 14–18-year-olds, and a substantial NAFE sector. One-year NAFE courses play some part in provision in Scotland for 16–17-year-olds (chapter 1 in this volume), but SCE courses in all-through, comprehensive, secondary schools constitute a much larger proportion of the total Scottish provision than do the counterpart courses outwith Scotland. The fifth-year Highers courses offered in Scottish secondary schools have therefore come to serve a wide mix of students.

An earlier study of the 1980 leavers in Scotland has identified a number of features of the 'mixed fifth year' that are pertinent to the present discussion (McPherson, 1984a). By the end of the 1970s, almost a third of the age group were voluntarily embarking on Highers courses in fifth year, even though the courses themselves were pitched at a level of difficulty that had originally been set with the potential university entrant in mind. Pupils tended to enter the fifth year uncertain whether they would then continue for a sixth year. Most wanted to take Highers, but such was the difficulty of the courses that most had also to settle for taking some of their fifth-year courses at the Ordinary rather than the Higher grade. Although they were guided in the number of Highers courses they started by their degree of success in the 'O' grade examinations of the previous summer, they tended, if anything, to pitch their aspirations high at the beginning of the year, and then to adjust them downwards in the light of the evidence of the Christmas preliminary examinations set by their schools. They might then decide to postpone Highers presentation in one or more subjects until a sixth year, or to present a subject only at the 'O' grade, or to reduce the overall number of examinable courses they were taking.

These features no doubt entailed some educationally undesirable consequences, and they certainly constituted a major impediment to the securing of parity of esteem for vocationally-based courses in fifth year (*ibid.*). But they also gave an open and non–determined character to the school fifth year that militated against premature and largely irrevocable decisions by pupils to opt out of academic courses that could lead them to qualify for higher education after what is now only one year of post-compulsory schooling. It is no accident that, by comparison with England and Wales, Scotland has for long had higher rates of post-compulsory schooling up to the end of the first post-compulsory year, lower rates in the second post-compulsory year, and higher rates of qualification overall (Wishart, 1980; SED, 1986b, annex C). This illustrates a point that we consider fundamental. It is that qualification rates, and school attainment generally, are sensitive to the precise phasing and character of the links between school certification and the market for qualifications. The point is not new. In the early 1960s, for example, the introduction of the fourth-year SCE 'O' grade had the effect of reducing, from two years to one, the gap between the minimum leaving age (then 15 years) and the first stage of public certification (in effect the SCE Higher taken at 17 years). There followed an immediate and substantial rise in certified attainment, much of it associated with an increased staying-on rate to 16 years (SED, 1965, p.32).

Conversely, however, future rates of qualification for higher education could be substantially depressed if the link between certification and the market for qualifications were to be mismanaged. In talking of 'mismanagement' we have several sorts of eventuality in mind. The first relates to the conditions that regulate the conduct of the examinations themselves. In Scotland, for example, we would envisage that there would *ceteris paribus* be some reduction in the proportions qualifying for higher education if the Standard grade were not to be widely offered in the fifth year, and especially if, in addition, a Credit award on the Standard grade were made a pre-condition for presentation at the Higher grade in the same subject. Such moves would have the effect of narrowing the 'slow lane' from fourth year to a first-time Highers presentation in sixth year. We understand that the present government firmly intends that no formal restriction of this type be imposed. Nevertheless, one might in practice emerge, for example in schools where there was no effective sixth year.[13]

A second eventuality is more intangible but also more potent. It relates to prestige. Policy makers can rarely legislate for prestige, but they do mismanage if they fail to have regard for the realities of prestige and for the limits of their ability to influence it. Realizing this, Government in Scotland badly wants to secure full university recognition of the Standard grade and the National Certificate, and wants also to find ways of planning the volume and character of university provision in the context of Scottish higher education as a whole. If it succeeds, there is a prospect that the National Certificate will supply, if only by *fiat*, much of the articulation between school and higher education that is currently provided by mixed courses comprising SCE 'O' grades and a limited number of Highers. But if it fails, and if in addition the schools were no longer encouraged to provide fifth-year courses that mixed the Higher and Ordinary (or Standard) grades, then qualification rates could well fall, because there would be little to offer the student of borderline potential for higher education.

Perhaps the worst scenario of mismanagement would be one in which students at 16 were directed into low-status National Certificate courses unless their performance at the Credit level of Standard grade had already marked them out for a school-based Highers course which itself remained the principal route towards higher education, and especially towards university. This would fix the upper limit to the pool of qualified leavers as early as the age of 14. In the context of falling school rolls and of parental choice, it could also see the six-year comprehensive school in lower-social-class areas revert in effect to four-year status, leaving viable six-year schools only in socially more favoured areas. Such a move might well dissipate the benefits that comprehensive reorganization has started to bring to levels of attainment up to 16 years. It would be socially regressive, and it would attenuate the link between higher education and secondary schooling. In all these respects it would damage features that for long have been considered essential characteristics of the national education system in Scotland. Such damage is already occurring, of course, in the waste of talent and decline in opportunity that has characterized higher-education provision in the 1980s.

The SED would doubtless argue, and not unreasonably, that it plans to deliver none of the more gloomy scenarios on which we speculate. We emphasize, however, that our analysis is concerned as much with the unintended consequences of policies, as with those that are intended. One presumes that no-one intended to damage the opportunities for higher education in the way that has occurred. Certainly there is no obvious rush of ministers or officials to claim such a policy for their own. On the contrary, the STEAC report of 1985 drew attention in its foreword to the 'traditionally high participation rates in higher education' that were a distinctive feature of Scotland's educational tradition, and it demanded that future policy should 'derive from, and be appropriate to, the Scottish system' (SED, 1985b, p.5). Was the Advisory Council aware that the system in the 1980s had started to move away from the traditional concern to provide opportunity? If it was aware, it did not say so. Perhaps it thought that opportunity would improve as the size of the 17-year-old age group fell. If, on the other hand, the Council was not aware that opportunity was declining (and the trend is now more apparent than it was), then perhaps the Council should be reconstituted on the grounds that changing circumstances have undermined a fundamental assumption on which its earlier recommendations were based.

Our point here is a simple one: it is not just management and policy that delivers provision, it is politics as well. Somehow or other, the SED must navigate its way between two potentially conflicting exigencies. One is the traditional Scottish demand, voiced by the STEAC, for access to higher education. Rightly or wrongly, however, many people currently believe that, if such a demand were conceded in generous measure, the concession would tend to depress the status of vocational education, unless it were also accompanied by a major restructuring of the universities along the lines indicated earlier. The other exigency is the preservation of the territorial and functional competence of the SED from encroachment by the MSC. If SED and MSC were to fight each other to a draw across the field of post-compulsory provision, one might be left, when the dust had settled, with any of the three scenarios sketched above or, indeed, with others. 'Disjointed incrementalism' has been a feature of post-compulsory provision in Scotland since 1945: that is, each party to policy change has tended to get a little of what it wanted, but has had, in the main, to accept a compromise. Perhaps we are coming to the end of a period of pluralist educational politics. But, even if we are, it is highly probable that the political and sociological 'context' of educational policies will continue to shape their actual outcomes in ways that their originators did not intend.[14]

Whilst some of the particulars of this discussion are Scottish, the general point has a wider application: namely that systems of certification are in a state of flux, and might settle in ways that could substantially depress or enhance the rate of qualification for higher education. Central government is now deeply involved in the restructuring of post-compulsory provision throughout the UK. It is not inappropriate, therefore, to regard the qualification rate for higher education as one of the indicators of the quality of its own policy performance. Parents are pouring cultural capital into the school system in the form of a rapidly rising level of parental education. They might reasonably expect, therefore, (to borrow from the language of current school reform) that policies improve their own levels of expectation, that underperforming policies be closed down, and that only the best policies survive. A realistic and attainable measure of the best is a qualification rate that is somewhat higher than the 21 per cent that was achieved for males and females in Scotland as early as 1982, or the 23 per cent rate that females had approached by the mid-1980s. Strangely, however, the 1987 White Paper rests content with the expectation that the *British* qualification rate for higher education will reach only 20 per cent by the end of the century (Cm.114, 1987, para.2.7).

One wonders why Scotland especially, and Britain as a whole, should be held back by this unrealistically low level of expectation. Perhaps the maximization of the rate of qualification for higher education has a lower priority for government in Scotland and the UK than its wish to restructure the type of higher education currently on offer. Perhaps, too, the government fears that its policies would be seriously compromised if the universities in their present form remained too full of students, and therefore too full of themselves. However, this chapter has shown that, to the extent that such a fear were based on the prospect of an emptying public sector, it would be exaggerated. The, longer-term effects of current policies on the rate of qualification have yet to be determined. They could be considerable. What is already abundantly clear, however, is that the educational provision of thirty years ago is still having effects on school attainment that could raise future rates of qualification way beyond current levels of expectation and performance, but only if current policies allow.

ACKNOWLEDGEMENTS

The results reported in this chapter arise from research funded in the Centre for Educational Sociology (CES) by the SED (grant JHH/219/1). Two further reports will cover trends in applications to higher education, and the influence on entry to higher education of parental intra-generational mobility. The dataset for the 1976–84 series drew on surveys that have been variously funded by the SED, the Manpower Services Commission, by other departments of central Government, and by the former Social Science Research Council. The construction of the series dataset was funded by the Economic and Social Research Council (ESRC) as part of its support for the CES as an ESRC Designated Research Centre (grant C00280004). The ESRC also funded the analysis of the data for 1986. We are grateful to officials of the SED for helpful comments on an earlier draft of this chapter, and also to Ian Diamond, Norman Elliott, Evelyn Ebsworth, Lynne Knowles, Angus Mackintosh and David Raffe. None of the sponsors nor any individual other than ourselves is responsible for the views we express or for any errors of fact that may have occurred.

NOTES

1   The fall for Britain as a whole over the same period will be about 32 per cent (calculated from DES, 1983, table 5). The Scottish figures are calculated from SED (1985b, annex H, table 1, pp,142–3). Unless stated otherwise, we label school sessions by the calendar year in which they terminate. In this context '1976' refers to the session 1975/76, and so on. When we refer to sessions in

higher education however, the year denotes the calendar year in which they commence. Thus '1976' in this context refers to the session 1976/77.

2   The GCE 'A' level is taken by small numbers of pupils in Scottish schools (but see note 8 below). University selectors take some account of courses and awards for the Certificate of Sixth Year Studies (CSYS) when making conditional offers to some applicants. But the practice here varies between universities and between faculties. The CSYS is not a recognized qualification for the General Entrance Requirement, in part because a Highers pass is a prerequisite for entry to the CSYS examination.

3   Some students whose formal qualifications consist of fewer than three Highers passes nevertheless enter higher education. In Scotland in 1984, such students comprised 6 per cent of all full-time higher education entrants, direct and indirect (SED, 1985b, p.32).

4   The missing information on parental education arises from 'don't know' responses which average around 10 per cent, and from item non-response which averages around 5 per cent. Both types of response were higher in 1984 and 1986 than in earlier years, especially in relation to the father. Where information on one parent was either missing or recorded as 'don't know', information on the other parent was retained in the construction of the composite measure of parental education.

5   In 1984, about one-third of the unclassified cases arose from item non-response, the majority of such cases reporting that they did not live with their father. The other two-thirds of the unclassified cases arose from inadequate descriptions of the paternal occupation, one third of such cases involving respondents who did not live with their father. Detailed detective work on the rise in the unclassified would be productive.

6   In table 3.4 the first column, headed 'deviance explained', represents a measure of the net contribution of each item in the model. These estimates are computed by removing each term in turn from the fitted model. The best-fit model for qualifying included three significant second-order interaction terms. These were: RG social class with parental education (reduction in deviance = 29 for 9 degrees of freedom, pr <.001); RG social class with sex (14 for 3 d.f., pr <.01) and parental education with sex (17 for 3 d.f., pr <.001). There were no interactions with year. The total deviance explained by the model with interactions was 95.4 per cent. However, for simplicity of exposition, the model described in the text is the main-effects model. This explains 93.8 per cent of the deviance using 15 degrees of freedom less than the best-fit model with interactions. The parameter estimates from the main-effects model are changed only trivially by the addition of the three interaction terms.

7   McPherson and Willms (1987) report a decline in the association between socioeconomic status (SES) and SCE attainment over the period 1976 to 1984. The absence in table 3.4 of a year/RG social-class interaction with qualifying is mainly owing to two differences between the two studies. First, McPherson and Willms used a composite measure of SES which included information derived from the father's occupation, the mother's education, and the number of siblings. Second, the dependent variable in the McPherson and Willms study was a continuous measure of SCE attainment at 'O' and 'H' grade. The study reported that, at the upper (i.e. Highers) end of this scale, there was no decline in RG social-class differences in attainment. The rise in female attainment is also more apparent when attainment is measured as a continuously distributed outcome (*ibid.*; Willms and Kerr, 1987).

8   The preferred models for all three dependent variables were the main-effects models. There were no significant interactions in the five-way tables analyzed. The higher probability of entry to university degree courses that was associated with having two parents schooled to 17 years or over probably reflects the fact that our measure of qualifying does not take account of passes at the GCE 'A' level. This examination is taken by a larger proportion of pupils in private-sector schooling than in maintained schools. Burnhill, Garner and McPherson (1988) summarize three alternative sets of four-way models corresponding to the three five-way models reported here. In the set for degree-level entry, and in the set for university entry, the net contribution of one or both of RG social class and parental education to the best-fit model was statistically significant. But the associated deviance was very small, and was judged to be of no substantive significance, given that qualifications were underspecified in the models. Neither family-background variable contributed significantly to a four-way model for entry to all higher education.

9   This is indicated by a calculation of the share of the total fall in entry that was borne only by the Scottish-domiciled (see SUCE, 1981, appendix C; and SUCE, 1985, appendix D). Logically, however, it cannot be conclusively demonstrated.

10   The shift in the argument of these two sentences from 'rate of qualification' to 'demand for [university] courses' is not intended to preclude the importance of potential students' preferences as evinced by whether or not they applied to higher education. However, our unpublished analyses of leavers' applications 1970 to 1984 demonstrate that 'demand', in the sense of applications, is largely a function of two factors endogenous to the education system: leavers' qualifications; and the supply of places in the previous year.

11   Some university faculties have admitted a small number of students who held Scotvec modules but whose SCE qualifications did not fulfil the General Entrance Requirements of the Scottish universities. However, these students were admitted under a waiver clause in the Requirements. See also CNAA (1986).

12   Nine Standard-grade subjects are currently available at Credit level. The universities currently accept seven of these as equivalent to the SCE Ordinary grade for the purposes of General Entrance Requirements, but sometimes with provisos. Also, individual universities may impose different or stricter provisos in respect of particular subjects, and recognition is provisional until some experience of the operation of Standard-grade examinations has been gained. Definitive syllabuses for the majority of Standard-grade subjects have not yet been published (as at January 1988). The universities also had fears that the revision of the SCE Higher-grade courses would involve a substantial increase in the proportion of the final grade that was contributed by internal assessment. The modularization of these courses that was implied by the original 1984 remit for the revision was thought to carry this risk. The government has since stated that the revisions to the Higher grade will be the minimum necessary to allow for smooth progression from Standard grade, and in particular, that traditional assessment methods should remain. This has involved some modification of the original remit, and a revised remit was promulgated by SED in 1987 (see also SIO, n.d.).

13   The remit that was given to the Higher Grade Joint Working Parties in August 1984 specified that 'a pupil who has obtained a Standard 1 or 2 award on a

Credit syllabus would be expected to gain at least a C on the Higher grade after one year's further study. A pupil with a Standard 3 on a general syllabus would be expected to gain at least a C on the Higher grade after two years' further study.' This wording was incorporated in a revised remit of 1987.

14   On the sociological 'context' of reform see Raffe (1984); and on its political context see McPherson and Raab (1988, chapter 13 and 20). On the conflicting interests of SED and MSC, and the implications of this conflict for fifth- and sixth-year provision, see McPherson (1984b, pp.164–73).

REFERENCES

BAKER, R.J. and NELDER, J.A. (1978) *The GLIM System: Generalised Linear Interactive Modelling* (release 3), Oxford, Numerical Algorithms Group.

BURNHILL, P.M., GARNER, C. and MCPHERSON, A.F. (1988) 'Parental education, social class and entry to higher education 1976–1986', Edinburgh, University of Edinburgh, Centre of Educational Sociology (submitted for publication).

COUNCIL FOR NATIONAL ACADEMIC AWARDS (CNAA) (1986) 'Changes in Scottish school/non-advanced further education examinations', mimeo, 1a/48, London, CNAA.

DEPARTMENT OF EDUCATION AND SCIENCE (DES) (1983) 'Future demand for higher education in Great Britain', *DES Report on Education*, no. 99, London, HMSO.

DEPARTMENT OF EDUCATION AND SCIENCE (DES) (1984a) 'Demand for higher education in Great Britain 1984–2000', *DES Report on Education*, no. 100, London, HMSO.

DEPARTMENT OF EDUCATION AND SCIENCE (DES) (1984b) *Technical Report* issued with *DES Report on Education*, no. 100, London, HMSO.

DEPARTMENT OF EDUCATION AND SCIENCE (DES) (1986) *Projections of Demand for Higher Education in Great Britain 1986–2000*, London, HMSO.

DEPARTMENT OF EDUCATION AND SCIENCE (DES) (1987) *Higher Education: Meeting the Challenge*, (Cmnd 114), London, HMSO.

FIENBERG, S.E. (1980) *The Analysis of Cross-Classified Categorical Data*, 2nd edn., Cambridge, MA, MIT Press.

MCPHERSON, A.F. (1984a) 'Post-compulsory schooling: The fifth year' in RAFFE, D. (Ed.) *Fourteen to Eighteen*, Aberdeen, Aberdeen University Press.

MCPHERSON, A.F. (1984b) 'Post-compulsory schooling: The sixth year' in RAFFE, D. (Ed.) *Fourteen to Eighteen*, Aberdeen, Aberdeen University Press.

MCPHERSON, A.F. and RAAB, C.D. (1988) *Governing Education: A Sociology of Policy since 1945*, Edinburgh, Edinburgh University Press.

MCPHERSON, A.F. and WILLMS, J.D. (1987) 'Equalisation and improvement: Some effects of comprehensive reorganisation in Scotland', *Sociology*, 21, 4, pp. 509–38.

MARSH, C. (1986) 'Occupationally-based measures of social class' in JACOBY, A. (Ed.) *The Measurement of Social Class*, London, Social Research Association.

MOSER, C.A. and LAYARD, P.R.G. (1964) 'Planning the scale of higher education in Britain: Some statistical problems', *Journal of the Royal Statistical Society*, Series A, no. 127, pp. 473–526.

OFFICE OF POPULATION CENSUSES AND SURVEYS (OPCS) (1970) *Classification of Occupations 1970*, London, HMSO.

OFFICE OF POPULATION CENSUSES AND SURVEYS (1980) *Classification of Occupations 1980*, London, HMSO.

RAFFE, D. (1984) 'The content and context of educational reform' in RAFFE, D. (Ed.) *Fourteen to Eighteen*, Aberdeen, Aberdeen University Press.

REDPATH, R. and HARVEY, B. (1987) *Young People's Intentions to Enter Higher Education*, London, HMSO.

RUDD, E. (1987a) 'Students and social class', *Studies in Higher Education*, 12, 1, pp. 99–106.

RUDD, E. (1987b) 'The educational qualifications and social class of the parents of undergraduates entering British universities in 1984', *Journal of the Royal Statistical Society*, Series A, 150, 4, pp. 346–72.

SCOTTISH EDUCATION DEPARTMENT (SED) (1965) *Education in Scotland in 1964*, (Cmnd 2600), Edinburgh, HMSO.

SCOTTISH EDUCATION DEPARTMENT (SED) (1983) 'Higher education projections', *Statistical Bulletin*, No. 7 J1/1983, Edinburgh, SED.

SCOTTISH EDUCATION DEPARTMENT (SED) (1985a) 'Revised higher education projections for Scotland', *Statistical Bulletin*, No. 6/C1/1985, Edinburgh, SED.

SCOTTISH EDUCATION DEPARTMENT (SED) (1985b) *Future Strategy for Higher Education in Scotland: Report of the Scottish Tertiary Education Advisory Council (STEAC) on Its Review of Higher Education in Scotland*, (Cmnd 9676) Edinburgh, HMSO.

SCOTTISH EDUCATION DEPARTMENT (SED) (1986a) 'School leavers qualifications', *Statistical Bulletin*, No. 10/E2/1986.

SCOTTISH EDUCATION DEPARTMENT (SED) (1986b) 'Staying-on rates', *Statistical Bulletin*, No. 9/C6/1986, Edinburgh, SED.

SCOTTISH INFORMATION OFFICE (SIO) (n.d.) 'Scottish Certificate of Education Standard Grade', *Factsheet 29*, Edinburgh, Scottish Office.

SCOTTISH UNIVERSITIES COUNCIL ON ENTRANCE (SUCE) (1981) *Report for 1980–81*, St Andrews, SUCE.

SCOTTISH UNIVERSITIES COUNCIL ON ENTRANCE (SUCE) (1985) *Report for 1984–85*, St Andrews, SUCE.

SCOTTISH UNIVERSITIES COUNCIL ON ENTRANCE (SUCE) (1986) *Report for 1985–86*, St Andrews, SUCE.

SCOTTISH UNIVERSITIES COUNCIL ON ENTRANCE (SUCE) (1987) *Entrance Guide 1988*, St Andrews, SUCE.

WILLMS, J.D. and KERR, P. (1987) 'Changes in sex differences in Scottish examination results since 1975', *Journal of Early Adolescence*, June (with an authors' correction in a subsequent issue).

WISHART, D. (1980) 'Scotland's schools', *Social Trends*, 10, pp. 52–60.

WRIGLEY, N. (1985) *Categorical Data Analysis for Geographers and Environmental Scientists*, London, Longman.

Chapter 4:

___

Has the Bottom Dropped out of the Youth Labour Market?

Michael A. Shelly

___

INTRODUCTION

Since the mid-1970s the level of youth unemployment has risen dramatically. This rise in the level of youth unemployment has affected less qualified young people in particular. The aim in this chapter is to use data from the 1977 and 1983 Scottish School Leavers Surveys to examine the link between school leavers' educational qualifications and their unemployment experience.

By way of introduction table 4.1 shows female and male school leavers' non-employment rates at each of fourteen levels of SCE (Scottish Certificate of Education) attainment in 1977 and 1983. Non-employment is here defined as participation on state schemes for the unemployed or unemployment. Non-employment rates are expressed as a percentage of school leavers from the previous session who were in the full-time labour market at the time of the survey in spring 1977 or spring 1983. Table 4.1 also shows unweighted sample numbers and the coefficients of variation between non-employment rates and SCE attainment.

Like all the tables in this chapter, table 4.1 is based on weighted data restricted to those school leavers in the labour market who came from state sector schools in four regions of Scotland, namely, Fife, Lothian, Strathclyde and Tayside. The restriction to just four regions of Scotland was necessitated by the fact that unqualified school leavers were not included in the other regions in 1977. The four regions contain about three-quarters of the population of Scotland. The restriction to state school leavers resulted from incomplete sampling arrangements for other schools in 1977 (see appendix 1). For the sake of comparability these restrictions are also applied to the 1983 data.

Table 4.1: Female and male school leavers' non-employment rates by qualification level, 1977 and 1983

SCE attainment	Females			Males		
	1977	*1983*	*Change 1977–83*	*1977*	*1983*	*Change 1977–83*
Unqualified	27.8	70.1	+42.3	33.1	67.8	+34.7
'O' grade at D–E only	15.1	61.2	+46.1	13.8	54.3	+40.5
1 'O' grade (A–C)	12.1	56.1	+43.9	14.3	47.0	+32.7
2 'O' grades	6.3	50.4	+44.1	6.7	33.0	+26.3
3 'O' grades	7.4	41.4	+34.1	5.6	29.6	+23.9
4 'O' grades	4.4	29.2	+24.8	8.1	29.1	+21.0
5 'O' grades	3.7	21.2	+17.5	5.1	20.7	+15.5
6+ 'O' grades	10.7	47.1	+36.4	6.0	27.3	+21.3
1 Higher	9.4	27.6	+18.2	11.5	33.2	+21.7
2 Highers	9.9	24.0	+14.1	7.3	32.2	+24.9
3 Highers	11.4	14.7	+ 3.2	3.1	30.1	+26.9
4 Highers	7.0	25.7	+18.7	13.0	20.9	+ 7.9
5 Highers	16.9	20.4	+ 3.5	30.0	36.4	+ 6.4
6+ Highers	0.0	66.1	+66.1	13.1	32.2	+19.0
Average, all levels of SCE attainment	10.9	39.7	+29.7	12.2	35.3	+23.1
Coefficient of variation	0.69	0.47		0.74	0.37	
Unweighted n	2383	1607		2628	1854	

Note: The average non-employment rates show the average of the fourteen rates shown, not the proportion of all school leavers without jobs.

The data are additionally restricted to those who gave full responses concerning their educational qualifications and post-school destinations. The measure of school leavers' educational qualifications utilized here is a fourteen-point scale of SCE attainment, ranging from one, for the unqualified, to fourteen, for those possessing six or more Highers. The data for the top points on this scale, for school leavers with several Highers, should be treated with caution. Few of these school leavers entered the labour market and the survey estimates are subject to considerable sampling error.

It can be seen from table 4.1 that non-employment rates noticeably varied with educational attainment in both 1977 and 1983, being particularly high for the unqualified and those possessing only D or E awards at 'O' grade (widely, if informally, regarded as 'fails'). Between 1977 and 1983, male school leavers' average non-employment rate (across the fourteen levels of SCE attainment) nearly tripled and female school leavers' average non-employment rate nearly quadrupled. This increase in school leavers' non-employment almost certainly reflected an increase in their involuntary non-employment, that is, their inability to find a job even though they were willing to work at the prevailing level of real wage rates.[1] For both genders large percentage point increases in the non-employment rate were experienced by the least qualified. It can be seen from table 4.1 that the coefficients of variation decreased in value for both genders between 1977 and 1983, reflecting the spread of above average non-employment rates up the SCE attainment scale.

To summarize, less qualified school leavers experienced higher rates of non-employment than their better qualified peers in both 1977 and 1983, and it was the least qualified who tended to experience the largest percentage point increases in their non-employment rates between 1977 and 1983.

TWO EXPLANATIONS

Introduction

Two main hypotheses have been proposed to explain why, in recent years, less qualified young people's non-employment has increased to a greater extent than that of their better qualified peers. These are the 'structural hypothesis' (NYEC, 1974; Ashton and Maguire, 1983; Roberts *et al.*, 1986) and the 'labour-queue' hypothesis (Main and Raffe, 1983a; Main, 1985; Raffe, 1986). In both hypotheses, the main role is attributed to changes on the demand side of the labour market. Where the hypotheses differ is in their emphasis as to the major cause of the changes in employers' relative demand for young workers with different levels of qualifications, and, consequently, in their expectations of the extent to which less qualified young people's particularly high rates of non-employment could be reduced by an increase in the general level of economic activity.

The Structural Hypothesis

According to the structural hypothesis, changes in the pattern of demand for goods and services, and changes in production techniques, have combined to cause (and will continue to cause) changes in the occupational structure of employment which have adversely affected less qualified young people's employment. These changes in the occupational structure of employment are not contended to be necessarily linked to the general level of economic activity, although they are believed to have accelerated in the recession after 1979. The changes include the shift from manufacturing to service industry employment, upskilling in the work process, the rise of industries based upon new technology, such as computing and biotechnology, and the mechanization of previously unskilled manual work, for example robots replacing workers in car assembly. These changes are held to have had the effect of reducing the number of unskilled and semi-skilled job openings for less qualified young people. At the same time, the number of trainee-managerial, trainee-professional, technical and skilled manual jobs, in which better qualified young people are often employed, is claimed to have increased. Consequently, Roberts *et al.* (1986, p. 23) argue that a growing structural mismatch has emerged between the composition of the demand for young people's labour and the composition of their labour supply, and that '(t)he bottom, but not the top, has fallen out of youth labour markets'.

Since this structural mismatch is believed to result from secular trends, and these trends are not held to be directly related to the general level of economic activity, an increase in the general level of economic activity cannot, it is claimed, be expected to remove this structural non-employment (Roberts *et al.*, 1986).

The major policy implication of the structural hypothesis is that, even if the general level of economic activity were to increase to such an extent as to significantly increase all ages' employment, measures would still be required to improve the quality, for example the educational attainment, of young people's labour supply. Specific measures would include: changing the education system so as to reduce the proportion of young people leaving school with few or no qualifications, training programmes designed to increase the attractiveness of young people to potential employers, and a reduction of unqualified and less qualified young people's labour supply via increased participation in continued full-time tertiary education.

The Labour-queue Hypothesis

The labour-queue hypothesis is based upon Thurow's (1976) 'labour-queue' model (Main and Raffe, 1983a; Main, 1985; Raffe, 1986). In the model, employers are assumed to offer 'training slots', with a fixed wage attached, to applicants. Applicants then compete for training slots on the basis of their expected training costs. Employers are assumed to use applicants' observable characteristics, such as educational qualifications, gender and age, as predictors of training costs. Employers are then assumed to rank applicants in their labour queues according to their expected training costs, with those with the lowest expected training costs nearest the front. Finally, it is assumed that employers proceed down their labour queues hiring workers until they meet their labour requirements, which are determined by firms' sales.

All applicants will have some chance of getting a job. This is because employers will differ among themselves as to which observable characteristics they believe to be good predictors of training costs and in their beliefs as to each observable characteristic's relative importance, and because jobs will differ in their training requirements. Furthermore, the observable characteristics which employers use in deciding which applicants to hire will, most probably, be positively correlated with applicants' minimum acceptable wage rates, so that applicants most favoured by employers will not apply for low paid jobs. Hence, employers offering low wage rates will have to form their labour queues from less attractive applicants. For all these reasons, even less attractive applicants stand some chance of securing a job, if not a well-paid job.

When firms experience a decline in their sales they will react by reducing the scale of their hiring and will not proceed as far down their labour queues as they did previously. This will especially reduce the employment chances of less attractive applicants, causing a change in the composition of employers' demand for labour in favour of more attractive applicants, for example the better qualified.

According to proponents of the labour-queue hypothesis, the recent changes in the qualification composition of the demand for young people's labour were the result of a deficiency in the aggregate demand for goods and services. They contend that these changes are not permanent and could be reversed by a Government-initiated increase in aggregate demand and hence economic activity, and this is their main policy conclusion.

Raffe (1986) has argued that much recent occupational upskilling is, in fact, the result of the uneven impact of aggregate demand deficiency across industries and occupations, which especially hit the manufacturing industries and unskilled and semi-skilled workers. Since the manufacturing industries previously employed a large number of manual workers, the decline in employment in such industries will have produced a shift towards non-manual occupations. Also, the unskilled and semi-skilled can be expected to have suffered particularly large job losses because they are cheaper to discharge than more skilled workers, since they have had little invested in their training by employers.

Summary

The proponents of both the structural and labour-queue hypotheses contend that there has been a change in the qualification composition of employers' demand for young people's labour which has adversely affected the unqualified and less qualified. The proponents of the structural hypothesis maintain that the change is irreversible. The proponents of the labour-queue hypothesis maintain that the change can be reversed by removing the deficiency in aggregate demand. The main difference between the two hypotheses lies in the relative importance they attach to changes in the occupational distribution of young people's employment in changing the qualification composition of employers' demand for young people's labour. The proponents of the structural hypothesis place great stress on occupational change, whereas the proponents of the labour-queue hypothesis emphasize the raising of hiring standards within occupations.

DECOMPOSING CHANGES IN SCHOOL-LEAVER NON-EMPLOYMENT, 1977–1983

This section discusses how changes in the level and composition both of the demand for school leavers' labour, and of its supply, combined to bring about the observed rise in school leavers' non-employment at each level of educational attainment. The demand for school leavers' labour is assumed to be represented by the level and composition of their employment. It is assumed throughout this chapter that school leavers' employment was demand-determined, so that changes in the demand for school leavers' labour were manifested as changes in their employment. This is consistent with the findings of the econometric studies reviewed in Shelly (1987), namely, that the youth labour market, as a whole, appears to have been in chronic disequilibrium for many years and that since the early 1970s it seems to have been characterized by excess supply.[2]

The proponents of both the structural and labour-queue hypotheses agree that the largest part of the rise in the overall level of youth non-employment was brought about by a decline in their total employment. They have little to say about changes in their total labour supply. Similarly, they attribute changes in the distribution of non-employment across qualification groups primarily to changes in the qualification composition of young people's employment, rather than to changes in the qualification composition of the labour supply. The aim in this section is to isolate the compositional changes in school leavers' employment and labour supply by use of a shift-share decomposition.

It is necessary to study the supply side as well as the demand side since school leavers' non-employment at each level of educational attainment is calculated as the gap between their labour supply and employment. Also, school leavers may adapt their labour supply behaviour in response to changes in their employment. For instance, school leavers may respond to the raising of employers' hiring standards by attempting to obtain more educational qualifications, thus changing the qualification composition of their labour supply, or they may choose to continue in further education rather than enter the labour market, thus changing their total labour supply. So although many of the changes on the supply side are responses to changes on the demand side, it is still necessary to take them into account.

Table 4.2: The estimated number of non-employed and employed school leavers at each level of SCE attainment in 1977 and 1983

SCE attainment	Females				Males			
	Non-employed		Employed		Non-employed		Employed	
	1977	1983	1977	1983	1977	1983	1977	1983
Unqualified	3898	6725	10137	2876	5605	9065	11354	4313
'O' grade at D–E only	581	2018	3270	1280	525	1897	3278	1595
1 'O' grade (A–C)	366	1680	2651	1316	621	1590	3737	1794
2 'O grades	155	750	2321	739	195	930	2705	1885
3 'O' grades	136	728	1718	1028	124	479	2080	1142
4 'O' grades	74	409	1592	992	131	462	1487	1124
5 'O' grades	36	150	940	559	68	217	1261	834
6+ 'O' grades	87	418	726	469	97	409	1516	1087
1 Higher	169	578	1624	1515	207	586	1590	1178
2 Highers	138	387	1256	1226	110	361	1401	761
3 Highers	95	226	738	1316	25	257	785	598
4 Highers	33	237	433	685	74	134	493	507
5 Highers	26	83	128	325	91	156	212	272
6+ Highers	0	70	23	36	7	17	49	36
All school leavers	5794	14459	27558	14353	7880	16559	31949	17126

Note: Estimates in this and the following tables are subject to rounding error in the survey estimates.

Table 4.2 shows the estimated number of non–employed and employed female and male school leavers, at each level of SCE attainment, in Scotland in 1977 and 1983. These figures are estimated by grossing up the estimates derived from the surveys to population levels. The table confirms that the number of non-employed school leavers rose at each level of SCE attainment between 1977 and 1983. However it also shows that the number of employed school leavers, while falling at most lower and middle levels of attainment, rose at the highest levels. Combining the non–employed and employed estimates for each year gives the supply of school leavers; this fell at the lower levels of attainment, but rose at the higher levels. These changes are analyzed further by means of a shift-share decomposition of the change in non–employment. This is reported in tables 4.3 (for females) and 4.4 (for males).

The first step in the analysis is to break the change in non-employment at each level of SCE attainment into two component changes; the change in supply (equal to employment plus non-employment) and the change in employment. (Note that increases in employment are represented by negative figures in the tables, since they contribute to a fall in non-employment. Falls in employment are represented by positive figures.)

The second step is to decompose both the change in supply and the change in employment at each level of SCE attainment into level and composition effects. The level effects are calculated by allowing for the

Table 4.3: The absolute change in female school leavers' non-employment decomposed into the level effect and composition effect, 1977–83

SCE attainment	The change in non-employment	The change in supply	Components of the change in supply		The change in employment	Components of the change in employment	
			Level effect	Composition effect		Level effect	Composition effect
Unqualified	+2827	−4443	−1911	−2533	+7270	+4858	+2413
'O' grade at D–E only	+1437	−553	−524	−28	+1990	+1567	+423
1 'O' grade (A–C)	+1314	−22	−411	+390	+1336	+1271	+65
2 'O' grades	+595	−987	−337	−651	+1582	+1112	+470
3 'O' grades	+591	−99	−252	+154	+690	+823	−133
4 'O' grades	+335	−265	−227	−39	+601	+763	−163
5 'O' grades	+114	−267	−133	−134	+381	+450	−69
6+ 'O' grades	+331	+73	−111	+184	+258	+348	−91
1 Higher	+409	+300	−244	+544	+109	+778	−669
2 Highers	+249	+219	−190	+408	+30	+602	−572
3 Highers	+131	+710	−113	+823	−579	+353	−932
4 Highers	+204	+456	−63	+520	−252	+207	−460
5 Highers	+57	+254	−21	+275	−196	+61	−258
6+ Highers	+71	+84	−3	+87	−13	+11	−24
All school leavers	+8665	−4540	−4540	0	+13205	+13205	0

Table 4.4: The absolute change in male school leavers' non-employment decomposed into level effects and composition effects

SCE attainment	The change in non-employment	The change in supply	Components of the change in supply		The change in employment	Components of the change in employment	
			Level effect	Composition effect		Level effect	Composition effect
Unqualified	+3460	−3581	−2616	−965	+7040	+5267	+1773
'O' grade at D–E only	+1372	−311	−589	+275	+1683	+1521	+162
1 'O' grade (A–C)	+969	−974	−672	−301	+1943	+1734	+209
2 'O' grades	+735	−85	−447	+362	+820	+1255	−435
3 'O' grades	+355	−583	−340	−244	+939	+965	−27
4 'O' grades	+331	−33	−250	+216	+364	+690	−327
5 'O' grades	+149	−278	−205	−74	+427	+585	−157
6+ 'O' grades	+312	−116	−249	+133	+429	+703	−275
1 Higher	+378	−34	−277	+244	+412	+738	−325
2 Highers	+251	−389	−233	−157	+640	+651	−10
3 Highers	+232	+45	−125	+170	+187	+365	−177
4 Highers	+60	+75	−87	+162	−15	+229	−243
5 Highers	+65	+125	−47	+172	−60	+98	−158
6+ Highers	+10	−3	−9	+6	+12	+23	−10
All school leavers	+8679	−6144	−6144	−1	+14823	+14823	0

changes in the levels of school leavers' total labour supply and total employment respectively whilst keeping their qualification compositions at their 1977 configurations. They show how school leavers' non-employment would have changed at each level of SCE attainment if there had been no qualification composition changes in labour supply and employment (that is, if supply and employment had changed by the same proportion at each level of SCE attainment). The composition effects are calculated as the actual changes minus the level effects and show the change in school leavers' non-employment, at each level of SCE attainment, attributable to the changes in the qualification composition of their labour supply and employment.

From tables 4.3 and 4.4, it can be seen that the change in the level of school leavers' total employment was the main cause of the rise in their total non-employment (for all levels of SCE attainment combined) between 1977 and 1983. However, the change in employment was not the major cause of the increase in non-employment at all levels of SCE attainment. At some of the upper levels of SCE attainment the change in supply was more important: for female school leavers with three or more Highers and male school leavers with four or five Highers, the increase in their non-employment was due to the increase in their supply exceeding the increase in their employment.

It can be seen from tables 4.3 and 4.4 that the employment qualification composition effect unequivocally added to the increase in non-employment experienced by the unqualified and less qualified and lessened the increase experienced by their better qualified peers. This effect was often offset, and occasionally overwhelmed, by changes in the qualification composition of school leavers' labour supply, with more better qualified and fewer less qualified leavers entering the labour market. However the changes in the qualification composition of school leavers' labour supply were insufficient fully to meet the increased qualification levels demanded by employers. Both sets of changes were greater for females.

To summarize: not only did the total level of employment fall between 1977 and 1983, but a larger proportion of the employment that remained went to the better qualified. Consequently the less qualified were most severely affected by the fall in employment. However this trend was partly offset by a fall in the number of less qualified school leavers entering the labour market, and a smaller increase in the number of better qualified entrants. It follows that the qualification composition of school-leaver *employment* changed much more than was reflected in the composition of *non-employment* since the latter was affected by this off setting change in the composition of *supply*. The next section examines the changing qualification composition of school-leaver employment.

DECOMPOSING CHANGES IN SCHOOL-LEAVER EMPLOYMENT, 1977–83

This section discusses the changes in school leavers' employment and examines the relative roles played by changes in employers' hiring standards (as stressed by the proponents of the labour-queue hypothesis) and changes in the occupational distribution of school leavers' employment (as stressed by the proponents of the structural hypothesis).

The analysis is based on the shift-share decomposition shown in tables 4.5 (for females) and 4.6 (for males). The first three columns of each table repeat part of the analysis in tables 4.3 and 4.4 (subject to small differences due to rounding of the survey data before grossing up to population estimates). The first column shows the change in employment at each level of SCE attainment. (Unlike tables 4.3 and 4.4, falls in employment are here represented as negative amounts.) The next column shows the level effect; this is the change in employment that would have been expected had employment fallen by the same proportion at all SCE attainment levels, that is, had the qualification composition of employment remained unchanged. The third column shows the effect of the changing qualification composition of employment.

This composition effect is then further decomposed into three components. Firstly, that component attributable to the changes in the shares of school leavers' employment *within* occupations accounted for by school leavers at each level of SCE attainment, holding fixed the occupational distribution of school leavers' employment at its 1977 configuration. That is, the first component represents that part of the change in the qualification composition of school leavers' employment that can be attributed to changes in employers' hiring standards within occupational categories. The second component represents that part of the change in the qualification composition of school leavers' employment attributable to occupational change, holding fixed employers' hiring standards within each occupational category. The final component represents that part attributable to the interaction of the first two components. These three components will be termed the qualification shift effect, the occupation shift effect and the interaction effect, respectively.[3]

From tables 4.5 and 4.6 it can be seen, firstly, that female school leavers' composition effects were larger in average absolute value than male school leavers', because their occupation shift effects were usually larger. In other words, the shift in the distribution of employment in favour of the better qualified was greater for females than for males, because it was more affected by occupational change. Secondly, for both genders, the unqualified and least qualified experienced negative composition effects, that is, lost jobs because

Table 4.5: *The decomposition of the observed change in female school leavers' employment, 1977–83*

SCE attainment	Observed change	Components of observed change		Components of composition effect		
		Level effect	Composition effect	Qualification shift effect	Occupation shift effect	Interaction effect
Unqualified	−7270	−4860	−2410	−1447	−1218	+254
'O' grade at D–E only	−1990	−1570	−420	−282	−120	−19
1 'O' grade (A–C)	−1336	−1272	−64	+91	+46	−201
2 'O' grades	−1582	−1111	−471	−418	+104	−156
3 'O' grades	−690	−824	+134	+78	+87	−31
4 'O' grades	−601	−764	+163	+72	+160	−69
5 'O' grades	−381	−446	+65	+45	+103	−83
6+ 'O' grades	−258	−349	+91	+33	+123	−65
1 Higher	−109	−777	+668	+337	+262	+69
2 Highers	−30	−601	+571	+291	+186	+94
3 Highers	+579	−353	+932	+668	+138	+126
4 Highers	+252	−209	+461	+329	+51	+81
5 Highers	+196	−60	+256	+199	+3	+54
6+ Highers	+13	−11	+24	+4	+2	+18
All school leavers	−13207	−13207	0	0	−73	+72

Note: The net shifts, qualification shift effects and occupation shift effects should sum to zero down the columns. The fact that they do not do so results from the fact that some cells which are filled in one of the SCE attainment by occupation matrices were empty in the other matrix.

Table 4.6: The decomposition of the observed change in male school leavers' employment, 1977–83

SCE attainment	Observed change	Components of observed change		Components of composition effect		
		Level effect	Composition effect	Qualification shift effect	Occupation shift effect	Interaction effect
Unqualified	-7440	-5273	-1767	-1632	-123	-11
'O' grade at D-E only	-1683	-1522	-161	-255	+23	+72
1 'O' grade (A-C)	-1943	-1738	-205	-285	+22	+57
2 'O' grades	-820	-1254	+434	+338	+90	+7
3 'O' grades	-939	-961	+22	+13	+8	+1
4 'O' grades	-334	-688	+324	+376	+23	-75
5 'O' grades	-427	-583	+156	+174	+42	-60
6+ 'O' grades	-429	-706	+277	+284	-61	+54
1 Higher	-412	-737	+325	+330	-7	+2
2 Highers	-640	-647	+7	+11	-12	+7
3 Highers	-187	-364	+177	+206	-38	+8
4 Highers	+5	-229	+224	+129	+22	+94
5 Highers	+60	-96	+156	+234	+8	-86
6+ Highers	-12	-21	+9	+43	+3	-37
All school leavers	-14821	-14819	-2	-34	0	+33

Note: See note to table 4.5.

of the changing qualification composition of employment. Conversely the better qualified increased their share of employment (experienced positive composition effects) although the pattern of this differed between the genders. In the case of female school leavers, it was those with Highers who benefited most; in the case of male school leavers, the benefits were more equally shared between those with 'O' grades and those with Highers. Thirdly, for both genders, the pattern displayed by the qualification shift effect was similar to that displayed by the composition effects. The less qualified lost their share of employment, and the better qualified gained, because employers recruited better qualified school leavers to given occupations. Fourthly, for both genders, the unqualified accounted for the largest part of the total negative occupation shift effects. In the case of unqualified female school leavers, the occupation shift effect was a major component of their negative composition effect. In other words occupational changes reduced the demand for school leavers in the lowest SCE attainment category, and accounted for a significant proportion (about half) of the job loss among female school leavers in this category. Finally, it can be seen that the qualification shift effect was usually more important than the occupation shift effect, especially for males. That is, more of the changing distribution of employment across SCE attainment levels can be accounted for by the raising of hiring standards within occupations than by occupational change.

These results indicate that the bottom did, to a certain extent, drop out of the female youth labour market. The types of occupations (such as seamstresses and textile workers) that were traditionally filled by unqualified female school leavers experienced large declines in employment between 1977 and 1983. This is shown in table 4.7 which shows large female declines in 'non-transferable craftsmen' occupations (mainly textile workers) and in 'other operatives' (semi-skilled and unskilled jobs in manufacturing). These employment declines were mainly associated with the ailing fortunes of one particular industry, clothing, footwear and leather goods, and were therefore a reflection of industrial change rather than of any upskilling within industries.

A closer examination of the link between the changes in the qualification composition of school leavers' employment and their occupations of employment (details not reported here) reveals that in the case of female school leavers the large negative, overall composition effect experienced by the least qualified school leavers was mainly accounted for by the manual occupations, wherein it mainly reflected the raising of hiring standards but also partly reflected the decline in employment in the clothing, footwear and leather goods industry. The large positive net shift experienced by female school leavers with Highers was overwhelmingly accounted for by white-collar occupations, wherein it was mainly due to the raising of hiring standards, though it was partly due to a shift towards white-collar employment. It appears that for female school leavers the higher their level of

Table 4.7: The occupational distribution of Scottish school leavers' employment, 1977 and 1983 (percentages)

Warwick Occupational Category	Females		Males	
	1977	*1983*	*1977*	*1983*
Managers and administrators	0.9	0.3	1.5	0.7
Education professions	0.0	0.1	0.2	0.0
Health professions etc	4.8	10.9	0.4	0.9
Other professions	0.1	0.3	0.4	0.1
Literary, artistic and sports occupations	0.7	0.4	0.7	1.2
Engineers, scientists, etc	0.0	0.5	0.5	0.8
Technicians, draughtsmen	1.0	1.0	4.4	1.4
Clerical occupations, etc	36.7	43.5	7.3	10.2
Sales occupations	14.9	13.9	4.5	5.4
Supervisors, foremen	0.0	0.0	0.0	0.0
Engineering craftsmen	0.9	0.8	27.4	27.2
Other transferable craftsmen	0.2	0.1	9.3	13.6
Non-transferable craftsmen	16.0	7.3	5.1	2.6
Skilled operatives	1.4	1.6	6.8	4.0
Other operatives	10.7	7.3	20.6	22.1
Security occupations	0.7	0.4	4.5	4.5
Personal service occupations	10.1	11.5	2.8	3.3
Other occupations	0.9	0.3	3.5	1.9
Unweighted n	2041	787	2203	920

SCE attainment, the lower the relative importance of changes in the occupational distribution of their employment and the greater the relative importance of the raising of hiring standards in bringing about the changes in the qualification composition of their employment.

The vast bulk of male school leavers' composition effects were experienced within the manual occupations, where the bulk of their employment was concentrated. The main trend within the manual occupations was for those with four or more 'O' grades to displace those with fewer qualifications in skilled manual occupations, such as engineering craftsmen and fitters, and for those with some qualifications to displace the least qualified in semi-skilled and unskilled occupations.

CONCLUSION

The examination in this chapter of the proximate sources of the change in the qualification composition of school leavers' employment showed that the raising of hiring standards within occupations was, usually, a more important factor than occupational change in explaining the shifts which so adversely affected the least qualified. Some evidence to support the structural hypothesis was provided by the fact that unqualified female school leavers experienced a large negative occupation shift; this was associated with the decline in employment in the clothing, footwear and leather goods industry.

The raising of hiring standards by employers was occasioned by the decline in the number of job openings available. Employers had fewer jobs to offer than there were applicants ready to fill them and had to apply a method of allocating the many applicants among the few job openings. With too many applicants chasing too few job openings a burst of qualification inflation took place.

Two policy implications arise from the evidence presented in this chapter. Firstly, it is to be anticipated that government-initiated expansionary economic policies would prove particularly efficacious in raising the employment prospects of less qualified young people inasmuch as they increased the number of job openings available and reduced the need for employers to 'ration' jobs via educational qualifications. Secondly, policies aimed at increasing young people's average level of educational qualifications may not have aided the less qualified since employers used educational qualifications as a relative, rather than an absolute, hiring criterion.

ACKNOWLEDGEMENTS

The author gratefully acknowledges financial support received from the Economic and Social Research Council (ESRC) and valuable research support received from the Centre for Educational Sociology (CES), University of Edinburgh, whose activities are sponsored, in part, by the Economic and Social Research Council. The chapter benefited from the comments of Professor Brian Main and Mr David Raffe.

NOTES

1   There are a number of reasons for assuming this. Firstly, there do not appear to be any *a priori* reasons for supposing that school leavers should have chosen to increase the extent of their voluntary unemployment between 1977 and 1983. Secondly, the increase in school leavers' non-employment is unlikely to be attributable to an increase in their frictional unemployment, since Raffe (1984) has produced evidence to show that Scottish school leavers had reduced their aggregate rate of job-changing between 1977 and 1983. Finally, since the evidence suggests (Wells, 1987) that young people's relative pay declined after 1979, it seems likely that none of the increase in their non-employment is due to the increase in their relative pay.

2   However, from table 4.1 it can be seen that some of the better qualified school leavers had very low rates of non-employment in 1977. These low rates are not

inconsistent with equilibrium in a youth labour market. But such school leavers experienced both an increase in their employment and their non-employment between 1977 and 1983. This suggests that between 1977 and 1983 their employment became demand determined. Therefore, the *changes* in their employment may be regarded as synonymous with the *changes* in the demand for their labour. When considering the demand for labour, it is usual to define it so as to include unfilled vacancies as well as employment. The survey data contain no information on unfilled vacancies and so unfilled vacancies will have to be ignored. Inclusion of such data would only have altered the results to the extent that the number of unfilled vacancies *changed* between 1977 and 1983. Evidence from the 1981 survey of Scottish school leavers (Main and Raffe, 1983b) suggests that by the spring of the year following that in which the sample left school, i.e. at the time when the survey was conducted, there were very few previously non-employed school leavers gaining jobs. This suggests that there were few unfilled vacancies for school leavers at that time and that the change in the number of unfilled vacancies between 1977 and 1983 was not very large.

3   A problem occurred in the calculations involved in the shift-share decomposition. It was found that some cells which were filled in the 1977 SCE attainment level by occupation matrix were empty in the 1983 matrix. This resulted from the fact that the 1983 matrix was constructed using a smaller sample than the 1977 matrix. The effects of this empty cell problem are, firstly, to prevent the composition effects, qualification shifts, occupation shifts and interaction effects from summing to zero across all SCE levels and, secondly, to allocate all of the net shift within an educational attainment level/occupational cell to either the qualification shift or occupation shift effect. The problems caused by sampling variation and the need to convert school leavers' occupations to a common classification (from the 1970 Classification of Occupations in 1977 and the 1980 Classification of Occupations in 1983) should also be borne in mind.

REFERENCES

ASHTON, D. and MAGUIRE, M. (1983) *The Vanishing Youth Labour Market*, London, Youthaid.

MAIN, B. (1985) 'School-leaver unemployment and the Youth Opportunities Programme in Scotland', *Oxford Economic Papers*, 37, pp. 426–47.

MAIN, B. and RAFFE, D. (1983a) 'The industrial destinations of Scottish school leavers 1977–1981', *Fraser of Allander Institute Quarterly Economic Commentary*, 8, 3, pp. 37–49.

MAIN, B. and RAFFE, D. (1983b) 'The "transition from school to work" in 1980/81: A dynamic account', *British Educational Research Journal*, 9, 1, pp. 57–70.

NATIONAL YOUTH EMPLOYMENT COUNCIL (1974) *Unqualified, Untrained and Unemployed*, London, HMSO.

RAFFE, D. (1984) 'The transition from school to work and the recession: Evidence from the Scottish School Leavers Survey, 1977–83', *British Journal of Sociology of Education*, 5, 3, pp. 247–65.

RAFFE, D. (1986) 'Change and continuity in the youth labour market: A critical review of structural explanations of youth unemployment' in ALLEN, S.,

WATON, A., PURCELL, K. and WOOD, S. (Eds) *The Experience of Unemployment*, Basingstoke, Macmillan.

ROBERTS, K., DENCH, S. and RICHARDSON, D. (1986) 'Youth employment in the 1980s', *Employment Gazette*, 94, 6, pp. 241–6.

SHELLY, M. (1987) *Scottish Young People's Post-School Destinations 1977–1983*, unpublished PhD thesis, University of Edinburgh.

THUROW, L. (1976) *Generating Inequality*, Basingstoke, Macmillan.

WELLS, W. (1987) 'The relative pay and employment of young people' in JUNANKAR, P.N. (Ed.) *From School to Unemployment? The Labour Market for Young People*, Basingstoke, Macmillan.

Chapter 5:

...But They Don't Want to Work, Do They? Unemployment and Work Ethics among Young People in Scotland

Andy Furlong

INTRODUCTION

According to Government statistics, the number of young people under 25 who are unemployed currently stands at over a million (*Employment Gazette*, 1987). This number is certainly an underestimate. In order to qualify for inclusion in these statistics young people must meet the rigid criteria which make them eligible for state benefits. Many fail to qualify because they do not register as unemployed (Roberts *et al.*, 1981), or because they have not been out of work long enough since leaving school. Many more are on Government-sponsored training schemes, under-employed, or have decided to remain in education while they are looking for work.

Statistics on unemployment are selective. While they exclude some young people who are genuinely looking for a job, they also convey the impression that unemployment is a minority experience. This is misleading, as unemployment statistics are 'snapshots' which do not usually show the numbers of young people who experience unemployment as part of the transition from school. Some commentators have suggested that the number of young people who experience unemployment is as much as three times the number who are unemployed at any one time (Roberts *et al.*, 1982) and when a youth unemployment rate reaches 20 per cent, the majority of young people will spend a period out of work.

Despite the enormity of the problem when unemployment becomes a normal part of the transition from school in many parts of the country, it is not uncommon to hear unemployed young people described as 'workshy'. Mention youth unemployment, and the response will often begin: 'the trouble with young people today is that they don't want to work...'. Such sentiments are not confined to the tabloid press, but are often echoed by government ministers in politically emotive speeches. Behind many of the policy initiatives aimed at the young unemployed is a fear that those experiencing unemployment during their formative years will become the long-term unemployed in future years. Yet if policy initiatives are to ease the problems caused by unemployment and prevent the formation of a hard core of unemployed, it is essential to understand fully the consequences of unemployment for young people.

Government reaction to youth unemployment has mainly taken the form of work experience and training schemes. However, both the Job Creation Programme (1975) and the Youth Opportunities Programme (1978) were widely criticized for providing little in the way of training for young people, while providing employers with a free source of labour (Stafford, 1981; Cohen, 1982; Watts, 1983). At this time the whole context of industrial training was at the forefront of debate due to the economic recession. In response to this debate, the Manpower Services Commission (MSC) developed its New Training Initiative which aimed to improve the training of the British workforce (MSC, 1981).

The Youth Training Scheme (YTS) was part of the New Training Initiative which was concerned to improve the training of young people by giving all young people the opportunity to enter post-16 education, training or a period of planned work experience which would include elements of off-the-job training. In practice, a compromise was reached when it came to implementing the new scheme. While MSC had envisaged YTS as a training initiative available to all young people whether employed or unemployed, the Government was primarily concerned with providing training for unemployed school leavers. Consequently, the emphasis of the scheme changed from what was intended as a comprehensive training scheme, to a measure which largely concentrated on the unemployed (Hockley, 1984).

Government reactions to youth unemployment must be seen in the context of these training schemes. With these schemes set up and with guarantees that all school leavers who remain unemployed by the Christmas after leaving school will be offered a place, those without a job who reject YTS are often regarded as 'workshy'. This has led to calls to make YTS compulsory for unemployed young people by refusing benefits to those turning down the offer of a training place.

In this chapter I will look at the characteristics of young people in Scotland who were unemployed at the time of the 1986 survey and examine their employment commitment and their job-search attitudes and behaviour. This survey covered young people who had been in the fourth year of secondary school in the academic year 1983/84. At the time of this survey, their average age was about 17 years and 9 months. Of this age cohort, 40 per cent were in full-time jobs at the time, 19 per cent were unemployed and 7 per cent were on YTS. Most of those who were on YTS at this stage would have joined at 17. At this time, 17-year-olds were only eligible to join YTS if they were unemployed. (Further details of their destinations are provided in chapter 1 of this volume). By looking at the characteristics of the unemployed and their employment commitment and job-search attitudes and behaviour, we should be able to learn more about youth unemployment and see if there are any grounds for describing unemployed young people as workshy.

CHARACTERISTICS OF THE UNEMPLOYED

Although unemployment has become a normal part of the transition from school, the social composition of the young people who are unemployed at this point in time merits further examination. Firstly though, it is important to note that the definition of unemployment used here is a self-reported one, defined in the questionnaire as 'unemployed and looking for work'.

In any examination of the unemployed, the first thing that becomes obvious is that they are not an undifferentiated group. Some had been continuously unemployed since leaving school, while others had spent time on YTS, had a previous job or done both. Table 5.1 highlights some of the characteristics of those who were unemployed at the time of the survey and contrasts them with those who were not unemployed at the time. A comparison across any of these items shows quite clearly that those who were unemployed were socially and educationally disadvantaged. In terms of social background, those who were unemployed were less likely to have a father employed in a professional or managerial occupation. The unemployed were also more likely to have a father who was unemployed or working on a part-time basis.

One of the reasons why unemployment often runs in families is that young people with a parent who is unemployed are less likely to be in contact with the social networks of the employed. Such networks have been shown to be important when it comes to finding employment in firms which recruit largely through word-of-mouth contact (Manwaring, 1984). When levels of unemployment rise, there is often a tendency for firms to increase their reliance on informal recruitment methods (Manwaring and Wood, 1984).

Unemployment also has a tendency to be concentrated within families due to the role of education in the social reproduction of inequality. There is a strong link between the level of educational certification achieved by young people and the types of work they are likely to find upon leaving school or

Table 5.1: *Social and educational characteristics by labour-market status*

	Father in class I or II[1]	Father unemployed or working part-time[1]	% in each group with:				
			Father in education at 17	Mother in education at 17	No SCEs by end of S4	No 'O' grades in bands A-C by end of S4	4+ 'O' grades in bands A-C by end of S4
Not unemployed	32	9	14	13	12	19	53
Unemployed (no job or YTS)	16	26	5	3	40	47	28
Unemployed (ex-job, no YTS)	19	15	3	5	37	45	19
Unemployed (no job, ex-YTS)	7	26	2	3	53	69	7
Unemployed (ex-job, ex-YTS)	6	20	3	2	52	64	7

Note: 1.Details of fathers' social class and employment status were collected at the time of the 1985 survey.

college (Gray *et al.*, 1983). Young people with poor educational qualifications have an increased chance of becoming unemployed. This is illustrated in table 5.1 where we can see that those who were unemployed tended to have lower educational qualifications than their peers. Further to this, there is a well documented link between low social class and poor educational achievement (Tyler, 1977; Reid, 1978; Halsey, Heath and Ridge, 1980). Again, table 5.1 demonstrates that the parents of those without jobs were less likely to have enjoyed an extended education themselves. As a result, they may not have been in a position to advise their children on the benefits of post-compulsory education.

Among those who were unemployed at this point in time, there were some important differences. These young people had a variety of post-school experiences, they had a range of qualifications and came from different social backgrounds. Those who were the most disadvantaged in social and educational terms did not necessarily have the greatest experience of unemployment. For example, a greater proportion of those who had been continuously unemployed had fathers in social class I or II than those who had had jobs and been on YTS. And those who had been continuously unemployed were more likely to have gained four or more 'O' grades at A–C than were those who had had jobs and been on YTS.

The most disadvantaged sections of the unemployed tended to be those who had spent some time on the Youth Training Scheme. Those with experience of YTS were the least likely to have had a father in social class I or II and the most likely to have gained no SCEs by the end of their fourth year at school. Those who had been continuously unemployed since leaving school and those who had had a job but not been on YTS had more favourable social and educational backgrounds.

EMPLOYMENT COMMITMENT

In modern industrial society work is central to the lives of most people. Indeed, work has often been regarded as central to the nature of man. (Marx and Engels, for example, described man as 'homo laborans'.) Much of our pre-adult lives are spent in preparation for future work roles, learning the skills and disciplines required in later life. Lifestyle, income and status are all strongly related to the sorts of work we do. Therefore it is not surprising to find that most young people have a strong commitment to work.

Yet to speak in a general sense of employment commitment can be misleading as people are committed to different aspects of work. For some people, work is a central part of their overall self concept. These young people tend to regard work as a central feature of their lives. Through work they achieve, and gain pleasure and satisfaction. Conversely, others do most of their living off the job (Lodahl and Kejner, 1965; Ashton and Field, 1976). Work is a peripheral part of their overall self-image, and may be regarded as an uncongenial and unsatisfying feature of life which supplies the material resources for enjoyment of leisure time.

The different aspects of work that young people regard as important are central to an understanding of work ethics, which are often defined in a form more appropriate to middle-class forms of work (Ashton, 1986). This 'middle-class work ethic' (*ibid.*) shares the assumptions of the Protestant work ethic in which work was regarded as a moral duty and as an activity which enabled self-fulfilment. This sort of employment commitment is illustrated by a back-page comment:

> I feel if I were offered a full-time job of a nature which interested me,
> my life would become more complete and worthwhile.

Yet many jobs are alienating and produce few rewards. In these circumstances satisfactions are not gained through work, but through material rewards or participation in shop-floor cultures and collective action. Commitment at this level is not necessarily linked to any of the inherent satisfactions which may be gained from work as an activity. Commitment to work may be simply due to the importance of the material rewards to be gained from employment, in which case lack of satisfaction from life without a job can often be tied to the importance of money. This is illustrated by a young person who was unemployed:

> I would like a job for money and to take up my spare time because it
> can be boring being unemployed.

In the 1986 survey, young people were asked to agree or disagree with four statements which probed their employment commitment: 'Having almost any job is better than being unemployed', 'I could easily get enough satisfaction out of life without a job', 'If you haven't got a job, life is rather pointless and a waste of time', and 'A person must have a job to feel a full member of society'. Table 5.2 shows the responses to these statements among the year group.

Firstly, it is important to note that in a general sense employment commitment among young people is high. The majority of young people agreed (63 per cent) that having any job is preferable to being unemployed, and most young people (56 per cent) felt that, without a job, they would be unable to lead a satisfying life; for some this would be because work is a central part of their identity, while for others it would be mainly because they needed money in order to use non-employed time satisfactorily. Even so, most (68 per cent) did not agree that without a job, 'life is rather pointless and a waste of time'.

Table 5.2:   Response frequencies for employment commitment scale items (percentages)

	Strongly agree	Agree	Not sure	Disagree	Strongly disagree
Having almost any job is better than being unemployed	25 n = 2573	38	13	18	5
I could easily get enough satisfaction out of life without a job	5 n = 2564	16	23	34	23
If you haven't got a job, life is rather pointless and a waste of time	7 n = 2569	12	12	40	28
A person must have a job to feel a full member of society	12 n = 2563	27	20	31	11

Yet many young people (42 per cent) did not feel that it was necessary to have a job in order to be accepted as a full member of society. In part, this attitude is a result of rising levels of unemployment which have had far-reaching effects on the youth transition. The transition from youth to adulthood used to be marked by the first wage packet. At this stage, young people would often regard themselves as full members of society, even though parents and older workmates often took longer to accept their claims to adult status. More recently, other stages in the process of becoming an adult have often been completed prior to economic independence through work (Roberts, 1985). Roberts has pointed out that the pattern of economic independence as a later stage of the transition, which has long been the normal pattern for those undergoing higher education, is becoming a more common experience.

It is important to be aware that the questions have only been used at one time point. Consequently, from this information, we are unable to distinguish cause and effect. While we may be able to identify a relationship between situational factors and attitudes, we cannot say with any certainty whether the situation is a result of the attitude, or the attitude is a result of the situation.

To aid interpretation of these findings, an employment commitment scale was constructed from the four statements in table 5.2. Responses were scored from 1 to 5 to indicate the strength of agreement or disagreement with a given item, the highest score being given to the most positive response. In all surveys the information collected suffers to some extent from measurement error. This is a problem which tends to be more acute in the collection of attitudinal data than is the case with more factual information (Cuttance, 1986). Checks on the reliability of responses to attitudinal questions are limited. When information is gathered using semi-structured interviews, responses to attitudinal questions which appear to contradict other responses may be probed. In postal surveys this sort of check is not possible. One method which is frequently used in dealing with attitudinal data is the use of scales. Grouping sets of related questions can help enhance reliability through avoiding dependence on one single question. Thus attitudinal scales are often regarded as being more reliable than are the single constituent elements of which the scale is composed (Thomas and Wetherall, 1974).

Table 5.3: Mean employment commitment scale values, by labour-market experience

	x̄	n
Job (no YTS)	12.8	531
Job (ex-YTS)	12.9	423
YTS	12.6	192
Unemployed (no job or YTS)	12.1	73
Unemployed (ex-job, no YTS)	12.5	65
Unemployed (no job, ex-YTS)	12.2	155
Unemployed (ex-job, ex-YTS)	12.7	87
All in the labour market	12.7	1526

ANOVA $p<0.05$

The employment commitment scale thus constructed varied only slightly with current labour-market status and experience, although the variation was statistically significant at the 5 per cent level (table 5.3). Two of the categories of unemployed young people (those who had past experience of YTS as well as employment, and those who had been employed but not been on YTS) had levels of employment commitment not much lower than those who were working. Those with the lowest levels of employment commitment were those who had never had a job; it made little difference whether their unemployment had been continuous or whether it had been interrupted by a spell on YTS.

As we have seen, those who were unemployed were socially and educationally disadvantaged in relation to the rest of the cohort. Yet these disadvantages were not directly related to low employment commitment. The group who were most disadvantaged in social and educational terms (those with experience of both a job and YTS) had a higher level of employment commitment than any of the other categories of unemployed. It is the group with no experience of full-time paid employment who had the lowest levels of employment commitment. Experience of YTS was only associated with relatively high levels of employment commitment in cases where a young person also had experience of a full time job.

The lack of a longitudinal dimension to this question means that from the available evidence we are unable to affirm that it is the experience of unemployment which leads to a reduced employment commitment. Yet if length of unemployment does lead to a reduced employment commitment it is unlikely to be because young people are discovering alternative and more enjoyable ways of filling their time. Studies which have looked at the ways in which unemployed young people spend their time have concluded that unemployment has a detrimental effect on leisure activities (Willis, 1985). Unemployed young people often spend much of their time 'in bed, watching television and listening to the radio' (Roberts, 1985). Unemployment benefit does not stretch very far, and even poorly paid jobs usually leave the young person better off financially than living from one 'Giro' to the next. The money earned through employment can enable a young person to lead a fuller life as it allows them to participate in more activities than would otherwise be the case. In addition, a job helps structure time by filling a day which may otherwise be empty. A young person who had recently lost his job illustrates these points:

> Now that I'm unemployed, I feel very depressed some of the time. Looking back I wish I was still working because I miss the money and I had something to do during the day, also I miss the laugh I get with the workmates.

For females a job may help prevent the isolation which often occurs as they are drawn into performing the household chores (Furlong, 1987b).

Rather than unemployment reducing employment commitment, it would seem more plausible to suggest that those gaining work experience in 'real jobs' increase their commitment as a result of their experiences. The biggest differences in employment commitment in table 5.3 are not between the employed and the unemployed, but between those who had had any experience of full-time employment and those who had not. Despite the emphasis which is placed on preparation for work roles in the family and school, throughout adolescence young people have given their lives meaning through experiences outside of the labour market, such as through school and leisure achievements. It is likely that work experience increases employment commitment as the young worker becomes habituated to the work role. However, work experience gained through YTS only tends to be associated with continued high levels of employment commitment in cases where the young person has found a job.

JOB-SEARCH ATTITUDES

On the basis of the evidence considered we have seen that most of the young people who were unemployed have a strong commitment to work, especially if they had had a job. Yet it is commonly suggested that young people do not look hard enough for jobs. In the 1986 survey, those who were unemployed or on YTS were asked to agree or disagree with three statements which were used to examine their job-search attitudes (table 5.4): 'I can't be bothered looking for a job any more', 'I'm looking for a job as hard as I've ever done' and 'It's not worth chasing after jobs nowadays'.

Table 5.4: Job-search attitudes of respondents who were unemployed or on YTS in spring 1986 (percentages)

	Strongly agree	Agree	Not sure	Disagree	Strongly disagree
I can't be bothered looking for a job any more	1 n = 555	6	8	45	40
I'm looking for a job as hard as I've ever done	24 n = 560	46	14	14	2
It's not worth chasing after jobs nowadays	4 n = 556	8	12	40	36

Responses to these statements show quite clearly that young people without jobs had positive attitudes when it came to looking for work. Very few of these young people agreed that they couldn't 'be bothered looking for work any more', a majority felt that they were looking for a job 'as hard as ever', and most did not feel that jobs are 'not worth chasing' these days. It was a small minority of young people who were sufficiently disillusioned as a result of their experiences to say that jobs were 'not worth chasing' or that they 'can't be bothered looking for a job any more'. Slightly more young people (but still only 16 per cent) admitted that they were not looking as hard as they had done previously.

In order to examine the job-search attitudes of the unemployed in more detail, an attitude scale was constructed from the responses to the three statements in table 5.4. Earlier we saw that those who were unemployed had a variety of labour-market histories which were associated with different levels of employment commitment. Similarly, table 5.5 suggests that there was some variation in the job-search attitudes of the unemployed, although not at a statistically significant level. Those who had had no employment

Table 5.5: Mean job-search attitude scale values of those unemployed in spring 1986, by past labour-market experience

	x̄	n
Unemployed (no job or YTS)	11.3	71
Unemployed (ex-job, no YTS)	11.6	64
Unemployed (no job, ex-YTS)	11.7	152
Unemployed (ex-job, ex-YTS)	11.5	86
Sample mean	11.6	373

ANOVA p = 0.554 (not significant)

experience since leaving school had less positive job-search attitudes than those who had worked or been on YTS.

Although not conclusive, this evidence suggests that prolonged experience of unemployment was associated with a less positive job-search attitude. One of the reasons for this is that lack of success in finding work can often lead to a situation in which young people become discouraged and reduce their job-search efforts (Banks, Ullah and Warr, 1984; Banks and Ullah, 1986). If we compare current status and past labour-market experience with the job applications young people had made in the last three months (table 5.6), we can see that job-search attitude is differentially reflected in job-search behaviour insofar as those who had not worked since leaving school had made fewer job applications over this recent period.

Table 5.6: Number of jobs applied for in the past three months, by labour-market experience of respondents currently on YTS or unemployed (percentages)

	None	1–2	3+
YTS	47	23	29
Unemployed (no job or YTS)	41	20	39
Unemployed (ex-job, no YTS)	23	29	48
Unemployed (no job, ex-YTS)	25	23	52
Unemployed (ex-job, ex-YTS)	29	21	51

n = 1159, Chi-Square = 65.6, df = 8, p<0.001

For some young people, low job-search attitudes are reactions which can be explained in terms of discouragement due to past experience, as well as in terms of the psychological stages of unemployment. As the unemployed face rejection in their attempts to find work, so they become more disillusioned as they start to feel that their efforts are futile.

Such feelings are highlighted by a comment written on the back page of the questionnaire by an unemployed young woman.

I am very depressed as I have not worked for five months. My careers office keeps telling me to come in but when I do its just the same old thing ('sorry we have no vacancies at the moment'). But when you walk in the rain and the snow and they tell you the same thing all the time I feel like killing myself.

In a study of unemployed men in the United States, Yancey (1980) illustrated how people may restrict their job search in order to protect their self confidence. Some of the men interviewed by Yancey limited their job-search activities to calling casually on firms in order to ask if they had any work. Being told that a firm had no vacancies was seen as less of a blow to the self-confidence than was being rejected for a known vacancy.

For other young people reactions are different. A reluctance to take the first job that comes along or to join the Youth Training Scheme cannot be taken as indicative of a breakdown in work ethics, as many of those holding out and turning down job offers often have a high work commitment and are holding out for work of a sort which they expect to find rewarding.

In a study of Birmingham school leavers, Jones (1983) discovered that those young people with the greatest confidence in obtaining the sort of job they wanted tended to persist in their attempts to find that job, whilst those with lower levels of confidence were more likely to accept the less desirable alternative. Similarly, MacKay and Reid (1972) classified a group of redundant workers as the 'stickers' who would hold out for the types of work they wanted, and the 'snatchers' who often took the first job which came along. The strategy adopted was found to have a significant influence on the subsequent period of unemployment, with the average period of unemployment of the 'stickers' being more than twice that of the 'snatchers'.

Evidence of this kind supports the contention that the intensity of the job search cannot be equated with a willingness to work. In a recent study of young people in Leicester (Furlong, 1987a and 1987b) it was discovered that many of the unemployed continued to seek their ideal choice of occupation in the short term, rather than settle for something they regarded as second best. The reason for persisting in attempts to fulfil earlier aspirations was explained in terms of the 'image maintenance strategies' adopted by young people in order to protect the occupational self-concepts which have been built up and reinforced over many years. When the occupational self-concept is central to the overall self-image, then the investment made will often mean that young people are unwilling to abandon an aspiration without a fight.

To understand the relationship between employment commitment and job-search attitude it is necessary to be aware of the different ways in which people are committed to employment. An awareness of the different forms of employment commitment also helps us to understand differential experiences of unemployment. In other words, orientations towards work can affect the ways in which unemployment is experienced (Ashton and

Field, 1976). For young people for whom work is a central part of their self concepts, unemployment can be distressing due to uncertainty about implementing their self-concept. For those young people for whom work is more peripheral to their overall self-concept, satisfaction often comes not from the work task, but from the material rewards of worker status.

CONCLUSION

The effects of unemployment on young people are far-reaching. In many areas most young people experience unemployment as a part of their transition from school, and even those who manage to avoid it may be forced to settle for second-rate jobs, may join a training scheme or may decide to stay in education longer than they had originally intended. The causes of youth unemployment are complex, but to blame the unemployed for their plight at a time when unemployment is becoming a common part of the transitional period is very misleading. As we have seen, most young people have a strong commitment to employment as well as having a positive job-search attitude which is supported by their pattern of job applications. To suggest that high levels of youth unemployment are partly a consequence of the poor work attitudes of young people is to turn the problem on its head. For some young people it is the disillusionment which unemployment breeds which eventually leads to despondency and may result in reduced efforts in the search for work.

Prolonged periods of unemployment are associated with less positive job-search attitudes. In turn this makes it more difficult for a young person to enter the labour market and creates a hard core of long-term unemployed. It is a vicious cycle. The longer they spend out of work, the more disillusioned young people get, and it becomes less likely that they will find a job.

Those who have never had a 'real job' since leaving school have the lowest levels of employment commitment. This is not because they were 'workshy' in the first place. Rather it is because they have never had a job that employment commitment has not developed. The young people who have never had a job but have had experience of the Youth Training Scheme have similar levels of employment commitment to those who have been continuously unemployed.

In this respect there is little value for youth training schemes or the community service schemes advocated by Marsland (1984) as it is doubtful whether enforced placement on schemes will strengthen employment commitment; it may have the reverse effect. In some cases participation on schemes may result in increased employment commitment. Yet there may be little benefit if the young person spends a long period out of work after the scheme. Indeed, in circumstances where schemes are little more than interruptions to a continuous cycle of unemployment, participation may be frustrating.

The use of the job-search attitude scale and the employment commitment scale helps us understand young people's work ethics more fully, and in particular they help us to see some of the less visible effects of the unemployment experience. Although the concepts are useful in this respect, it is important that analysis is not constrained by the concepts but moves beyond them. The employment commitment scale, for example, does not recognize the different forms of commitment which may result in the same overall level of commitment.

The evidence examined in this chapter suggests that it would be worthwhile to look more closely at employment commitment, especially longitudinally. The analysis presented here has also shown the importance of examining current status in relation to labour-market biography. As unemployment becomes more commonplace, it is important not to treat the unemployed as an undifferentiated mass, but to look at the experiences prior to unemployment which are often more revealing.

ACKNOWLEDGEMENTS

I would like to thank David Raffe for his helpful comments on an earlier draft, as well as the other members of the Centre for Educational Sociology (CES) with whom I have discussed the issues raised in this chapter.

REFERENCES

ASHTON, D.N. (1986) *Unemployment Under Capitalism: The Sociology of British and American Labour Markets*, Brighton, Wheatsheaf.

ASHTON, D.N. and FIELD, D. (1976) *Young Workers*, London, Hutchinson.

BANKS, M. and ULLAH, P. (1986) *Youth Unemployment: Social and Psychological Perspectives*, Research Paper No. 61, London, Department of Employment.

BANKS, M., ULLAH, P. and WARR, P. (1984) 'Unemployment and less qualified urban young people', *Employment Gazette*, 92, 8, August, pp. 343–6.

COHEN, P. (1982) 'School for dole', *New Socialist*, January/February, pp. 43–7.

CUTTANCE, P. (1986) 'Towards a typology of information to aid reliability of response in social surveys', *Quality and Quantity*, 20, pp. 27–52.

Employment Gazette, (1987) 95, 7, September.

FURLONG, A. (1987a) 'Coming to terms with the decline in demand for youth labour' in BROWN, P. and ASHTON, D.N. (Eds) *Education, Unemployment and Labour Markets*, Lewes, Falmer Press.

FURLONG, A. (1987b) *The Effects of Youth Unemployment on the Transition from School*, unpublished PhD thesis, University of Leicester.

GRAY, J., MCPHERSON, A.F. and RAFFE, D. (1983) *Reconstructions of Secondary Education: Theory, Myth and Practice since the War*, London, Routledge and Kegan Paul.

HALSEY, A.H., HEATH, A.F. and RIDGE, J.M. (1980) *Origins and Destinations: Family Class and Education in Modern Britain*, Oxford, Clarendon Press.

HOCKLEY, J. (1984) *The Implementation of the Youth Training Scheme in Three Local Labour Markets*, report to the Department of Employment (unpublished).

JONES, P. (1983) 'Effects of rising unemployment on school leavers', *Employment Gazette*, 91, 1, January, pp. 13–16.

LODAHL, M.M. and KEJNER, M. (1965) 'The definition and measurement of job involvement', *Journal of Applied Psychology*, 49, pp. 24–33.

MACKAY, D.I. and REID, G.L. (1972) 'Redundancy, unemployment and manpower policy', *Economic Journal*, 82, pp. 1256–72.

MANPOWER SERVICES COMMISSION (1981) *A New Training Initiative; A Consultative Document*, London, Manpower Services Commission.

MANWARING, T. (1984) 'The extended internal labour market', *Cambridge Journal of Economics*, 8, 2.

MANWARING, T. and WOOD, S. (1984) 'Recruitment and the recession' in BEARDSWORTH, A. (Ed.) 'Employers and recruitment: Explorations in labour demand', *International Journal of Social Economics*, 11, 7.

MARSLAND, D. (1984) 'Youth unemployment: Ideology, policy and social action', paper presented to the annual conference of the British Sociological Association, Bradford.

REID, I. (1978) *Sociological Perspectives on School and Education*, London, Open Books.

ROBERTS, K. (1985) 'Youth in the 1980's: A new way of life', *International Social Science Journal*, 37, 4.

ROBERTS, K., DUGGAN, J. and NOBLE, M. (1981) *Unregistered Youth Unemployment and Outreach Careers Work: Final Report, Part One, Non-Registration*, London, Department of Employment.

ROBERTS, K., DUGGAN, J. and NOBLE, M. (1982) 'Out-of-school youth in high unemployment areas: An empirical investigation', *British Journal of Guidance and Counselling*, 10, 1, pp. 1–11.

STAFFORD, A. (1981) 'Learning not to labour', *Capital and Class*, 15.

THOMAS, R. and WETHERALL, D. (1974) *Looking Forward to Work*, London, HMSO.

TYLER, W. (1977) *The Sociology of Educational Inequality*, London, Methuen.

WATTS, A.G. (1983) 'Skill transfer and post-YTS realities', *Lifeskills Teaching Magazine*, 2, 2, April, pp. 13–16.

WILLIS, P. (1985) *The Social Condition of Young People in Wolverhampton in 1984*, Wolverhampton, Wolverhampton Borough Council.

YANCEY, W.L. (1980) 'Intervention as a strategy of social inquiry: An exploratory study with unemployed Negro men' in ZURCHER, L.A. and BONJEAN, C.M. *Planned Social Intervention*, Scranton, USA, Chandler Publishing.

Chapter 6:

A Tale of Four Cities: Social and Spatial Inequalities in the Youth Labour Market

Catherine Garner, Brian G.M. Main and David Raffe

SOCIAL AND SPATIAL INEQUALITY

When social inequalities are the subject of public debate in Britain they are often depicted in spatial terms. Thus social divisions within the country are frequently portrayed in terms of the contrast between the (depressed) north and the (prosperous) south, notwithstanding significant pockets of southern poverty or northern prosperity, or the internal heterogeneity of Scotland, a part of the north (see chapter 1 in this volume). Similarly, the problems of the most disadvantaged members of society are often discussed in terms of the 'inner cities', despite rural poverty and the fact that much of the worst urban deprivation is to be found not in the centre of large cities but on their peripheral housing estates.

Geography does matter. Several recent studies of the youth labour market have demonstrated large differences in the fortunes of young people seeking jobs in different areas (Ryrie, 1983; Ashton and Maguire, 1986; Coles, 1986; Roberts *et al.*, 1987). Other studies, based on single areas, have implicitly reflected this insight by situating their research clearly within its local context and its specific social and economic features (Wallace, 1987; Hutson and Jenkins, 1987; Lee *et al.*, 1987). At the same time, these studies show that many inequalities affecting young people's transition from school and their progress within the labour market cannot be expressed solely in spatial terms. They reveal substantial inequalities *within* areas, associated with gender, class, ethnicity, education or other dimensions of social differentiation. Moreover they sometimes suggest that the same factors, unequally distributed as they are (except for gender) across areas, may explain at least some of the observed inequalities *between* areas.

The spatial representation of inequality in public debate can be understood in at least two ways. On the one hand spatial concepts can be used as code for other correlated aspects of inequality that may lack the same political acceptability or legitimacy. Thus, the 'north' often appears to be code for 'working class', and the 'inner city' code for 'black'. The implication is that spatial inequalities are merely derivative of other 'social' inequalities, for example those associated with class or ethnicity. On the other hand the spatial dimension, and the variation in access and opportunity it represents, may matter in its own right; the opportunities and advantages of otherwise comparable people may depend directly on where they live.

These two interpretations of spatial inequality yield testable empirical propositions. The first predicts that spatial inequalities, being derivative of 'social' inequalities, would disappear in an analysis that controlled for them. Conversely, the second predicts that spatial inequalities would still be found even among people with the same social characteristics. However, which proposition is valid might depend on the context. It might depend, first, on the criterion of inequality: spatial inequality in (say) access to education might require a different explanation from spatial inequality in employment and unemployment. Second, it might depend on the range and type of spatial variation. We might need different explanations for spatial inequalities within local labour markets than for inequalities between them. This chapter explores the relation of social to spatial inequality within and between labour markets with respect to the post-school destinations of school leavers.

THE 'LOCAL VARIATIONS' PROJECT

Our analysis looks at inequalities in respect of three outcomes: entry to full-time post-school education; entry to employment; and entry to a 'skilled' occupation. For each of these it explores the relationships between four types of inequality, respectively: differences between cities; gender differences; differences between areas within each city; and differences associated with other aspects of social and educational status. We use data on the experiences of 1979/80 school leavers from Scotland's four large cities: Aberdeen, Dundee, Edinburgh and Glasgow. The data were analyzed in the course of a research project whose main aim was to explain differences in the employment chances of school leavers from different areas of a large city. In other words, we wanted to find out whether and why school leavers from the 'inner city', or other deprived urban areas, were disadvantaged. We used data from the 1981 Scottish School Leavers Survey, which covered an exceptionally large sample and thus gave us the opportunity for more focused analysis within each city. We also used small-area statistics from the

1981 Census. Not only was the Census carried out within a few weeks of the survey, but the small-area statistics provided, at a detailed local level, indicators of a range of characteristics of areas that we hypothesized to be associated with advantage and disadvantage among school leavers. Full details of the study are reported by Garner *et al.* (1987a); selected analyses and conclusions, focusing mainly on Glasgow, are presented by Garner *et al.* (1987b and 1988).

THE FOUR CITIES

Scotland has four cities with populations over 100,000. Glasgow has a population of three-quarters-of-a-million, as at the 1981 Census; Edinburgh has just over 400,000 and Dundee and Aberdeen have less than 200,000 each (OPCS, 1984). The demographic structure of the population is remarkably similar in all four cities with an approximate 47 per cent to 53 per cent male–female split and around 20 per cent of their populations of school age and younger. In terms of the Registrar General's Social Class composition, however, there are significant differences among the four, with Aberdeen and Edinburgh having 22.1 per cent and 26.2 per cent respectively in classes I and II compared with only 11.6 per cent and 18.1 per cent respectively for Glasgow and Dundee. Not surprisingly, there is a similar variation across the four cities in the proportions of men and women with higher educational qualifications.

Glasgow and Dundee are more heavily involved in the energy, manufacturing and construction industries with 35.8 and 40.2 per cent of their employed residents working in these three areas compared with 31.7 per cent in Aberdeen and 25.4 per cent in Edinburgh. Aberdeen has three times as much employment in energy-related industries as any of the other cities and also a higher proportion employed in the distribution and catering trades, 24.1 per cent compared with around 19 per cent in Dundee, Edinburgh and Glasgow. Edinburgh has a markedly higher proportion of employment in the service sector than the three other cities: 47.5 per cent in comparison with around 35 per cent in the others.

Not only do employment structures vary, but so too do levels of unemployment. At the 1981 Census this stood at 24.3 per cent of all 16–64-year-old males in Glasgow, 17.7 per cent in Dundee, 11.1 per cent in Edinburgh and 8.1 per cent in Aberdeen, while the British average stood at 11.6 per cent. Female unemployment rates (for women aged 16–59) ranged from 13.2 per cent in Glasgow through 13 per cent in Dundee to 6.2 per cent in Edinburgh and 4.9 per cent in Aberdeen. This compared with a British average of 7.7 per cent. The range in female unemployment rates broadly mirrors the range in the male rates, but the ratio of male to female rates suggests that Glasgow and Edinburgh may be relatively biased towards female employment, and Dundee towards male employment.

SCHOOL LEAVERS FROM THE FOUR CITIES

For the purposes of our study we redefined the boundaries of the four cities to approximate the likely local labour market for young people. The scope of the main city bus service was our main criterion in judging this. As a result we studied areas which were generally larger than the administrative units on which the Census figures reported above were based. Allowing for this, the social and educational backgrounds of school leavers from the four cities in the 1981 survey reveal similar differences. The proportion with fathers in social classes I and II was highest in Aberdeen and Edinburgh (28 per cent each) and lowest in Dundee (17 per cent) and Glasgow (16 per cent). The percentage who described their fathers as either unemployed or unable to work ranged even more widely, from 6 per cent in Aberdeen through 8 per cent in Edinburgh to 14 per cent in Dundee and 24 per cent in Glasgow.

The educational attainments of school leavers varied rather less across the cities. The percentage leaving school with Higher grade passes was highest in Edinburgh (36 per cent), but varied little between Aberdeen (28 per cent), Dundee (26 per cent) and Glasgow (25 per cent). However educational differences measured by a single benchmark may be misleading. For example Aberdeen had easily the highest proportion of school leavers with four or more 'O' grades but no Highers, suggesting that its relatively buoyant labour market encouraged many well-qualified pupils to leave school at 16 rather than attempt further qualifications. In the decisions about staying on at school, 'push' factors (such as Aberdeen's favourable social composition) may be balanced by 'pull' factors (such as the local opportunities for employment).

Table 6.1 summarizes the destinations of school leavers in relation to the first two aspects of inequality listed above: city and gender. It covers a representative sample of all young people who left school, at any age, in or at the end of the 1979/80 session; and it describes their status at the time of the survey the following spring, typically in April or May 1981.

The first two columns show the percentage of male and female school leavers in full-time education. This includes not just university and other higher education but also non-advanced courses at colleges of further education. In each city more girls than boys were in full-time education. The differences between cities were small, particularly among boys. Edinburgh, with the best qualified and most middle-class school leavers, had the highest

Table 6.1: *School leavers' destinations in spring 1981, by city and gender*

	% in full-time education		% of labour-market entrants in employment		% of employees in 'skilled' job	
	Males	*Females*	*Males*	*Females*	*Males*	*Females*
Aberdeen (n = 881)	19	23	88	87	63	69
Dundee (n = 555)	18	29	63	57	62	53
Edinburgh (n = 1521)	22	30	74	81	66	64
Glasgow (n = 3741)	18	21	55	61	64	63

participation in full-time education, but there was little variation among the other three cities except for Dundee girls whose participation was a mere percentage point behind Edinburgh. As with respect to school attainment, the social and educational push factors may not always coincide with the labour-market pull; the high female participation in Dundee may reflect their relatively poor employment prospects, just as the low participation in Aberdeen (relative to school leavers' social and educational backgrounds) may reflect the rival attraction of a more favourable labour market.

Most of the school leavers who did not continue in full-time education entered the labour market. The middle two columns of table 6.1 show the proportions of male and female labour-market entrants who were in jobs in spring 1981. At this time the Youth Opportunities Programme (YOP), the predecessor of the Youth Training Scheme, was only available to unemployed school leavers; YOP trainees are counted as being in the labour market but not in jobs. Employment rates ranged from 88 per cent of boys in Aberdeen to 55 per cent of boys in Glasgow. The variation in employment rates across the four cities therefore reflects the variation in all-age (un)employment rates reported earlier in this chapter. Girls had higher employment rates than boys in Edinburgh and Glasgow, and lower in Dundee – again reflecting a tendency we noted in respect of the all-age data. Not only do school leavers' employment chances vary across cities, but the variation closely resembles the concurrent variation in adults' chances.

The last two columns of table 6.1 show, for males and females respectively, the proportion of employed school leavers in 'skilled' jobs. These were defined to include self-employed, non-manual (except sales), supervisory and skilled manual occupations, using the Registrar General's Socio-Economic Groups (OPCS, 1981) as the main reference. At best this is a crude measure of skill level and should be regarded as providing a rough indication of occupational differences. The proportion of boys in 'skilled' jobs varied considerably less across cities than their employment levels. There was slightly more variation among girls: Aberdeen had the highest proportion in 'skilled' jobs, and Dundee the lowest. Dundee's position can be largely attributed to the relatively small proportion (36 per cent) of girls in clerical and related occupations, compared with around 50 per cent in the other three cities.

INEQUALITIES WITHIN AND BETWEEN CITIES

We now turn to the other two types of inequality listed earlier. That is, we consider spatial variation within cities in addition to variation between them; and we examine how far either type of spatial inequality can by explained by what we shall term 'personal' advantage or disadvantage, that is by correlated inequalities in the educational and family backgrounds of school leavers. In other words, to what extent do the chances of comparable school leavers (that is, with like educational and family backgrounds) vary between advantaged and disadvantaged areas of each city? and how do these chances vary between the four cities?

In the course of our research we used multivariate (probit) techniques to estimate the 'effects' of various family and educational characteristics of school leavers, and various characteristics of the areas they lived in, on the three outcomes in table 6.1 – entry to full-time education, employment, and having a 'skilled' job. We produced our estimates separately for each city and, for Edinburgh and Glasgow, separately for males and females. (The smaller sample numbers in Dundee and Aberdeen compelled us to pool the sexes, with gender included as a separate but additive predictor in the model.) Full details of these analyses are presented elsewhere (Garner *et al.*, 1987a); here we summarize their conclusions by presenting the 'expected' outcomes of different 'stereotyped' school leavers from each city. These 'expected' outcomes are based on the probit analyses and are expressed in probabilistic form: they show the expected probability of a school leaver with certain characteristics being in full-time education, in employment or in a 'skilled' job respectively. They are shown in tables 6.2, 6.3 and 6.4.

For each city and each gender we identify four stereotypes, based on the permutations of 'advantaged' and 'disadvantaged' personal (educational and family) characteristics and 'advantaged' and 'disadvantaged' areas within each city.

Our 'personally advantaged' school leaver was defined in a standard way for each city. He or she left school from fifth year with one to three Highers passes, had a non-manual father who was not unemployed, had fewer than four siblings, and both parents educated beyond 15. Note that in some respects this school leaver does not represent the extreme of educational 'advantage'; an even more 'advantaged' school leaver might have left from sixth year and gained more than three Highers passes, but would have been unlikely to enter the labour market. By contrast our 'personally disadvantaged' school leaver had no qualifications and at least four siblings; both parents had left school at 15, and the father used to have a semi-skilled or unskilled manual job but was currently unemployed.

It proved inappropriate to devise standard stereotypes of advantaged and disadvantaged areas within each city, since the range of area characteristics varied between cities. Therefore we defined stereotyped 'advantaged' and 'disadvantaged' areas separately for each city, based on examples of areas at the extremes of the existing range within each city. However in each city the 'advantaged' area tended to have less overcrowding, fewer single-parent families, fewer 16–19-year-olds in the economically active population, and more owner-occupation, more travelling to work by car and more service sector employment.[1] School leavers' home addresses were used to identify the area of the city they came from.

Table 6.2 shows the estimated probability that each of our school-leaver stereotypes would be in full-time education in spring 1981. Probabilities are expressed on a range from zero to one: a probability of zero means that the school leaver would certainly not have been in full-time education, a probability of one means that he or she certainly would have been.

Whatever their gender, and wherever they lived, personally advantaged school leavers were substantially (and significantly, in statistical terms) more likely to be in full-time education. By far the most important aspect of personal advantage that influenced this outcome was the level of school qualifications, but social class appeared to have an additional effect. The probability of advantaged school leavers being in full-time education varied

Table 6.2: *Estimated probability of being in full-time education in spring 1981: 1979/80 school-leaver stereotypes*

		Males		Females	
		Personally advantaged	*Personally disadvantaged*	*Personally advantaged*	*Personally disadvantaged*
Aberdeen	advantaged area	.11	.01	.18	.03
	disadvantaged area	.10	.01	.17	.03
Dundee	advantaged area	.41	.02	.59	.05
	disadvantaged area	.21	.00	.38	.02
Edinburgh	advantaged area	.23	.01	.24	.05
	disadvantaged area	.14	.00	.08	.01
Glasgow	advantaged area	.46	.01	.47	.04
	disadvantaged area	.53	.01	.57	.06

across cities, being much higher in Glasgow and Dundee than in Edinburgh and Aberdeen. In this context it must be remembered that our 'advantaged' school leaver left from fifth year with one to three Highers passes; he or she would have been a marginal entrant to post-school full-time education, and in many cases would have entered a non-advanced course at college rather than higher education. It is likely that the decisions of these marginal school leavers on whether to continue full-time education were strongly influenced by the availability of desired jobs in the labour market, with the result that many more were attracted away from full-time education in Glasgow and Edinburgh rather than in the other two cities with weaker labour markets. An analysis which produced estimates for an intermediate category of advantaged school leavers, who left from fourth year with one to three 'O' grades, showed a similar variation across cities. However, among the personally disadvantaged, especially boys, the probability of full-time education was in all places negligible.

In Dundee and Edinburgh school leavers from advantaged areas of the city were more likely to continue in full-time education than those from disadvantaged areas. (The apparent difference between areas within Glasgow is not statistically significant.) This was somewhat unexpected: when we chose area characteristics to include in the analysis our main concern was to represent the factors most likely to influence success in the labour market, not in education. It is possible that the location of colleges and universities, or some aspects of their admissions procedures, resulted in more school-leaver entrants from some areas than from others. A more likely explanation is that 'area' variables served in our analysis as proxies for unmeasured (or imperfectly measured) variation in school leavers' educational or social background. In particular, young people from more advantaged areas may have attended schools where school leavers with given levels of attainment received more help and encouragement to continue in full-time education.

Table 6.3 is restricted to school leavers who entered the labour market, and shows the probability of employment for each of our stereotypes. Once again personally advantaged school leavers were substantially (and significantly) more likely to be employed, whatever their gender or location. Again, qualifications were the single most important aspect of personal advantage, with father's unemployment also having a significant (negative) influence on the employment of school leavers. There are several possible reasons why fewer school leavers with unemployed fathers were in jobs (Payne, 1987); among other things they were less likely to find jobs through informal 'word-of-mouth' recruitment channels.

Controlling for personal advantage, as in table 6.3, does not substantially affect the differences between cities observed from the aggregate comparisons in table 6.1. Both tables show that Aberdeen was the most

Table 6.3: Estimated probability of labour-market entrants being in employment in spring 1981: 1979/80 school-leaver stereotypes

		Males		Females	
		Personally advantaged	*Personally disadvantaged*	*Personally advantaged*	*Personally disadvantaged*
Aberdeen	advantaged area	.98	.72	.98	.69
	disadvantaged area	.98	.67	.97	.63
Dundee	advantaged area	.87	.38	.88	.38
	disadvantaged area	.90	.42	.89	.40
Edinburgh	advantaged area	.99	.50	.97	.61
	disadvantaged area	.97	.32	.95	.53
Glasgow	advantaged area	.90	.39	.86	.28
	disadvantaged area	.87	.33	.85	.27

favoured city, followed by Edinburgh, with Dundee and Glasgow the least favoured. In other words, variations between cities in school leavers' employment rate were not primarily the product of different levels of personal advantage. (The one exception concerns the relative employment rates of girls in Glasgow and Dundee. The aggregate figures in table 6.1 show Glasgow with the marginally higher rate, whereas the control for personal advantage in table 6.3 gives Dundee the higher rate.) The difference between cities emerges most clearly in relation to the personally disadvantaged. This is partly because the data are presented in terms of probabilities of employment rather than unemployment (a difference between employment probabilities of .90 and .99 may seem small, whereas that between unemployment probabilities of .10 and .01 is proportionately much greater). But the data are also consistent with a labour-queue model of occupational allocation in which qualifications and other personal indicators are used to identify each individual's position in the queue of job-applicants; employers recruit from the front of the queue and if jobs are scarce those near the back remain unemployed (Thurow, 1975). Thus, most personally advantaged school leavers find employment whichever kind of labour market they live in, whereas the disadvantaged are vulnerable to the state of the local labour market which affects whether employment levels are sufficient to recruit sufficiently far to the rear of the labour queue.

Table 6.3 also shows that in none of the four cities were comparable school leavers from advantaged areas of the city significantly more likely than those from disadvantaged areas to find employment. The main apparent exception concerns personally disadvantaged males in Edinburgh, but the area difference was not statistically significant: it could, in other words, have been a chance result of the sampling process. Area effects on employment within cities were a main concern of the project, which attempted alternative ways of representing them in the analysis for each city. None of these attempts revealed an area effect independent of the personal (educational and family) characteristics of school leavers from each area, so we are confident in our conclusion that no area effects of any size existed.

Table 6.4: Estimated probability of employees being in a 'skilled' job in spring 1981: 1979/80 school-leaver stereotypes

		Males		Females	
		Personally advantaged	*Personally disadvantaged*	*Personally advantaged*	*Personally disadvantaged*
Aberdeen	advantaged area	.86	.22	.89	.29
	disadvantaged area	.90	.30	.90	.33
Dundee	advantaged area	.83	.27	.67	.13
	disadvantaged area	.86	.30	.84	.28
Edinburgh	advantaged area	.98	.61	.98	.38
	disadvantaged area	1.00	.89	.95	.23
Glasgow	advantaged area	.99	.54	.74	.25
	disadvantaged area	.94	.21	.83	.35

Finally, table 6.4 shows the estimated probabilities of stereotyped school leavers who were in employment being in 'skilled' jobs. Once again personally advantaged school leavers were significantly better off, with qualifications the principal contributor. Among males, the comparisons of school leavers with the same personal characteristics reveal more differences between cities than the uncontrolled comparisons in table 6.1: Edinburgh boys were most likely to be in skilled jobs, followed by Glasgow, with boys from Aberdeen and Dundee the least likely. However it must be remembered that the probability of being in any job varied sharply between cities, particularly for the less advantaged. Employed boys in Glasgow were more likely to be in skilled jobs if they came from advantaged areas. This finding was not robust: it did not hold for all the different ways in which area effects were modelled in the analysis; and when job level was represented by a different measure (the Hope-Goldthorpe scale: Goldthorpe and Hope, 1974) no significant area effect was found. Apart from this somewhat equivocal finding none of the area effects within cities was statistically significant; indeed several were in the reverse direction to expectation, with more school leavers from disadvantaged areas in skilled employment.

DISCUSSION

Earlier in this chapter we distinguished spatial inequalities that were, in effect, derivative of other social inequalities, from inequalities where spatial factors mattered directly in their own right. We also distinguished spatial inequalities within local labour markets from those between them.

Neither distinction is conceptually straightforward. The social and the spatial are not empirically or logically independent: the spatial dimension is an essential constituent of social relationships (Massey, 1984). For example, when comparing the fortunes of stereotyped school leavers in different cities we standardized their fathers' (un)employment and occupation, treating these as aspects of personal advantage or disadvantage; yet especially in between-city comparisons these may be seen as outcomes of cities' local labour markets, and thus to reflect spatial advantage or disadvantage.

Distinguishing inequalities within local labour markets from those between them assumes that the boundaries of such markets can be identified. Yet in reality there are few clear boundaries: the effective 'local labour market' for a given worker may be very different from that of another worker living at the same address. We prefer Cheshire's (1979) concept of the effects of labour–market changes 'rippling out' from their source, becoming progressively weaker as they get further away. It follows that the distinction between inequalities within and between local labour markets is essentially one of degree. This point is probably less important with respect to cities than to other local labour markets. Our conclusions about spatial inequalities within cities would probably need to be qualified in relation to larger and less densely populated travel-to-work areas, where the geographical distances tend to be much greater and the identification of local labour markets more problematic.

Subject to these reservations, we draw two main conclusions from our study. The first is that inequalities between local labour markets (cities) are not merely derivative of other social inequalities; the spatial element matters in its own right. Thus, we found substantial variation between cities in the educational and employment chances of comparable school leavers. This was most evident with respect to employment: comparable school leavers seeking employment were much more likely to find it in Aberdeen and Edinburgh than in Dundee and Glasgow, and the differences were most clearly visible with respect to personally disadvantaged leavers. Differences with respect to the probability of skilled employment were smaller, and harder to interpret in terms of our stereotypes because of the different probabilities of school leavers finding a job. More surprisingly, perhaps, there were substantial differences between cities in the probabilities of comparable school leavers entering some kind of full-time post-school education. These differences appeared to reflect the availability of employment: school leavers in Glasgow and Dundee, with fewer employment opportunities, tended to opt for further education instead. If this interpretation is valid, it follows that the differences between employment opportunities in the four cities were greater than the survey employment rates suggest, since there were more 'discouraged workers' in Glasgow and Dundee who entered education rather than the labour market. Moreover, if entry to full-time education is partly a response to the scarcity of suitable employment, and if as we suspect vocational courses are the most affected, this raises questions about the articulation between full-time vocational education and the labour market. It suggests that entry to vocational education may be greatest in precisely those labour markets where employment opportunities, and presumably also the demand for vocationally qualified students, are most limited.

The second main conclusion from this study is that spatial inequalities within cities are more likely to be attributable to other social inequalities. Thus, we found no significant effect of area factors within cities on entry to employment, or on the skill level of job obtained – with the somewhat equivocal exception, in the latter case, of male school leavers in Glasgow. In two of the four cities entry to full-time education did seem to be influenced by area of residence. It is possible that this apparent effect merely reflects the influence of absent or imprecisely measured aspects of personal advantage; but given other survey evidence that both school and area factors may influence educational outcomes (McPherson and Willms, 1986; Garner, 1988) it is possible that there was indeed a genuine area effect on entry to full-time education, either direct or mediated by the school. However any area effect would have been tiny compared to the massive influence of school leavers' educational attainments and social background; it would still be fair to conclude that most of the spatial variation within cities was attributable to these other aspects of social inequality.

Our findings were most clear-cut with respect to the probability of employment – which was, after all, the main focus of our study. Spatial inequalities within cities were very largely derivative of social inequalities; area factors had no significant direct effect on school leavers' employment chances. As far as school leavers were concerned each city appeared to function as a single labour market, probably segmented by gender but not by spatial boundaries.

It follows that the policy implications of spatial inequality are different for inequalities between and within cities respectively. (Subject to our earlier reservation, the same goes for inequalities between and within other types of local labour markets.) Inequalities between labour markets are at least in part directly attributable to the spatial dimension and to the differences in access and opportunity that this represents. The imagery of the north/south divide may inadequately represent this dimension, but at least it correctly identifies the spatial aspect of the problem. A policy which equalized opportunities across local labour markets would not eliminate all social inequalities but it would remove a significant source of them. Our research further hints that some of the educational inequalities affecting school leavers in different cities are in fact derivative of labour-market inequalities.

However, a different set of policy prescriptions applies to inequalities within local labour markets, and especially within cities, where the spatial dimension is of less direct importance. The problems of young people in 'disadvantaged' localities of a city do not primarily result from their distance from the available employment opportunities, from problems of travel or access, or even from employers' stigmatization of job-applicants from particular districts. Instead they mainly reflect the deficiency of employment opportunities in the city as a whole, coupled with recruitment and selection processes which distribute the scarce jobs in ways which penalize young people with no qualifications, with limited access to word-of-mouth recruitment networks, or with other 'disadvantaging' personal characteristics.

A policy to redress disadvantage within an urban youth labour market may attack one or more of three targets. It may seek to raise the total level of employment within the city as a whole; it may seek to enhance the personal characteristics of disadvantaged young people, for example by helping them gain more skills and qualifications; or it may seek to reduce the extent to which labour-market selection processes disadvantage young people with particular attributes, for example by fighting social or racial discrimination. All these approaches recognize the problem of urban disadvantage as primarily social not spatial. There is a danger that because the problem is so often defined politically in spatial terms, most notably in terms of the 'inner city', spatial policies will be adopted despite (or conceivably because of) their failure to tackle the underlying social problems. Relocating employment opportunities within a large city would have little effect on these problems, since the city tends to function as a single labour market. Intervention through housing policy may produce other benefits but it would not solve the labour-market problem; the disadvantage associated with 'personal' attributes would remain, even if the individuals concerned were redistributed across the city. At its worst such a policy would merely hide the problem by gentrifying the inner city and decanting the disadvantaged to remote and less visible housing estates. Spatial terminology may provide a convenient label for the problems of inequality within cities, but it provides no guide to their solution.

ACKNOWLEDGEMENTS

The research reported in this paper was carried out as part of the project on Local Variations in School Leaver Employment and Unemployment within

Large Cities, funded by the Economic and Social Research Council (grant no. D00232070). Small-area statistics from the 1981 Population Census, and the postcode directory used in linking data, were made available by the University of Edinburgh Data Library. We are grateful to the careers officers and local and central government officials who gave help and advice to the project. The interpretations and opinions in the chapter are the authors'.

NOTE

1. The exception is Aberdeen, where despite the help of the local careers service it proved impossible to identify advantaged and disadvantaged areas of sufficient size to meet the requirements of the analysis. Consequently the 'advantaged' and 'disadvantaged' areas of Aberdeen identified in this chapter tended to have similar socioeconomic profiles.

REFERENCES

ASHTON, D.N. and MAGUIRE, M.J. (1986) *Young Adults in the Labour Market*, Research Paper No. 55, London, Department of Employment.

CHESHIRE, P.C. (1979) 'Inner areas as spatial labour markets: A critique of the inner area studies', *Urban Studies*, 16, pp. 29–43.

COLES, R. (1986) 'School leaver, job seeker, dole reaper: Young and unemployed in rural England' in ALLEN, S., WATON, A., PURCELL, K. and WOOD, S. (Eds) *The Experience of Unemployment*, London, Macmillan.

GARNER, C. (1988) 'Educational attainment in Glasgow: The role of neighbourhood deprivation' in BONDI, L. and MATTHEWS, M.H. (Eds) *Education and Society: Studies in the Politics, Sociology and Geography of Education*, London, Croom Helm.

GARNER, C.L., MAIN, B.G.M. and RAFFE, D. (1987a) *Local Variations in School Leaver Employment and Unemployment Within Large Cities*, Edinburgh, University of Edinburgh, Centre for Educational Sociology.

GARNER, C.L., MAIN, B.G.M. and RAFFE, D. (1987b) 'Local variations in school-leaver unemployment within a large city', *British Journal of Education and Work*, 1, 2, pp. 67–78.

GARNER, C.L., MAIN, B.G.M. and RAFFE, D. (1988) 'The distribution of school-leaver unemployment within Scottish cities', *Urban Studies*, 25, 2.

GOLDTHORPE, J.H. and HOPE, K. (1974) *The Social Grading of Occupations*, Oxford, Clarendon Press.

HUTSON, S. and JENKINS, R. (1987) 'Coming of age in South Wales' in BROWN, P. and ASHTON, D. (Eds) *Education, Unemployment and Labour Markets*, Lewes, Falmer Press.

LEE, D., MARSDEN, D., HARDEY, M., RICKMAN, P. and MASTERS, K. (1987) 'Youth training, life chances and orientations to work: A case study of the Youth Training Scheme' in BROWN, P. and ASHTON, D. (Eds) *Education, Unemployment and Labour Markets*, Lewes, Falmer Press.

McPherson, A. and Willms, J.D. (1986) 'Certification, class conflict, religion and community: A socio-historical explanation of the effectiveness of contemporary schools' in Kerckhoff, A. (Ed.) *Research in Sociology of Education and Socialization*, Volume 6, Greenwich, CT, JAI Press.

Massey, D. (1984) *Spatial Divisions of Labour: Social Structures and the Geography of Production*, London, Macmillan.

Office of Population Censuses and Surveys (1981) *Classification of Occupations 1980*, London, HMSO.

Office of Population Censuses and Surveys (1984) *Key Statistics for Urban Areas, Scotland; Localities*, London, HMSO.

Payne, J. (1987) 'Does unemployment run in families? Some findings from the General Household Survey', *Sociology*, 21, 2, pp. 199–214.

Roberts, K., Dench, S. and Richardson, D. (1987) *The Changing Structure of Youth Labour Markets*, Research Paper No. 59, London, Department of Employment.

Ryrie, A.C. (1983) *On Leaving School: A Study of Schooling, Guidance and Opportunity*, Edinburgh, Scottish Council for Research in Education.

Thurow, L. (1975) *Generating Inequality*, New York, Basic Books.

Wallace, C. (1987) 'From generation to generation: The effects of employment and unemployment upon the domestic life cycle of young adults', in Brown, P. and Ashton, D. (Eds) *Education, Unemployment and Labour Markets*, Lewes, Falmer Press.

Chapter 7:

Does It Pay Young People to Go on YTS?

Brian G.M. Main and Michael A. Shelly

INTRODUCTION

In April 1983 the Youth Training Scheme (YTS) was introduced by the Manpower Services Commission (MSC) to replace the Youth Opportunities Programme (YOP). The change marked an attempt to move away from the temporary counter-cyclical job-creation activities that had characterized YOP to a more constructive long-run manpower policy that would enhance the productivity of participants through the provision of both on-the-job and off-the-job training. The aim in creating YTS was to fulfil Objective Two of the New Training Initiative agreed by the Government and the MSC in 1981 (Gray and King, 1986). Objective Two of the New Training Initiative was to move toward a position where all under-18-year-olds had the opportunity either to continue in full-time education or enter training or a period of planned work experience which incorporated vocational training and education, that is enter a manpower programme. After consultations with representatives from the CBI, TUC, local authorities, voluntary agencies and careers services, the one-year YTS was introduced to fulfil Objective Two. This chapter attempts to gauge the success of YTS when judged as a manpower programme.

Broadly speaking, a manpower programme attempts to improve the attractiveness of an individual to employers by providing participants with new skills and/or work experience. In economic terms, this can be thought of as enhancing the human capital, that is the stock of acquired education and training, of those going through the programme. The expected result of such an experience should be an increase in the probability of participants finding a job, and an improved chance of their finding a good job, whether good jobs are measured by rate of pay or by occupational classification. In what follows, each of these considerations will be addressed using the experience of a group of young persons from the Scottish Young Peoples Survey who left school during the 1983/84 school year. By way of providing a control group, analysis will be presented both for those who had experience of YTS and those who had no experience of YTS. During the period under consideration, YTS was operating as a one-year scheme, although since 1986 it has been upgraded to a two-year scheme.

In the next section of the chapter, the impact of YTS on school leavers' chances of employment is examined. The third section takes up the issue of wages in employment, and the fourth section analyzes the occupational and industrial distribution of former YTS participants' employment. The chapter ends with a summary of the main findings and a discussion of their policy implications.

FINDING A JOB

The data used in this chapter came from the cohort arm of the Scottish Young Peoples Survey. In spring 1985, the Scottish Young Peoples Survey covered a random 10 per cent sample of all young people in the fourth form at school during the 1983/84 school year and of all school leavers from the 1983/84 school year. A subset of this sample, those in the fourth form in 1983/84, was contacted again a year later. The analysis below is restricted to fourth-form leavers who were continuously in the labour market from October 1984. Fourth-form leavers constitute around two out of five of all school leavers, a figure which would be higher were not some students required to stay on at school until the Christmas leaving date of their fifth form, owing to the minimum school-leaving age regulations.

Table 7.1 utilizes this data to examine routes through the labour market for those who had entered the labour market on leaving school and who had remained in the labour market until April 1986. By this date some 64.4 per cent of the males and some 64.9 per cent of the females were in employment. Almost all of the remainder were unemployed save 1.7 per cent who were on YTS schemes. For those in employment, almost three-fifths had found employment after being on a YTS scheme. For the school leavers involved in these surveys, YTS was in its original one-year form. It was not extended to two years until the spring of 1986. The more traditional routes to employment, i.e. entering a job either directly after leaving school or after some unemployment during which the school leaver engaged in job search, accounted for 42 per cent of both employed males and employed. females. The YTS-assisted mode is, therefore, seen to be the dominant route to employment for young people leaving school at age 16.

Table 7.1: Routes through the labour market

A Routes to employment in April 1986

Biography	Percentage of the employed in April 1986	
	Males	Females
(1) Traditional mode 1: continuous employment, no experience of YTS (a)	34.3	37.6
(2) Traditional mode 2: some unemployment, no experience of YTS (b)	7.5	4.6
(3) YTS-assisted mode: some experience of YTS (c)	58.2	57.8
(1) – (3)	100.0	100.0

B Routes to unemployment in April 1986

Biography	Percentage of the unemployed in April 1986	
	Males	Females
(1) Some employment, no experience of YTS	11.1	14.2
(2) No employment, no experience of YTS	13.7	10.0
(3) No employment, some experience of YTS	59.0	51.7
(4) Some employment, after experience of YTS	14.6	22.7
(5) Some employment, before experience of YTS	1.6	1.4
(1) – (5)	100.0	100.0

Notes: (a) Continuous employment is defined as being in employment at each of four dates: October 1984, April 1985, October 1985, and April 1986.
(b) Some unemployment is defined as being unemployed at at least one of the four dates.
(c) Some experience of YTS is defined as being on YTS at at least one of the four dates.
(d) This table does not include the twenty-one individuals who were on YTS in April 1986.

Among those in table 7.1 who were not in employment, 73 per cent of the males and 62 per cent of the females had never had a job, even twenty-one months after leaving school. Also, of all the unemployed only one-quarter had never been on a YTS scheme. It is clear, then, that YTS is the dominant labour-market experience of school leavers whether they were employed or unemployed in April 1986. Finally, a worrying 14 per cent of unemployed male school leavers and 10 per cent of females had remained continuously unemployed since leaving school. Already experiencing very long term unemployment less than two years after leaving school, this group of school leavers provide testimony to the failure of YTS to reach all those school leavers experiencing employment difficulties.

Table 7.2: Labour-market state in April 1986 by labour-market state in October 1984

Labour-market state in October 1984	Labour-market state in April 1986			Percentage by state in October 1984
	Employed	*YTS*	*Unemployed*	
Employed	85.1	0.2	14.7	33.0
YTS	61.9	1.3	36.8	49.4
Unemployed	33.7	5.7	60.6	17.6
Percentage by state in April 1986 Unweighted n = 1326	64.6	1.7	33.7	100.0

Table 7.2 presents the observed labour-market transitions made by school leavers between October 1984 and April 1986. From the table it is clear that YTS appears to have successfully led to employment for the majority of its participants. Of the half of our sample of school leavers who were on a YTS scheme in October 1984, three-fifths were in regular employment some eighteen months later. This contrasts with the fate of the 18 per cent who were unemployed in October 1984, of whom only one-third were in employment in April 1986.

It is possible, of course, that those recorded as unemployed in October 1984 would later join a YTS scheme or, in fact, may have already been on a YTS scheme but left early. Table 7.3 attempts to control for this possibility by examining the labour-market transitions made by those school leavers who never had experience of YTS, and those who by April 1986 had had

Table 7.3: Labour-market state in April 1986 by labour-market state in October 1984, by whether ever been on YTS

Labour-market state in October 1984	Labour-market state in April 1986		Percentage by state in October 1984
	Employed	*Non-employed*	
(i) Never on YTS			
Employed	87.2	12.8	79.0
Non-employed	36.2	63.8	21.0
Percentage by state in April 1986 Unweighted n = 482	76.6	24.4	100.0
(ii) Have been on YTS			
Employed	73.4	26.6	7.8
Non-employed	56.7	43.3	92.2
Percentage by state in April 1986 Unweighted n = 844	58.0	42.0	100.0

some experience of YTS, respectively. In this case the labour-market states are distinguished as employed and non-employed. The main conclusion to be drawn from this table is that YTS seems to have increased the probability of a non-employed person being in a job by April 1986 by 20.5 percentage points (that is, the difference between 36.2 per cent and 56.7 per cent). Main and Shelly (1987) have shown that this employment-enhancing effect of YTS remains even when the personal characteristics of the YTS participants and non-participants are controlled for via the use of multivariate statistical analysis. This 20.5 percentage point job-finding advantage which is attributable to YTS participation is significantly lower than the approximately 60 per cent 'success rate', that is job placement rate, generally claimed by the MSC. This disparity in findings is due to the failure of MSC measures to compare the job placement rate of YTS participants with that of a control group of young people who had never been on YTS. In table 7.3, therefore, an MSC-equivalent measure of the job placement rate would be that 56.7 per cent, i.e. near to 60 per cent, of those non-employed young people who participated in YTS were found to be in jobs in April 1986. The MSC's measure does not allow for the fact that of the non-employed who did not go on YTS some 36.2 per cent were in jobs in April 1986. It is, of course, the difference between the figures for ex-YTS participants and non-participants that provides a measure of the effectiveness of YTS in assisting young people to find jobs.

But not even table 7.3 is totally free of ambiguity. It contrasts the experience of those who have been on YTS with those who have not been on YTS. It is well known, however, that in some cases the first year of regular jobs was arranged to qualify for support under YTS. To all intents and purposes, therefore, people in such arrangements had already found employment although they may have reported themselves as being on YTS at the time of the April 1985 survey. One way to allow for this possibility is to remove from the comparison all people who subsequently went on to be employed by their YTS sponsor. While this is certainly an exaggeration of the pervasiveness of the arrangement such an approach would tend to produce a 'lower bound' estimate of the employment effect of YTS to contrast with the 20.5 per cent result reported above which may well be, for this reason, an 'upper bound'. It is found that such an approach produces a 'lower bound' estimate of the employment effect of YTS of some 11.8 per cent.

So, for our sample of school leavers, YTS had become a pervasive intermediate state between the education system and the world of work. Our evidence suggests that experience of YTS served to increase the employment prospects of those who were initially without a job after leaving school, that is, non-employed in October 1984. The question arises as to how YTS enhanced young people's employment prospects. On the positive side, it may reflect the employment of apprentices. Or it may be due to the training explicitly or implicitly, for example through the acquisition of 'industrial discipline', provided by YTS sponsors, or the opportunity YTS gives employers to 'screen' young people. On the negative side, it may be that since YTS trainees are cheaper than straightforward employees, employers have, to some extent, used YTS trainees in place of the young people they would have otherwise chosen to hire or in place of workers from other labour market groups. Finally, it may be that employers were retaining some YTS trainees under the auspices of The Young Workers Scheme.

WAGE RATES

Having established that participation in YTS exerts a positive influence on school leavers' employment prospects, we now inquire whether there are any measurable influences of YTS participation on the subsequent rates of pay in employment. If YTS is to be judged as a manpower programme, rather than just a counter-cyclical job-creation scheme, then it would be expected that participation in the scheme would have enhanced the human capital stock of its participants via the training received, and that this will have made participants more productive in employment than they would have been prior to participation. As noted in the previous section, there is some evidence that employers give a certain amount of preference to former YTS participants *vis-à-vis* non-participants in their recruitment. As argued above, this is certainly consistent with YTS increasing the productivity of participants to a level higher than that of otherwise identical school leavers. But the question remains whether this higher productivity is reflected in terms of higher wages being paid to ex-YTS participants.

The assumption being made here is that workers are paid wages which reflect the value of their marginal products. There is the complication that young workers may be receiving further training, and hence their current productivity (and wage) may not reflect their productive potential. This issue is addressed below.

Table 7.4: Basic hourly earnings (gross) in April 1986

	£	Unweighted n
Never on YTS	1.55	303
Ever on YTS:	1.44	421
(i) Found employment with		
scheme provider	1.29	136
(ii) Found employment elsewhere	1.51	285

Table 7.4 reports the basic gross (before deductions for income tax and national insurance) hourly earnings[1] of employed school leavers according to whether or not they had been on YTS. Those who had been on YTS received, on average, a rate of pay that was some 7 per cent less than that received by those who had never been on YTS. This result is consistent with the findings of Main and Shelly (1987) wherein variations in personal characteristics such as age and educational credentials are controlled for via the use of multivariate statistical techniques. In particular, the result holds even when an allowance is made for training by controlling for whether or not school leavers claimed that they were continuing to receive training. The training aspects of employment are particularly problematic as during training an individual's productivity, and hence wage, will not reflect that person's productive potential. Implicit in most notions of training is the idea that the person involved is either taking time out from the formal productive process in which to receive instruction, or that the person is essentially 'practising' in the sense of performing the production activity but in a way that consumes more inputs and/or produces less output than would be so in the case of a fully trained person. Such situations imply that the current productivity is less than it could be in a process which involved no learning or training opportunities, and hence, no such distractions. The loss of productivity and hence earnings during training represents the individual's investment in training, and is usually compensated by the later higher productivity and earnings that result from training.

The MSC had attempted to ensure that apprenticeships could be brought under YTS in order to fulfil Objective One of the New Training Initiative, to develop apprenticeships in such a way as to allow young people to attain agreed common standards, and this raises the possibility that former YTS participants continued to receive extensive training at the end of their YTS scheme. It is clear that the self-reported training descriptor, available from the survey and mentioned above, may be a very poor way of controlling for this possibility. Some evidence to support the contention that young people continued to receive training is provided in that part of table 7.4 wherein ex-YTS participants are considered separately according to whether or not they had found employment with their scheme sponsor. Other things being equal, those who continue with their scheme sponsor should enjoy higher wages than those who do not, because remaining with the YTS sponsor at the end of their period of training implies that school leavers will be able to utilize all the training gained during the YTS scheme – both that which is specific to the employer, and therefore not portable, and that which is general (that is, generally applicable) and hence portable. Those who change employers will only be able to utilize the general training that they gained from YTS. Great emphasis was placed on the general, and flexible, aspects of training in the design of YTS, with three months being spent by YTS participants in off-the-job training, usually in a technical college, but it would have been impossible to eliminate all specific aspects from YTS training. It can be seen from table 7.4 that those who found employment with their scheme sponsor received some 15 per cent less than those who found employment elsewhere. This does suggest that ex-YTS participants who remained with their scheme-providing employer were engaged in further training.[2]

In addition to information pertaining to subsequent employment with YTS sponsors, we are also able to estimate the duration of each school leaver's experience of YTS.[3] This information is contained in table 7.5 along with the subsequent earnings of YTS participants. From table 7.5 it can be seen that those who had left YTS early enjoyed higher hourly earnings than those who had remained for the full period. This may, of course, be of some comfort to the MSC, who have been concerned by the high attrition rates on YTS schemes caused by early leavers. However, it raises a question concerning the subsequent training of early leavers. If they left YTS to take jobs in which they would maximize their existing earnings by fully exploiting their current productive potential, then there would have been little scope for training. The only exception would be training involving costless 'learning by doing'.

Table 7.5: Basic hourly earnings (gross) by estimated duration of YTS experience

Duration of YTS experience	£	Unweighted n
Up to five months	1.64	77
More than five months and less than one year	1.48	128
One year or more	1.39	221

It seems, therefore, that the outcome whereby early leavers from YTS are seen to be earning particularly high wages is inconsistent with the overall aim of the YTS programme 'to develop and maintain a more versatile, readily adaptable, highly motivated and productive workforce...' (MSC, 1982, para. 4.3). This conclusion is suggested because these high wages open the possibility that early leavers from YTS were entering jobs that have little or no scope for further training.

So, although participation on YTS appears to have improved YTS participants' employment prospects, it did not improve their wages. However, this may not be a bad thing, since the lower wages earned by those who had been on YTS may be a reflection of the fact that they were continuing to undertake training, and this may explain the particularly low wages of those retained by their sponsors. If young people continued to undertake training after YTS, this might suggest that YTS was raising the level of youth training even outwith its own auspices. The lower wages earned by ex-YTS participants may, however, be a reflection of the fact that many of these individuals had experienced periods of non-employment and that they therefore earned a lower wage because of this break in their employment experience. In a statistically complex analysis that makes allowance for YTS participants having different but unmeasured productive characteristics from other school leavers, Main and Shelly (1987) do find some evidence of a positive wage effect owing to YTS participation.

TYPE OF JOB

In addition to influencing school leavers' chances of employment and their earnings in employment, YTS may influence the type of employment that a school leaver finds. By type of employment we mean here the industrial and occupational classification of employment. Table 7.6 shows the occupational distributions of employment of two groups of school leavers at two points in time. The first group comprises those who were in employment in April 1985 who were also in employment in April 1986 and who had no experience of YTS. We will label this group the 'continuously employed', and their occupational distributions of employment in April 1985 and April 1986 are presented in columns 1 and 3, respectively, of table 7.6. The second group comprises those who were on YTS schemes in April 1985 and who were in employment in April 1986. Columns 2 and 4 of table 7.6 compare the YTS occupations of the YTS group with their subsequent employment occupations. The information provided in table 7.6 neglects other types of labour-market experience.[4] In both pairs of columns, therefore, we are looking at the same individuals, i.e. those in employment in both April 1985 and April 1986 who have no experience of YTS are in columns 1 and 3 and those on YTS in April 1985 who subsequently were found in employment in April 1986 are in columns 2 and 4. Those without adequate industrial or occupational descriptors at any point are excluded from the analysis.

Inspection of table 7.6 reveals that, in terms of the Warwick Occupational Categories[5] used, the occupational distribution of YTS trainees in April 1985 was somewhat different from that of the continuously employed. The index of dissimilarity[6] value of 2.3 reported at the foot of table 7.6 measures this difference. The YTS group were, compared to the continuously employed, more heavily represented in sales occupations, engineering craftsmen and transferable craftsmen, and less heavily represented in clerical occupations, non-transferable craftsmen, skilled operatives, other operatives, security and personal services. Between April 1985 and April 1986 the

Table 7.6: *The occupational distribution of continuously employed school leavers and YTS participants in April 1985 and April 1986*

Warwick Occupational Category	Continuously employed April 1985	YTS group April 1985	Continuously employed April 1986	ex-YTS group April 1986
Managers and administratrors	0.9	0.3	0.8	0.3
Education professions	0.0	0.0	0.0	0.4
Health professions, etc	0.4	0.0	0.2	0.5
Other professions	0.0	0.0	0.0	0.0
Literary, artistic and sports occupations	1.0	0.0	0.4	0.3
Engineers, scientists, etc	0.2	0.6	0.4	0.6
Technicians, draughtsmen	0.0	0.0	0.3	0.0
Clerical occupations, etc	12.1	11.0	11.2	9.5
Sales occupations	7.5	14.1	8.5	10.4
Supervisors, foremen	0.0	0.0	0.0	0.0
Engineering craftsmen	10.2	17.5	13.2	13.8
Other transferable craftsmen	11.9	17.6	10.7	16.7
Non-transferable craftsmen	9.7	5.4	9.8	5.8
Skilled operatives	4.6	3.6	4.5	5.8
Other operatives	21.9	15.1	18.5	20.6
Security occupations	3.7	0.0	4.9	0.7
Personal service occupations	13.4	11.6	13.4	10.9
Other occupations	2.4	3.2	3.3	3.5
Unweighted n	385	230	385	230

Index of dissimilarity:
Employed/YTS group 1985   2.3
Employed/ex-YTS group 1986   1.5
Employed 1985/employed 1986   0.7
YTS group 1985/YTS group 1986   1.2

differences between the occupational distributions of the YTS and continuously employed groups' employment decreased; this can be seen by noting that the index of dissimilarity between the occupational distribution of employment of the continuously employed and the former YTS participants was 1.5 in April 1986. Both groups experienced occupational mobility between 1985 and 1986 but the movement was most marked for the YTS group. This can be seen from the index of dissimilarity figures relating to each group's employment in April 1985 and April 1986. The figures are 0.7 for the continuously employed and 1.2 for the YTS group. The YTS group tended to move out of clerical occupations, sales occupations and engineering craftsmen and into skilled operatives and other operatives. The continuously employed tended to move out of other transferable craftsmen and other operatives, and into sales, engineering craftsmen and security occupations.

It appears from table 7.6 that the continuously employed were more likely to be found in the better (white-collar and skilled) occupations than the YTS group, but there was not a large difference. However, to some extent, the YTS group tended to gain ground on completion of their schemes,

Table 7.7: *The occupational distribution of continuously employed school leavers' and YTS participants' employment in April 1985 and April 1986*

Occupational category	Continuously employed April 1985 (%)	YTS group April 1985 (%)	Continuously employed April 1986 (%)	wage	ex-YTS group April 1986 (%)	wage
White-collar occupations	14.5	11.9	13.2	£1.64	11.7	£1.56
Sales occupations	7.5	14.1	8.5	£1.41	10.4	£1.40
Skilled manual occupations	10.2	17.5	13.2	£1.54	13.8	£1.39
Intermediate manual occupations	26.3	26.6	24.9	£153	28.3	£1.43
Unskilled manual occupations	41.5	29.9	40.1	£1.48 All	35.8	£1.50 All
	100.0	100.0	100.0	£1.55	100.0	£1.44
Unweighted *n*	385	230	385		230	

Index of dissimilarity:
Employed/YTS group 1985   5.7
Employed/ex-YTS group 1986   2.3
Employed 1985/employed 1986   1.6
YTS group 1985/YTS group 1986   3.0

moving up the occupational ladder out of intermediate and unskilled occupations. This picture is made somewhat clearer in table 7.7, which repeats the analysis of table 7.6 in terms of a more aggregate classification of occupations. Table 7.7 also provides the average (gross) basic hourly earnings for both groups in each aggregate occupational category in April 1986. In white-collar, skilled manual and intermediate manual occupations, the YTS group was earning markedly less than the continuously employed group. This difference may be due either to the lack of on-the-job experience among the YTS group or to the greater prevalence of continuing training among the YTS group. Both explanations are consistent with the absence of any wage differential between the continuously employed and the YTS group in the large unskilled manual occupational category.

Finally table 7.8 repeats the above analysis in terms of industrial categories. In terms of final employment, i.e. employment in April 1986, the YTS group were more likely than the continuously employed group to be in construction and less likely to be in manufacturing. These differences were quite large, and, to a large extent, reflected the industrial distribution of YTS schemes in 1985; there was a relatively large number of schemes in construction and a relatively low number in manufacturing. Between 1985 and 1986, the YTS group's employment tended to shift towards construction and manufacturing, thus reducing their presence in mining and utilities and

Table 7.8: The industrial distribution of continuously employed school leavers' and YTS participants' employment in April 1985 and April 1986 and wages in April 1986

Industrial category	Continuously employed April 1985 (%)	YTS group April 1985 (%)	Continuously employed April 1986 (%)		ex-YTS group April 1986 (%)	
			(%)	wage	(%)	wage
Agriculture, forestry and fishing	4.2	3.5	4.8	£1.28	3.2	£1.73
Mining and utilities	1.2	3.2	0.7	£1.59	1.5	£1.66
Manufacturing	29.3	15.1	27.0	£1.64	18.7	£1.74
Construction	17.6	23.8	17.6	£1.48	27.4	£1.31
Services	47.8	54.4	49.9	£1.49	49.2	£1.38
Unweighted n	385	230	385		230	

Index of dissimilarity:
Employed/YTS group 1985	5.9
Employed/ex-YTS group 1986	4.2
Employed 1985/employed 1986	1.1
YTS group 1985/YTS group 1986	2.9

in services. The continuously employed group displayed greater constancy in the industrial distribution of their employment.

So, YTS schemes do not appear to have been restricted to a narrow range of either industries or occupations. Furthermore, YTS participants do not appear to have been 'locked into' certain occupations or industries by the specificity of the training they received. By April 1986, the occupational and industrial distributions of employed ex-YTS participants had come to resemble more closely those of the continuously employed. In April 1986, the main differences that remained between the two groups were the greater concentration of ex-YTS participants in the construction industry and the greater concentration of the continuously employed in the manufacturing industries.

SUMMARY AND POLICY DISCUSSION

From the evidence presented above, it seems clear that in terms of the labour-market experience of early school leavers, YTS is extremely important. It is important in the quantitative sense that the vast majority of school leavers who enter the labour market will eventually acquire some experience of YTS. It is also important in the sense that such experience seems to enhance the employment prospects of participants by increasing their probability of being in employment, some 21 months after leaving school, by around 20 percentage points. This increase in the probability of employment suggests that YTS makes participants more attractive to employers. To the extent that some YTS places are, to all intents and purposes, the first year (and since 1986, the first two years) of regular jobs, then the above estimate will exaggerate the effect of YTS.

In terms of subsequent earnings in employment, the effects of YTS are much less clear. It seems that former YTS participants earn wages in employment that are some 7 per cent less than those earned by similar employed school leavers who have not been on YTS. The issue is clouded by the uncertainty about the extent of further training being received by former YTS participants and the operation of the Young Workers Scheme. If ex-YTS participants are more likely than other employed school leavers to continue to receive training, then this wage discount may merely be a reflection of such training. The evidence that those school leavers who continue in employment with the YTS sponsor receive lower wages than those who move to different employers can be viewed as lending support to this interpretation. Similarly, the operation of the Young Workers Scheme in this period provided a natural extension to one-year YTS, whereby a wage subsidy of £15 per week was paid to employers of 17-year-olds as long as their wages were no more than £50 per week. If a disproportionate number of YTS participants ended up in this scheme, then their wages would tend to be lower than the wages of those who had not been on YTS, owing to the imposition of this upper earnings limit.

YTS participants were more likely than the continuously employed to end up in sales and some craftsman occupations and in the construction industry. They were less likely than the continuously employed to end up in white-collar, non-transferable craftsmen and other operatives occupations and less likely to end up in the manufacturing industries. Overall, the wages of YTS participants seemed to be lower in most occupations than those of the continuously employed. The variation of wages with industry of employment was more equivocal.

There is little doubt that YTS exerts a pervasive influence on the youth labour market. It may seem that, compared with those school leavers who avoid YTS, either by being fortunate enough to secure continuous employment or by simply enduring unemployment while searching for employment, the advantages gained by YTS participants in terms of wages are modest; but this may have reflected YTS participants' greater participation in continued training. Of course, if all those who went through YTS had, instead, entered directly into the job-seeking process, and joined the unemployed, then the employment prospects facing all young persons in the labour market would have been a lot worse than they actually turned out to be. That is, YTS may also have improved the employment prospects of those unemployed school leavers who avoided YTS by reducing the competition. Furthermore, the fact that YTS took many school leavers out of the competition for jobs may have served to maintain the wage rates of those school leavers who found employment at a level higher than that which might have been observed if YTS had not existed. On the other hand, the presence of essentially free YTS labour may have held down wages paid to young people in employment.

The change to a two-year YTS may produce further concrete benefits to YTS participants. The evidence discussed above, concerning one-year YTS, suggests that it is likely that for these benefits to be forthcoming it will be necessary to maintain or improve tha quantity, quality and marketability of the training received by participants.

ACKNOWLEDGEMENTS

The authors gratefully acknowledge valuable research support received from the Centre for Educational Sociology (CES), University of Edinburgh, whose activities are sponsored, in part, by the Economic and Social Research Council. This research project was funded by a grant from the Leverhulme Foundation.

NOTES

1.   Basic hourly earnings are computed using reported gross weekly earnings and hours of work. The assumption is made that hours over forty hours a week are paid at time and a half. The results are not sensitive to this assumption.
2.   This finding may also reflect the possibility that such school leavers had been retained by their former employer within the auspices of the Young Workers Scheme, which was introduced in 1982 and phased out on 31 March 1986. As from 1985, the scheme covered 17-year-old young people only and it provided for the payment of £15 per week per young person to employers if that young person's wage was below £50 per week.
3.   This measure is only approximate as we do not have an exact YTS leaving date for respondents. We do, however, know the date on which they started their YTS scheme and also their employment status in October 1984, April 1985, October 1985 and April 1986. This is sufficient to allow us to estimate the approximate duration of each individual's YTS experience.
4.   For example, those who were unemployed in April 1985 but who were in employment in April 1986, or those who were on YTS in April 1985 but who were unemployed in April 1986.
5.   The Warwick Occupational Categories were developed by Peter Elias and others at the University of Warwick, for the purpose of analyzing occupational trends using data from the 1961, 1966 and 1971 Population Censuses (Lindley, 1976; Elias, 1981). They are based on the 223 Occupational Unit Groups of The

1970 Classification of Occupations and take no account of employment status. The schema is intended to reflect differences in the extent of industrial training for manual jobs and in the level of professional qualifications and/or vocational training associated with non-manual occupations (Elias, 1985). The condensed categories of table 7.7 are formed from the following aggregation of WOC: 1 = (1,2,3,4,5,6,7,8); 2 = (9); 3 = (10,11); 4 = (12,13,14); 5 = (15,16,17,18).

6. The index of dissimilarity measures the average absolute percentage difference between the two distributions in question.

REFERENCES

ELIAS, P. (1981) 'The MRG/EOC Occupational Classifications', University of Warwick, Institute for Employment Research.

ELIAS, P. (1985) 'Changes in occupational structure 1971–81', University of Warwick, Institute for Employment Research.

GRAY, D. and KING, S. (1986) *The Youth Training Scheme: The First Three Years*, YTS Evaluation Series No. 1, Sheffield, MSC.

LINDLEY, R.M. (1976) 'The problem of choosing occupational groups for a medium-term manpower assessment', University of Warwick, Manpower Research Group.

MAIN, B.G.M. and SHELLY, M.A.(1987) 'The effectiveness of YTS as a manpower policy', University of Edinburgh, Centre for Educational Sociology Working Paper (July).

MANPOWER SERVICES COMMISSION (1982) *Youth Task Group Report*, London, MSC.

Chapter 8:

Modules and the Strategy of Institutional Versatility: The First Two Years of the 16-plus Action Plan in Scotland
David Raffe

INTRODUCTION: THE STRATEGY OF INSTITUTIONAL VERSATILITY

The Scottish Model

Since 1984 post-compulsory education in Scotland has been transformed by the Scottish Education Department's 16-plus Action Plan (SED, 1983). Nearly all non-advanced vocational courses have been replaced by a system of modules, each of notional forty hours' duration, available in schools, colleges and in a small but increasing number of private centres. Students may study modules in more than one institution, and credits are transferable. All modules are accredited by a single National Certificate, issued by the Scottish Vocational Education Council (Scotvec). The certificate records the modules completed but gives them no formal group title. In principle, at least, the notion of a 'course' is superseded and a student's commitment to the system is open-ended; the system has multiple entry and exit points and not only the content but also the pacing of a student's learning are flexible.

The Action Plan responds to several problems shared with the rest of the UK (SED, 1979). These include low participation in post-compulsory education; the perceived irrelevance of much of the curriculum to economic demands; the need to adapt to changing skill demands, as well as to problems raised by youth unemployment; the need to reduce the complexity of the jungle of vocational courses and qualifications; and the need for coordination and integration, particularly in the context of new and changing institutional forms such as the Youth Training Scheme (YTS). Moves towards modularization are found in many other countries, but rarely in the thoroughgoing form in which it has been applied in Scotland. Consequently the Action Plan has attracted considerable interest internationally, as well as in England and Wales.

It is tempting but misleading to treat the Action Plan simply as a test case of 'modularization'. In the first place the success of the Scottish reform depends critically on the support of those charged with its implementation. This support is significantly influenced by the political context in which it was introduced, and would not necessarily be replicated elsewhere (Raffe, 1985). Second, the Action Plan was about much more than modularization; it also introduced reforms in the curriculum (with more emphasis on competencies), in pedagogy (with the development of more student-centred, or at least activity-based styles) and in assessment (which is criterion-referenced, continuous and largely internal). Third, and perhaps most importantly, the Action Plan introduced only one of several possible models of reform.

The Scottish modular system has several distinctive features. Each module is specified by a module descriptor, the most important element of which is a list of learning outcomes. To complete a module, a student must achieve all the learning outcomes to a level specified by performance criteria also included in the descriptor. Passes are not graded; a module is either completed or not completed. Certification is wholly modular, in that the certificate records the modules completed and does not give them any group title (although as a transitional measure systems of equivalence have been published which relate modules to pre-existing group certificates and to other UK qualifications, and certificates may be endorsed with these equivalences). There are no formal general distinctions of level and status among modules, although modules vary widely in level or 'difficulty' and within subject areas there may be clearly defined patterns of progression between modules. Subject to this, the Action Plan aimed to remove arbitrary entry requirements and barriers to access.

However, the features described above may simply indicate that the logic of modularization and, relatedly, of criterion-referencing has been applied more rigorously in Scotland than elsewhere (see Roberts, 1987). The feature — or aspiration — of the Scottish model that most clearly distinguishes it from most other modular reforms is what I shall refer to as its institutional versatility. By this I mean the ability to cover a diverse range of institutions (using the term in its broadest sense, to embrace not just school and college but also education and training that is full- and part-time, pre-employment and in-service, education-based and work-based, and MSC and local initiatives) with a single, integrated and coordinated framework. Thus modules are available at school, at college or elsewhere: modules offered by one institution may be available to students based at another; they are available to full- and part-time students and, relatedly, to students who have not yet entered the labour market, to employees studying part-time and to the intermediate category of YTS trainees; they may be used in conjunction with national initiatives such as the Technical and Vocational Education Initiative (TVEI), and YTS and the Job Training Scheme (JTS), with innovations based on a single school or college, and with other developments, for example in work-based learning. Yet the modular framework remains a national one, with the module descriptors designed to a uniform specification and with a central apparatus for moderation and validation. In principle this allows for integration and coordination across these diverse initiatives and institutional bases, and provides a common system of currency to underwrite curricular planning and to serve as the basis of progression. Terminology in this area is notoriously loose: but it may help to distinguish between the integration and coordination across diverse institutions *within* the modular system, and the 'external articulation' of this system with other sectors of education or with the labour market (Taylor *et al.*, 1986). It is the first of these that is most distinctive of the Scottish Action Plan.

The Action Plan reform, therefore, cannot be regarded merely as an experiment in 'modularization'; nor can the results of this experiment necessarily be applied directly to other countries. In one respect, however, the Scottish experience may have lessons that are directly applicable elsewhere in Great Britain. Under the two-year YTS, all trainees have the opportunity to acquire or work towards recognized vocational qualifications. It is too soon to evaluate the effects of this policy on the attitudes, learning and educational and labour-market progression of trainees, especially in England and Wales where the final structure of qualifications is still being determined. However many Scottish YTS trainees took Scotvec modules under the one-year scheme; their experience may point towards the eventual implications of the extension of certification in YTS across the whole of Great Britain.

Rationales and Strategy

The rationales for the Action Plan include, first, the *extension of choice and opportunity* for the individual student. Because students can select individual modules rather than courses, they have a much wider choice of study programmes; they may have a wider choice of institutions wherein to study; they have more flexibility in determining the pacing of study, by varying the number of modules taken in each year; the length of a programme of modules is similarly flexible; and changes of specialism can more easily be accommodated, since credit for relevant general modules can be transferred. The Action Plan also attempts to reduce arbitrary barriers to educational participation and movement, by relaxing entry criteria and by widening the range of institutions in which given curricula can be followed.

Second, the Action Plan is intended to *increase participation* in post-compulsory education and training in general, and in more vocational areas in particular. This is assumed to follow, in part, from the extension of choice and opportunity: people wishing to study can more easily do so. But the plan also aims to increase the opportunities and incentives for educational progression once students have entered the modular system. Because a single certificate and system covers provision in a range of institutions and contexts, there is both more scope for students to progress educationally and more incentive for them to do so, particularly as they move between institutions and contexts, for example from school to YTS or from YTS to employment. The possession of some modules may provide an incentive to build on them and gain more. There is an analogy with a marketing strategy which makes introductory Lego sets freely or cheaply available to potential customers. Not only may this whet people's appetites for more, but the possession of the introductory set enhances the value of any further sets that are bought and thus provides an additional incentive to purchase. In the Action Plan the analogues of the introductory Lego sets are the modules studied at school (including those taken by fifth-year winter leavers)[1] or on YTS, often more as a matter of happenstance rather than through conscious educational plans. Once acquired, these modules may provide an incentive to come back for more. A further incentive to participation is supplied, in the Action Plan rationale, by the greater marketability of the modules.

Third, the Action Plan is intended to *enhance the economic contribution* of post-compulsory education and training. Not only is the increased participation itself of economic benefit, but the modular system improves the efficiency of the 'market' for vocational education and training, and thus enhances the relevance of what is purchased in this market. It does this in two ways. First, it provides convenient, flexible and standard 'units of currency' (Squires, 1985) for this market, which can serve as the basis for negotiations with employers and other customers. Second, the choice of programmes is broadened; modular programmes can more easily be constructed to cross traditional subject, departmental or even occupational boundaries — for example to accommodate changing combinations of skill demands. They can respond to upskilling, deskilling or other changes in the level of skill demands, since the length and level of modular programmes is flexible as well as their content (Ainley, 1985). The curriculum remains responsive: change is more easily incorporated by changing a single module than by revising a whole course.

Fourth, the Action Plan seeks to *rationalize and facilitate planning* within the education system itself. It replaces the 'FE jungle' of courses and qualifications with a single framework. Common elements of different group certificate courses are replaced by single modules; duplication between courses and between institutions is reduced. The modules are convenient units for planning the curriculum, particularly in new initiatives such as TVEI (Pignatelli, 1987), or for groups for whom longer courses may be inappropriate, such as fifth-year winter leavers or YTS trainees. Modules provide access to national certification, form part of a single framework with opportunities for progression, and provide a basis for integration across diverse initiatives and different contexts; this makes them particularly useful in such situations.

The foregoing account describes the rationales for the Action Plan; it makes no judgment on their theoretical and empirical validity, although a tentative and early assessment will be offered at the end of this chapter.

The perspectives implied by these rationales are diverse. Some regard the student primarily as a client or citizen, whose needs and rights are the prime justification for education; others regard the student more instrumentally as a decision-maker whose behaviour may be influenced, through various incentives, in pursuit of societal aims such as economic growth. Other rationales are oriented primarily to other decision-makers, notably employers, or to the organizational needs of educational providers. Part of the initial attraction of the Action Plan lay in its ability to appeal to a wide range of educational and political opinion (Raffe, 1985). The corollary is that the relative emphasis given to different rationales may vary. For example, recent literature on the Action Plan appears to emphasize the economic rationale more than the extension of choice and opportunity for the individual student, although this may be a largely tactical reflection of the need to address (and win support from) particular audiences (SED, 1986).

At all events, the varied rationales suggest that people based in different parts of the system may have very different understandings of what the Action Plan is essentially about. Moreover, although these rationales embrace many of the arguments for modularization found in the wider literature (Mansell *et al.*, 1976; Spencer, 1984; Squires, 1986; Jonathan, 1987; Roberts, 1987; Watkins, 1987), notably those concerning choice, flexibility and the responsiveness of the curriculum, even these arguments take a particular shape in the context of the Action Plan. For this literature, reflecting the actual experience of modularization outside Scotland, mainly describes modular systems that are institutionally bounded. Many of these systems are based on a single institution, such as a school, college or university; others are based on a single sector, such as secondary education, further education or industrial training, and usually on a clearly delimited subsector of this.

By contrast, the rationales for the Scottish Action Plan depend critically upon its strategy of institutional versatility: of covering a diverse range of institutions (using the term in the broadest sense) with a single, integrated and coordinated framework. For example, the first rationale, increasing choice and opportunity, depends in part on the range of institutional bases from which modules are offered. It also depends on modules having value in a common system of currency wherever they are studied. The second rationale (increasing participation) depends, in terms of the introductory-Lego-set strategy described above, on the very wide dissemination of introductory sets: to TVEI students, to traditional and non-traditional school stayers, and above all to fifth-year winter leavers and to YTS trainees. It also assumes that the Lego pieces will fit together wherever they are acquired. In the third (economic) rationale modules provide a curricular currency to smooth the workings of the education and training market; this presupposes a central monetary authority to defend the value of the currency and to regulate the market. Above all, the fourth rationale of the Action Plan — to do with rationalization and planning within the education system — is wholly dependent on the institutional versatility of the Scottish model: on a modular framework which allows for initiative, responsiveness and adaptability to suit varied local demands and situations and varied institutional bases, but which preserves integration, coordination and (to a degree) control from the centre.

The reference to control reminds us that the strategy of institutional versatility is essentially a political one. It is certainly easier to implement in the relatively centralized Scottish system than in that of England and Wales where the centres of power and initiative are more dispersed. Yet paradoxically the Action Plan's strategy is fundamentally a response to the *limits* of central, and especially SED, power. The SED's freedom of manoeuvre is circumscribed in several ways. Its capacity for institutional reform in the post-compulsory sector is limited, not only by the autonomy of the university system, but also by political constraints and by the professional and vested interests associated with schools and colleges. The SED may also be reluctant to encroach upon local responsibility for the institutions of post-compulsory education: far better to let local authorities incur the political costs of change. The SED also has limited influence over employees' training activities or their recruitment and selection practices. Above all, it has little direct influence over the activities of the MSC such as YTS, JTS and (to a lesser extent) TVEI.

Hence the need for a strategy which eschews institutional reorganization but which seeks to maximize central (SED) control over a diverse range of institutional forms. However the versatility of the system must also relate to unknown future institutional variation, as well as to known existing variation: MSC initiatives are nothing if not unpredictable. Within Scotland the Action Plan has been widely perceived as an SED attempt to control if not pre-empt MSC incursions into Scotland. As the foregoing indicates, this is not the whole story, but it is a part of it. (Two alternative conspiracy theories should be noted: first, that the SED would have introduced its reforms anyway but used the MSC bogey to attract support; and second, that the whole episode was orchestrated by the MSC in order to set up Scotland as a testbed for future developments. There may be some truth in the first of these but the second is implausible: conspiracy theories presuppose a degree of consistency and coherence on the part of the conspirators.)

In its early days the Action Plan was widely perceived as a kind of comprehensive reform of post-16 education (McPherson, 1984a and 1984b). Significantly, the reform remains only two-thirds complete: the different level of (non-advanced) vocational education are combined within the modular system, but academic Highers courses retain their separate identity and status. However in an important sense the Action Plan is an alternative to comprehensive (or other) reforms at 16+. Modularization facilitates a shift in the focus of policy debate and reform, from institutions to curricula and qualifications (Squires, forthcoming). The strategy of institutional versatility is a direct alternative to institutional restructuring of the kind which secondary education experienced after 1965. Rather than change institutions, the strategy pursues a framework that is consistent with a wide variety of institutional forms, but which can rationalize, integrate, coordinate and (to a point) control them. In the rest of this chapter I present data on the initial impact of the Action Plan and offer a tentative assessment of the strengths and weaknesses of this strategy.

THE FIRST YEAR GROUP

This chapter describes young people who had been in the fourth year of secondary school in 1983/84. A 10 per cent sample was surveyed first in spring 1985 and again in spring 1986; the chapter uses data collected from both surveys. Further details of the surveys are given by Nils Tomes in appendix 1. In August 1984, when Scotvec modules came on stream, these young people were entering the fifth year or its non-school equivalent; they therefore comprised the first school year group to have the opportunity to study Scotvec modules at 16.

Three caveats should be noted. First, these young people were the pioneers of the Action Plan, and are likely to have suffered the various teething problems involved in its implementation. In 1984/85, when the first sample members took modules, modularization was incomplete; equivalences had yet to be agreed with the City and Guilds of London Institute; the use of modules on YTS had yet to be boosted by the extension of certification opportunities under the two-year scheme; and the introduction of modules into schools, initially very swift, was soon interrupted by industrial action which lasted more than two years. Perhaps most critically, many employers were still poorly informed about the new certificate. Later year groups are likely to take more modules and to experience a more settled system.

Second, the chapter does not compare this year group with previous year groups in order to measure the changes that accompanied the introduction of the Action Plan. Not only are there no directly comparable samples – the present year group being the first to be surveyed longitudinally by the Scottish Young Peoples Survey — but comparing data collected before and after Action Plan would in any case face conceptual problems: the Action Plan has changed many of the terms in which such data must be collected. The aim of the chapter is rather to describe the operation of the Plan in terms of its own logic, and to attempt some assessment of how far this logic is effective in practice. However, it must be recognized that many of the problems revealed by the chapter may have existed before the Action Plan. They may not all be problems *of* the modular system, even if they are problems *for* it.

Third, there are considerable difficulties in collecting accurate data on the Action Plan reforms in a postal questionnaire. Postal surveys tend to presuppose relatively simple and stable categories whose names and boundaries are agreed by respondents and researchers. The Action Plan broke down or blurred familiar boundaries. Institutional differences became more complex; convenient concepts such as 'course' became, at least in principle, redundant. Above all, the modular system was new and a shared and settled terminology to describe it had yet to emerge by spring 1985 when the Scottish year group was first surveyed. One consequence was that many young people doing modules — especially those at school, on YTS or in employment for whom modules were not their main activity — had difficulty in describing what they were doing. The 1985 questionnaire was despatched before any certificates for the new modules had been issued. When respondents taking post-school courses were asked if their main courses included any Scotvec National Certificate modules, four in ten responded 'don't know'.

By the following year, sample members appeared more familiar with the new system. Thirty per cent answered 'yes' to a question which asked: 'Have you *ever* started any Scotvec National Certificate modules?' However 5 per cent did not answer, and it is probable that the item underestimates the total experience of modules. A further 7 per cent of the sample gave an answer to at least one question in at least one (1985 or 1986) questionnaire which implied that they had at least started a Scotvec module. Although still imprecise, the resultant total of 37 per cent is taken in this chapter to represent the proportion of the year group who had experienced Scotvec modules by 1986. Reference to a variety of items in both questionnaires made it possible to identify the statuses in which 34 out of the 37 per cent had studied modules. Thus, 15 per cent had done module(s) while at school, 12 per cent while on YTS, 8 per cent while full-time students not on YTS, and 5 per cent while part-time students not on YTS. These figures sum to more than 34 per cent because some young people had taken modules while in more than one status, over the period (of rather less than two years) covered by the data. Once again, these figures may be subject to some imprecision.

Because of the way the data have been extracted from different questionnaire items, the information on subjects studied and on the number of modules taken or completed is complex, sometimes incomplete and will not be presented here. It is important to note, however, that the number of modules taken varied sharply across the different statuses. Respondents were asked how many modules they expected to have completed in each status by July 1986. Nearly half of those who gave a positive number for school modules expected to have completed just one module; the median was two modules. The median number of modules expected to have been completed in the other statuses were: four while on YTS; twenty while a full-time student; and seven while a part-time student.

EXPERIENCE OF SCOTVEC MODULES BY SPRING 1986

The educational and labour-market experiences of the year group have been described in chapter 1 of this volume, and I will not describe them again here. However one point from that chapter bears repetition as it lies at the heart of the strategy of institutional versatility. Between August 1984 (when year group members could first take Scotvec modules) and the spring 1986 survey there was considerably more movement between different institutional statuses among the Scottish year group than among the equivalent year group in England and Wales. Some of this movement was associated with school-leaving arrangements which required three in ten of the year group to stay on to December of the fifth year, when many became winter leavers. Other movements were associated with the pattern of one-year courses in Scottish post-compulsory education and the associated transition point at 17 years, when many young people moved within full-time education, from school to college or higher education, or out of full-time education to YTS or employment. Over this period, more than half the year group (54 per cent) occupied two or more of the main statuses in which they might study modules: school, YTS, full-time further education and employment. One in eight (12 per cent) occupied three or more of these statuses. All this movement serves to increase the need for coordination, integration and lines of progression between the different institutional contexts in which education is offered. It suggests that the Action Plan's strategy of institutional versatility may particularly suit the institutional as well as the political circumstances of Scotland.

Table 8.1: Experience of modules by spring 1986 (year group)

	% reported any module(s)	% studied module(s) while...				
		at school	on YTS	FT student	PT student	n
All	37	15	12	8	5	(5292)
Sex						
Males	36	14	13	5	7	(2598)
Females	37	16	11	11	3	(2694)
S4 'O' grades						
4+ A–C awards	31	17	6	7	5	(2498)
1–3	45	18	14	11	6	(1433)
D–E awards	48	17	19	11	5	(417)
None	31	8	16	5	3	(932)
Father's social class						
I	26	16	5	4	1	(279)
II	32	17	7	8	5	(1132)
IIInm	39	19	10	10	7	(356)
IIIm	39	14	14	8	6	(1667)
IV	41	17	13	9	5	(655)
V	34	12	14	8	3	(185)
Status in spring 1986						
School	20	20	0	*	0	(1333)
FT higher education	11	6	0	4	0	(165)
FT further education	78	19	3	69	3	(338)
FT job	40	13	14	6	10	(2007)
YTS	55	28	33	8	2	(390)
Unemployed	33	10	19	3	2	(802)
Others	26	11	7	5	4	(165)

Note: Young people who studied modules in more than one status are counted separately in each status. The 37 per cent who reported taking modules includes about 3 per cent whose status when they took them could not be reliably identified. Asterisk denotes less than half of 1 per cent.

Table 8.1. summarizes the consequences of these transitions for the epidemiology of Scotvec modules. As discussed above, 37 per cent of the year group reported starting at least one module; the table also shows how many had done modules in each status. (All references to 'modules' in this chapter are to Scotvec National Certificate modules.)

Similar proportions of males and females had done modules. However the statuses wherein modules were taken were clearly gendered, and ranged on a continuum from full-time further education (the most feminine) through school and YTS to part-time further education (the most masculine). The incidence of modules across levels of fourth-year attainment resembled an inverted 'U', with nearly half young people in the middle ranges having studied a module. However this distribution varied across the different statuses, with YTS showing a relatively 'downward' skew and school and part-time further education a relatively upward skew.

Further analyses, not reported in the table, help to explain the distribution of modules by fourth-year attainment. Scotvec modules were only available to school students in their fifth or sixth years. Young people with good fourth-year attainments were much more likely to stay on into fifth year; however among the stayers those with lower fourth-year attainments were more likely to do modules. This was substantially due to the large take-up of modules (more than 30 per cent) among those who stayed on compulsorily to the winter of fifth year, who tended to be less qualified. The downward skew of YTS modules in relation to fourth-year attainment was due to the larger proportion of the less qualified who had been on YTS; among YTS trainees, the better-qualified were slightly more likely to have done modules. Among year group members in full-time jobs the better-qualified were substantially more likely to have done modules as part-time students. A majority of full-time further education students had done modules, whatever their fourth-year qualifications. Girls in full-time further education were more likely to have done modules than boys; this probably reflects the different pace of modularization across subject areas.

The social class distribution of young people who did modules also resembled an inverted 'U'.

The proportion who had done modules varied across the current (spring 1986) statuses of year group members, ranging from 11 per cent of the early entrants to higher education to 78 per cent of students in full-time further education (table 8.1). More striking, perhaps, is the extent to which young people had studied modules in some earlier status. For example, a third of current YTS trainees had studied modules while on YTS; but nearly as many (28 per cent) had studied modules at school, and others had studied them as full-time or (in a few cases) part-time students.

Young people in full-time jobs had, in a sense, come nearest to completing their post-16 transitions, and this is reflected in the range of statuses in which they had done modules. Altogether 40 per cent had at least started a module, slightly above the average for the year group. Six per cent had studied modules in full-time further education, and 10 per cent in part-time further education. But the two largest sources of modules for full-time employees were school (13 per cent) and YTS (14 per cent). Both will increase in importance as more modules are offered to school students following the resolution of the teachers' industrial dispute in 1987, and as modules are used to certificate two-year YTS. Altogether about 40 per cent of young people in full-time jobs in spring 1986 had stayed at school for at least the first term of fifth year, and 49 per cent had been on YTS; 73 per cent had done one or other of these things. Among the whole year group the corresponding percentages are 57 per cent, 42 per cent and 83 per cent. This gives some indication of the potential market for modules even if institutional patterns remain constant, and shows the scope for the strategy of institutional versatility in the Scottish system.

Table 8.2 shows that young employees with Scotvec modules were well spread across occupational areas, with security and protective services (mainly armed forces) the only major exception. In large part this reflects the wide occupational spread of young employees with modules from YTS or (to a lesser extent) from school. By contrast young people with modules gained as part-time or (to a lesser extent) full-time students tended to be concentrated in particular occupational areas. There was a similar spread across industrial sectors (table not shown), again with the exception that young people with part-time modules tended to be concentrated in particular industries, notably construction and metal goods, engineering and vehicles.

The data so far presented suggest that the strategy of institutional versatility is an effective way of exposing young people to modules; with current developments in school and YTS a majority of each year group may soon study at least one module. Many may have only one or two modules, and many may have modules that are only indirectly relevant to their educational or occupational ambitions. However the strategy of institutional versatility, and especially what I have described as the introductory-Lego-set strategy, assumes that young people who have gained experience of a few modules in one status, particularly at school or on YTS, are thereby encouraged to take more modules in subsequent statuses. This is explored in the next section.

EDUCATIONAL PROGRESSION

Perceived Encouragement to Progression

Asked whether the modules they had studied had 'made [them] want to take more courses at college', 10 per cent of young people who had done modules replied 'very much', 15 per cent 'somewhat' and 57 per cent 'not at all'. The remaining 18 per cent were 'not sure'. Thus, one in four (10 + 15 = 25 per

Table 8.2: Experience of modules, by occupation: all in full-time jobs in spring 1986

	% started any module(s)			% (males + females) studied modules while...			
	All	Males	Females	at school	on YTS	FT student	PT student
Professional, managerial and related	35	(54)	21	5	10	10	15
Clerical and related	40	31	42	17	14	8	6
Selling	35	34	36	20	12	4	2
Security and protective services	19	19	*	10	2	2	2
Catering, cleaning, hairdressing and other personal services	41	(30)	43	16	16	6	8
Farming, fishing and related	48	50	*	14	20	2	13
Materials processing, making and repairing (exc metal and electrical)	40	49	29	8	17	4	10
Processing, making, repairing and related (metal and electrical)	49	50	*	9	10	7	27
Painting, repetitive assembling, product assembling, product inspecting, packaging and related	36	(43)	(27)	11	16	4	8
Construction, mining and related not identified elsewhere	27	27	*	8	12	6	7
Transport operating, materials moving and storing and related	35	37	*	6	12	5	7
Miscellaneous	(37)	(39)	*	(15)	(14)	(8)	(5)
NK/inadequately described	41	44	37	13	15	7	8
All	40	42	37	13	14	6	10

Note: Brackets indicate base n less than 50; asterisks denote base n less than 20.

cent) appeared at least 'somewhat' encouraged to pursue educational progression, with the proportion ranging from 20 per cent of young people who had studied modules at school to 34 per cent of those who had studied them as full-time students. YTS and part-time students each scored 27 per cent.

Progression from School

Wanting to take more courses is one thing; actually going ahead and taking them may be another. The first part of table 8.3 covers young people who had started fifth year (and therefore could have done modules at school) but had left school by spring 1986. The table distinguishes between those who left in the winter of fifth year and those who left later, mainly at the summer of fifth year; 31 per cent of the former and 24 per cent of the latter had studied modules while at school. Within each group there was no significant difference between those with and without school modules in the proportion subsequently taking modules as full-time students. However the figures for later leavers in table 8.3 conceal a minority - those with high fourth-year attainments - who were significantly more likely to take modules in full-time education if they had done modules at school (see chapter 9 in this volume). We cannot tell from the data if these young people were encouraged to enter further education by their experience of school modules, or encouraged to take modules at school by the same vocational aspirations which attracted them into further education.

Among the later leavers who were in full-time jobs in spring 1986, those with school modules were rather *less* likely to study modules as part-time students than those with no school modules. However this difference can be explained by the lower fourth-year attainments of employees with school modules; young workers with higher fourth-year attainments were much more likely to study modules as part-time students.

The main positive evidence of progression from school concerns YTS. School leavers with modules were more likely to enter YTS and, if they did, they were more likely to take modules on YTS. Different qualification levels explain some of these differences, especially among the later leavers: school leavers with modules tended to have lower SCE attainments, and school leavers with lower SCE attainments were more likely to enter YTS. But the association between school modules and YTS, and that between school modules and YTS modules, are both statistically significant even when SCE qualifications (including Highers) are controlled for.[2] The data therefore suggest a link between school modules and YTS. However this effect may be the result of differential reporting of school modules; sample members who

Table 8.3: Educational progression from school and from YTS: summary (percentages)

	With school/ YTS modules	Others
Left school between autumn 1984 and spring 1986		
% took modules as FT student		
Winter S5 leavers	5	6
Later leavers	14	13
% took modules as PT student		
(base = current FT employees excluding		
former YTS trainees)		
Winter S5 leavers	(13)	11
Later leavers	7	13
% entered YTS		
Winter S5 leavers	78	62
Later leavers	41	29
% took modules while on YTS		
(base = YTS entrants)		
Winter S5 leavers	37	28
Later leavers	34	27
YTS entrants		
% in further education in spring 1986	2	2
% took modules as PT student		
(base = current FT employees)	13	7
% took modules as PT student		
(base = remained unemployed after YTS)	3	2

Note: Brackets indicate base n less than 50.

entered YTS, and especially those who took modules on YTS, may have been more aware of Scotvec modules and more likely to recall and report those they had studied at school. Against this, it can be noted that sample members who took modules as full- or part-time students do not appear to have been affected by this differential reporting of school modules; but in view of the problems of collecting data, especially in 1985, the possibility that the school/YTS effect is spurious cannot be discounted.

Completing YTS

Comparisons between YTS trainees who did and did not do modules are complicated by differences in the occupations for which they were training. Those doing modules were overrepresented in farming, fishing and related occupations and in catering, cleaning, hairdressing and other personal services; they were underrepresented in selling, and in processing, making, repairing and related (metal and electrical) occupations, However, these occupational differences do not account for the finding that YTS trainees who did modules were more likely than other trainees to complete their scheme. This difference remains statistically significant even controlling for gender, school attainment, and occupation.[3] Of year-group members on YTS in spring 1985, 76 per cent of those doing modules completed their schemes compared with 67 per cent of the others (table not shown). Most of the very early leavers from YTS had already left by spring 1985, so the difference is unlikely to be due to non-completers not staying long enough on YTS to take any modules. Nor is it substantially due to higher proportions of trainees with modules being kept on by scheme sponsors (see table 8.6 below). One interpretation of these data is that providing trainees with opportunities for nationally recognized certification encourages them to complete their schemes. The implication is that drop-out rates may fall as such opportunities are extended to all YTS trainees. However this encouragement does not depend on the modular nature of the certification (which may even encourage dropping-out, since drop-outs are credited for what they have already achieved). If these data represent a success of the Action Plan, this is because modularity and the strategy of institutional versatility make it easier to offer certification on YTS.

Progression from YTS

Of the year-group members who had entered YTS and left it by spring 1986, 27 per cent had studied modules while on the scheme. The proportion who were in full-time further education in spring 1986 was small (2 per cent) and identical for those with and without YTS modules (table 8.3). Indeed nearly twice as many young people had 'progressed' from full-time further education to YTS as from YTS to full-time further education over this period.

Among YTS trainees who entered employment, those who had done modules on YTS were nearly twice as likely to take further modules as part-time students (13 per cent compared with 7 per cent: see table 8.3). This difference is statistically significant, even controlling for gender, SCE qualifications and current occupation.[4] However, it is doubtful whether this is an 'effect' of YTS modules on subsequent educational progression, following the logic of the introductory Lego set; for this logic tends to assume that the decisions on progression were taken by the individual student. Yet 89 per cent of former YTS trainees in jobs studying modules as part-time students said they had been sent on their course by an employer, with no significant difference between those who had and had not done modules on YTS. It is conceivable, if perhaps unlikely, that employers might themselves have responded to the incentive of the introductory Lego set, and been encouraged to send their employees for part-time study if they already had modules from YTS to build on.

Among those who remained unemployed after YTS any decisions about educational progression are likely to have been made by the individual student. The proportion who took further modules was tiny, and not significantly influenced by the experience of modules on YTS.

Summary

These data describe the first year group to be affected by the Action Plan; new patterns of progression may only develop when the new system is more widely understood and accepted. The data suggest that members of this year group who did modules at school may have been more likely to enter YTS and to take modules there; and that a minority – high attainers who left at the end of fifth year — may have been encouraged by school modules to enter full-time education. YTS trainees who did modules on YTS were more likely to complete their schemes, and they were more likely to take further modules as part-time students if they entered employment. There were few other signs of educational progression being encouraged by modules. Modules may have encouraged many young people's willingness to progress; their actual behaviour, we speculate, too often either depended on the decisions of others such as employers, or responded to other educational or labour-market incentives that proved stronger than the incentive of the introductory Lego set.

MODULES AND ENTRY TO EMPLOYMENT

Perceived Help in Finding Jobs

Young people who had done modules were asked if their modules had helped them when looking for a job. Table 8.4 shows the responses of those who were either in jobs or unemployed (those still on YTS may not have looked for jobs yet) and distinguishes between modules studied in different statuses. Most of these young people who had taken modules at school, on YTS or full-time at college would have looked for jobs since taking their modules; conversely, many of those who had studied modules part-time may have started them since entering their current jobs.

This is reflected in table 8.4. Few part-time students thought their modules had helped them find jobs. Modules studied in full-time further education appeared most helpful; two-thirds of the former full-time students said their modules had helped at least somewhat, compared with a little more than a third of those with modules from school or YTS. It should be

Table 8.4: *Have the modules you've studied helped you when looking for a job? (percentages)*

	Studied modules....				
	at school only	*on YTS only*	*as FT student only*	*as PT student only*	*All*
In full-time jobs or unemployed in spring 1986:					
very much	16	18	38	11	18
somewhat	20	20	28	7	17
not at all	57	48	24	53	49
not sure	8	15	11	30	16
Total	101	101	101	101	100
n	(70)	(112)	(37)	(59)	(389)
In full-time jobs in spring 1986:					
very much	13	26	40	9	20
somewhat	19	19	29	7	17
not at all	60	43	18	54	46
not sure	9	13	13	30	17
Total	101	101	100	100	100
n	(52)	(74)	(30)	(57)	(297)

Notes: 'All' includes multiple or unknown statuses. Based on random subsample receiving relevant questionnaire version.

remembered that full-time students typically had a programme of some twenty modules to show to employers, compared with medians of two modules from school and four modules from YTS.

The second half of table 8.4 is restricted to young people currently in full-time employment, but shows few changes from the data discussed above.

It is open to question whether the data in table 8.4 describe a level of 'helpfulness' of modules that is high or low in absolute terms. Arguably the finding that only two-thirds of former full-time students said their modules had helped even 'somewhat', and less than four in ten said they had helped 'very much', is low for what were, in most cases, one-year full-time programmes with explicitly vocational aims. However we do not know how earlier students taking traditional group certificate courses would have replied to equivalent questions.

Comparative Data

An alternative perspective on whether modules helped people find jobs is gained by comparing the actual experiences of young people with and without modules. Table 8.5 shows net transitions of year-group members between spring 1985 and spring 1986. Where sample numbers are large enough the table compares young people who had and had not done modules while in their spring 1985 status.

Among students still at school in Spring 1985, those with modules were less likely to be still at school or in higher education in spring 1986, and more likely to be on YTS. The first two differences can be explained in terms of their different levels of SCE attainment but the apparent YTS effect, as we have seen, is greater than qualification differences can account for. The proportions entering employment were similar between the two groups.

Among those in full-time further education in spring 1985 those doing modules were more likely than the others to be still in full-time further education in spring 1986 but less likely to be in employment (27 per cent compared with 49 per cent). However, the difference between the groups may largely reflect different subject areas, as some areas were modularized earlier than others. The more worrying statistic is the low absolute figure in employment in spring 1986: 27 per cent of those with modules. Since 65 per cent had left further education by then this represents an employment rate among college leavers with modules of below 50 per cent. These young people, most of whom entered college after fourth year, are not typical of all full-time students; twice as many students entered full-time non-advanced further education from fifth year as from fourth year. But the data,

Table 8.5:*Status in spring 1986, by status in spring 1985 and whether studied modules (percentages)*

Status in spring 1986	School	FT HE	FT FE	FT job			YTS	Unemp	Others	NK	Total	n
				Same occ as 1985	Diff occ	85 or 86 occ NK						
Status in spring 1985												
School:												
studied school modules	42	2	10	–	–	21	16	5	3	2	101	(591)
others	49	7	9	–	–	19	10	4	3	0	101	(2092)
Full-time further education:												
studied modules as FT student (not on YTS)	0	3	35	–	–	27	18	10	5	2	100	(148)
others	0	0	14	–	–	49	15	8	14	0	100	(34)
Full-time job:												
studied modules as PT student (not on YTS)	0	0	1	72	6	13	0	3	4	0	99	(101)
others	0	0	1	56	17	11	1	12	2	0	100	(707)
YTS:												
studied modules or YTS	0	0	2	35	10	12	2	36	4	*	101	(365)
others	0	0	2	30	17	10	2	35	4	*	100	(657)
Unemployed	0	0	2	–	–	25	9	53	12	*	101	(448)
Others	0	0	3	–	–	26	3	29	39	1	101	(80)

Notes: Sample numbers of 'unemployed' and 'others' who studied modules as part-time students too small for reliable inference. Same/different occupation – based on the 16 Orders of the OPCS 1980 schema. Occupational moves within an Order count as the same occupation. Note that reported occupational mobility is inflated by unreliable or inadequate reporting of occupations or inconsistent coding procedures between surveys.

reinforcing a pessimistic interpretation of table 8.4, still raise questions about how well full-time vocational education articulates with patterns of recruit-ment and selection in the labour market (see Raffe and Tomes, 1987, pp. 43–5).

Among young people in full-time jobs in spring 1985, those who did modules as part-time students were relatively likely to be well qualified and to receive training in their jobs. This may explain why those with part-time modules were not only more likely to be still in full-time employment a year later, but also more likely to be in the same occupation. A similar trend is evident in respect of YTS: trainees who took modules while on their schemes were significantly more likely to find subsequent employment in the same occupation, although they did not have a higher employment rate overall than trainees without modules.

Table 8.6: *Destinations after YTS: young people on YTS in spring 1985 who had left it by spring 1986*

	Studied modules while on YTS	Others	All
Full-time job with YTS employer or sponsor:			
before completing scheme	6	7	7
on completing scheme	29	25	27
Full-time job elsewhere:			
before completing scheme	9	13	11
on completing scheme	7	9	8
later	16	12	13
Unemployed on leaving YTS and in spring 1986	31	29	30
Others	3	5	4
Total	101	100	100
n	(337)	(595)	(932)

Table 8.6 provides further details of the post-scheme employment histories of young people who had been on YTS in spring 1985. Those who had done modules were slightly more likely than the others to be taken on by scheme sponsors on completing their schemes; they were less likely to find employment at a later date. However, the differences in table 8.6 are not statistically significant (p = .109). Among YTS trainees in full-time jobs in spring 1986, those who had done modules were significantly more likely to be employed in the same occupation as their YTS scheme (see table 8.5); interestingly, this was more true of those who had been kept on by scheme sponsors (91 per cent compared with 79 per cent) than of those who had not

(55 per cent compared with 46 per cent: this latter difference is not significant, but is based on smaller sample numbers). The processes by which YTS modules are associated with occupational stability may have more to do with the internal than the external labour market.

Indeed, the role of YTS modules in the external market seems doubtful. Former trainees who had done modules on YTS were slightly *less* likely than other trainees to agree that 'being on a YTS scheme helped (them) to get (their) present or most recent job'. Among trainees who had found jobs in the external labour market, 34 per cent with YTS modules replied 'yes' compared to 40 per cent of the others. (Among trainees kept on by their YTS sponsors there was, predictably, near total agreement from both groups.) We have seen in table 8.4 that fewer than half the trainees with YTS modules — even among those who found jobs — felt their modules had helped them 'very much' or 'somewhat' when looking for a job. A similar proportion felt they had helped 'not at all'. If we distinguish between those who found jobs with their scheme sponsor and those who found jobs elsewhere, we find that similar proportions of each group felt their modules had helped 'very much' or 'somewhat', but nearly twice as many of those recruited in the external labour market felt their modules had helped 'not at all'.[5] The difference is not statistically significant (p = .103) but is consistent with other data reported above.

There is one slightly more optimistic conclusion from the analysis of YTS. Table 8.6 showed that YTS trainees who had done modules were more likely to find jobs some time after leaving their scheme, even if they first became unemployed. Among trainees who found jobs at this stage those with modules were more likely to say that being on a YTS scheme helped them to get their jobs (47 per cent compared with 30 per cent). Neither difference is statistically significant, but two non-significant findings may have greater credibility if they point in the same direction. They suggest that the value of YTS lasts longer when accompanied by modules.

Summary

The number of students saying their modules had helped them find jobs appears low, although lack of a comparative standard makes such judgments subjective. Comparisons between young people with and without modules yield little evidence of a positive effect on employment, beyond a suggestion that modules might prolong the effect of YTS. If anything the data suggest that modules may have been more closely associated with movements in the internal than in the external labour market: for example they were associated with occupational stability among employees and also among YTS trainees kept on by their sponsors. The data lend indirect support to the tentative suggestion of Taylor *et al.* (1986) that employers have reacted more positively to modules in their role as direct 'purchasers' of part-time programmes for their employees, than in their role as selectors of young recruits with National Certificate qualifications.

These are early data; it may take time for modules to acquire currency in the external labour market. But even if they do it may be insufficient to remove the question mark which this analysis has left against the role of full-time further education as a route into employment for 16-year-olds.

CHOICE OF MODULES

A random subsample of those who had done modules were asked how they had chosen which modules to do (table 8.7). The fixed-choice answers were worded so as to be applicable across a range of contexts, and are somewhat imprecise in meaning. Nevertheless the broad-brush data they yield point to two fairly clear conclusions. First, except at school students often had limited choice of individual modules. Each of the last five responses in table 8.7 may indicate a degree of constraint. Thirty per cent of school students ticked at least one of these items, compared with 95 per cent of YTS students, 100 per cent of full-time college students and 90 per cent of part-time students. These figures may exaggerate the lack of choice: being 'told which modules to do' may reflect guidance rather than direction. Nevertheless, they are consistent with other evidence that college students tend to be offered course-like off-the-peg programmes with limited choice of individual modules (Hart *et al.*, 1987). The second, and related, conclusion is that young people's reasons for taking and choosing modules varied with their institutional base. The strategy of institutional versatility cannot abolish these differences.

Some of the weaknesses as well as strengths of a modular system are related to the scope for choice, and are likely to be diminished accordingly as this choice is limited (Jonathan, 1987). For example, the risk of students choosing poorly integrated or imbalanced programmes is reduced if students in fact have little choice (although there is no guarantee that those who choose for them, such as employers, will choose more wisely). At least three-quarters of students agreed either 'very much' or 'somewhat' that their modules 'fitted together well to make a good course overall', and that they gave them 'enough variety in [their] course' (table not shown). In both respects full-time students showed most agreement; integration and balance may be easiest to achieve in full-time programmes, and college staff designing programmes for full-time students may attach higher priority to integration and balance than managing agents or employers selecting modules for YTS or part-time programmes.

Table 8.7: How did you choose which modules to do? Tick all that apply: Whole year group (percentages)

| | Studied modules | | | | |
	at school only	on YTS only	as FT student only	as PT student only	All
I picked the modules I was interested in	74	12	17	12	31
I picked the modules I would need for a future job	29	10	18	15	18
I picked the modules which went with my other school subjects	11	0	1	0	4
I was told which modules to do by my teachers	15	14	21	9	14
I was told which modules to do by my employer or YTS managing agent	1	56	1	45	27
I took the modules that were part of my college course	3	32	75	33	35
I wanted the modules that were the same as the old course in that subject	2	0	1	1	1
I didn't have any choice	17	43	50	42	36
Unweighted n	(209)	(165)	(135)	(66)	(748)

Notes: 'All' includes multiple and unknown statuses. Based on random subsample receiving relevant questionnaire version, and ticking at least one response.

However, the restricted scope for choice may have resulted in some students taking modules at an inappropriate level. Nearly three in ten felt their modules had been 'very' easy, and six in ten that they had been 'not at all' difficult. In principle the modular system allows programmes to be designed so that students will be sufficiently stretched; in practice, it seems, this did not always happen.

RELEVANCE TO EMPLOYMENT

The argument that modular provision will enhance the economic contribution of education rests on a view about market structures that individual data can only indirectly address. Table 8.8 shows the responses of young people in full-time jobs to questions which touch, if indirectly, on the 'relevance' of their modules to employment. A majority felt their modules had been at least 'somewhat' useful to them; usefulness can be defined in various ways but it is likely that most current employees defined it at least partly in relation to employment. The proportion responding 'very much' ranged from less than a third of those who had done modules at school, to nearly two-thirds of those who had done them as part-time students. School modules were least likely, in the eyes of respondents, to have helped them 'to understand the world of work'. Most respondents felt their modules had helped them 'to learn new skills', although the strength of agreement varied, being greatest among full-time students. Responses to the fourth question, whether modules 'trained you for the job you wanted to do', varied most across the different statuses, although the two-dimensional character of the question makes interpretation difficult: did part-time students receive the best training, or were they merely lucky enough to be preparing for the jobs they wanted to do?

Table 8.8: Selected attitudes to modules, by status when studied them: All in full-time jobs (percentages)

| | Studied modules | | | | |
	at school only	on YTS only	as FT student only	as PT student only	All
Have the modules you've studied...					
...been useful to you?					
very much	29	34	51	64	44
somewhat	46	39	29	25	37
not at all	21	19	12	3	12
not sure	3	8	8	8	7
Total	99	100	100	100	100
n	(55)	(73)	(33)	(60)	(314)
...helped you to understand the world of work?					
very much	12	26	34	29	27
somewhat	38	38	45	45	43
not at all	45	31	19	16	25
not sure	5	5	2	10	5
Total	100	100	100	100	100
n	(52)	(75)	(32)	(58)	(309)
...helped you to learn new skills?					
very much	54	47	73	61	57
somewhat	27	40	28	31	33
not at all	18	11	0	6	9
not sure	2	2	0	2	2
Total	101	100	101	100	101
n	(52)	(73)	(31)	(59)	(308)
...trained you for the job wanted to do?					
very much	14	28	48	65	36
somewhat	22	28	28	22	25
not at all	59	34	20	9	31
not sure	5	10	4	4	7
Total	100	100	100	100	99
n	(53)	(74)	(31)	(59)	(310)

Notes: 'All' includes multiple or unknown statuses. Based on random subsample receiving relevant questionnaire version.

The main conclusion from these data is simply that the perceived vocational or other relevance of modules varied according to the institutional base from which they had been taken. In part this may reflect the different motives for taking modules: school students may not have expected or wanted their modules to help them understand the world of work or to train them for a job. In part it may reflect the different relation to labour-market selection: most part-time students had already entered their jobs before doing modules, so it is not surprising to find a closer match with their current employment. The more general point is simply that the experience and evaluation of modules varied systematically across the different statuses wherein they were studied. The strategy of institutional versatility may attempt to straddle institutional differences; it cannot expect to abolish them.

Comparisons of YTS trainees who had and had not done modules reveal little clear effect of modules on the perceived relevance of YTS. A question asking whether their YTS scheme had prepared them for many, several, one or no kinds of work found no significant difference between the two groups. In response to a question asking whether what they learned on YTS had helped them to do their present or most recent jobs, those with YTS modules were rather less likely to say that it had 'helped a lot' (38 per cent compared with 43 per cent) but much more likely to say that it had 'helped a little' (43 per cent compared with 28 per cent) and less likely to say that it had 'not helped at all' (19 per cent compared with 30 per cent).

SUMMARY AND DISCUSSION

Evaluating the Rationales

At the beginning of this chapter I outlined four rationales for the Action Plan. The first of these, which refers to extending opportunity and choice, is partly vindicated by these data. Modules can be taken from a wide range of institutional bases, and because of this the Action Plan has extended opportunities for certification and increased the range of options open to many students. Opportunities may be widened further, as more modules are made available to school students following the end of industrial action and the extension of TVEI, and as modules are extended through the two-year YTS. However in many contexts the scope for student choice of individual modules is limited. Possibly the Action Plan has extended individual opportunity and choice, less by the process of modularization *per se* with its implications for options within programmes, than by the strategy of institutional versatility which has made modules available to young people in a wide range of institutions and situations.

The second rationale for the Action Plan concerned the effect on participation. The Action Plan has increased the number of young people gaining certification; whether it increases total levels of participation in education and training rests, in part, on the success of what I have called the introductory-Lego-set strategy. The institutional versatility of the Action Plan makes the first stage of this strategy highly successful, since it distributes the introductory sets to a large number of young people in a wide range of settings. On the second stage of the strategy — the purchase of further Lego sets — the data are more equivocal. Young people who studied modules at school were more likely to enter YTS and to do modules there, although there remains a suspicion that this finding merely reflects the differential recall and reporting of school modules. Some higher-attainers with school modules may have been encouraged to enter further education. YTS trainees who took modules were more likely to complete their schemes, possibly responding to the incentive of certification. They were also more likely to take further modules as part-time students in their subsequent jobs, although this seems to have rested on the decisions of their employers rather than of the students themselves. There were few other signs of educational progression encouraged by the introductory-Lego-set strategy. However the analysis raised at least one basic question concerning this strategy; to what extent does it assume that decisions on educational progression are taken by the individual student following an essentially educational logic? In practice such decisions may be taken by others, or they may be taken by the student but anticipating a logic dictated by the labour market.

The third Action Plan rationale concerned the educational contribution to economic performance. The Plan is a part, if a small one, of a general drive to improve the 'supply side' of the British economy. Evaluating its contribution to this drive is extremely difficult. On one criterion, the value of modules in the external labour market, the evidence is not encouraging. Many young people felt their modules had not helped them very much when looking for jobs. Less than half of young people leaving full-time further education with modules found jobs. There was no association between doing modules at school and finding a job later on. Modules taken on YTS were not associated with a higher overall probability of employment, although they may have helped to prolong the impact of YTS on subsequent employability.

However these pessimistic conclusions must be qualified in at least three ways. First, the evidence in this chapter does not tell us whether the pre-existing vocational qualifications fared any better in the external labour market. Earlier vocational certificates were also affected by employers' preferences for academic qualifications and/or for recruitment at 16. Scotvec modules may be merely the latest victims of the British youth labour market's chronic failure to support a significant full-time technical or vocational sector for the post-compulsory age group (Raffe and Tomes, 1987). Second, our year group was the first to take Scotvec modules: in time employers may become more familiar with the new certificate and attach more value to it. Third, and most fundamentally, it is inappropriate to judge the economic contribution of the Action Plan on the basis of indicators generated by a highly distorted market. The relative employment rates of young people leaving different education or training programmes should be seen as constraints upon, rather than indicators of, the programmes' relative success and development (Raffe, 1987). They are none the less important for that.

Indeed there is more encouraging evidence on the success of modules in the internal labour market. Taylor *et al.* (1986) report generally favourable reactions from employers who use modules for in-service provision for their apprentices and employees. They go on to suggest that employers have reacted more favourably to modules in this role, as direct consumers, than when acting in the external labour market and selecting young people for employment. Many of the showcase examples of the success of the Action Plan concern the use of the modular currency to negotiate training packages for large employers (SED, 1986). The survey data have less to say about internal labour markets than about external ones, but they show that part-time students tended to find their modules most useful, and most valued the training they provided; and the link between modules and occupational stability, particularly in relation to YTS, appears to reflect processes in the internal labour market more than in the external one. At the same time the data confirm that employers' use of modules for part-time programmes for their employees has been heavily skewed by gender and concentrated in particular occupations and industries.

The last of the Action Plan rationales referred to rationalization and planning within the education system. The need for this is enhanced not only by the institutional variety within Scottish post-compulsory education, but also by the frequent transitions that characterize this stage. In contrast to some other systems Scotland does not have parallel streams at the post-compulsory stage, but rather a variety of options which may be taken as alternatives, in sequence or sometimes even in combination. There is a need for a framework that can rationalize, coordinate and integrate across these options, although the need is premised on the assumption that institutional reforms to simplify the options and their permutations are either impracticable or undesirable.

Young people with modules were well scattered across different statuses in spring 1986, both in and out of the labour market, and many of them had studied modules in previous statuses. However the data cannot comment directly on the effectiveness of the rationalization, coordination and integration provided by the Action Plan framework. Reviewing the implementation of modular programmes, Roberts (1987, p. 244) notes that 'a satisfactory outcome is extremely difficult to achieve, especially in cross-boundary situations'. His comment refers primarily to subject and departmental boundaries within institutions; it may be even more pertinent in relation to the Action Plan, where there are so many more boundaries to cross.

Limitations of the Strategy of Institutional Versatility

The data show that the organizational and political arguments for the strategy of institutional versatility are reinforced by the institutional structure of post-compulsory education and training in Scotland and by the frequent transitions to which this gives rise. But the data also remind us that while the strategy of institutional versatility may attempt to straddle institutional differences it cannot expect to abolish them. Differences in the sociological character of institutions, in their relation to selection and differentiation in education and the labour market, and in their status and ethos, persist. And the characteristics of young people taking modules, their reasons for choosing them, their expectations, their reactions, and even the consequences of taking modules vary according to their institutional base and status when they take them.

This gives rise to three limitations of the strategy of institutional versatility under the Action Plan. The first is simply that the institutional range, although broad, is incomplete, and in particular that it excludes SCE courses and therefore much of post-compulsory provision at school. The reasons for this are varied, and partly reflect the other two limitations described below. The consequences are to start Scotvec modules in a position of relatively low status in a hierarchical system, and to inhibit their potential role in occupational and educational selection.

The second limitation is that the *intrinsic logic* of modularization tends to be overlaid by, and subordinate to, the *institutional logic* of the context in which the modules are delivered. Before the Action Plan, young people's movements into, within and out of full- and part-time education, training, YTS, employment and so on responded to various social and economic pressures and incentives. This is what I mean by institutional logic. The 'intrinsic logic' of modularization refers to the ways in which individual decisions on whether, what, how, when and where to study are influenced by incentives arising from the modular system itself. It embraces the textbook arguments for modularization, particularly those concerning motivation, choice, flexibility and progression. This logic tends to be most significant in respect of choices and behaviours within a single institution, or at least a single type of institution, because the institutional logic is largely controlled for. By contrast the Action Plan attempts to spread modularization across a diverse range of institutions. In this situation there is no insulation from institutional logic which tends to be much more powerful.

This subordination of intrinsic to institutional logic is well illustrated by the issues of progression and credit transfer. The introductory-Lego-set strategy is founded on the intrinsic logic of modularization; it assumes that students respond to a structure of incentives defined in terms of the common currency of modules. Yet the student may in practice respond to a different set of incentives, determined by selection practices in higher education or the labour market, or by systems of financial support; or the effective decision on participation may not in any case be the student's, but rest with employers or YTS managing agents. Above all, institutional logic threatens the common currency of modules, an essential condition of progression (as of coordination and integration) in the Action Plan. There are numerous stories of colleges' refusal to recognize school-based modules as having equal value to those delivered at college; and there are stories of the value of an individual's modules depending on the period over which they were taken, or on where they were studied, or by which method. In other words the value of modules may depend on their institutional context. The effect is to undermine the common currency of modules and thus invalidate the intrinsic logic of modularization. This is one reason why the validity and credibility of assessment are so important for the Action Plan strategy. But valid and credible assessment is only a necessary, not a sufficient, condition for the intrinsic logic of modularization to be sustained.

One corollary of this point is that the modular system as implemented is likely to fit in with some institutional logics better than others. This introduces the third limitation of the strategy of institutional versatility, which is that no single framework can be infinitely versatile. A single modular framework must be designed to fit in with a variety of institutional logics with different demands. Design features that make the framework well suited to one of these contexts may make it less well suited to another.

To illustrate this point I refer to a distinction in an earlier paper between 'pre-employment' and 'in-service' markets for modules (Raffe and Tomes, 1987). Students themselves are the main customers for modules in the pre employment market, although their decisions tend to anticipate the later selection decisions of employers or of further or higher education. This market covers most modules studied by school or full-time college students. In the in-service market the immediate customers tend to be employers purchasing off-the-job education or training for their apprentices or employees, or approved training organizations purchasing the off-the-job components for YTS schemes. Thus this market covers most modules studied on part-time courses or on YTS (although in some respects YTS comprises an intermediate market). The distinction between the two markets is related to the distinction between external and internal labour markets. Demand for modules in the pre-employment market is strongly influenced by their perceived currency as selection criteria in the external labour market; employers' use of modules for in-service education or training will reflect the organization of their internal labour markets.

The function of education is very different in the two markets. In the pre-employment market the main economic function of education is to screen for employment; differentiation is hierarchical, and based on diffuse, social as well as intellectual, criteria; specific present competencies matter less than general future potential; education embraces socialization. The 'market signals' generated for students are distorted and tend to reinforce traditional academic status distinctions (Raffe, 1987). In the in-service market the main function is closer to training; the emphasis is on competencies rather than potential; the emphasis on socialization is weaker; differentiation occurs on several dimensions.

The two markets make different demands on certification. In the pre-employment market this is used primarily as a criterion for selection; the main demand is that certificates can rank students in a single, if diffuse, hierarchy of attainment. In the in-service market certification is used more for accounting than for selection purposes; it must guarantee the quality of the units of curriculum purchased by customers, and define its content in terms of criterion-referenced competencies; grades or levels that enable overall levels of attainment to be identified are not wanted, and may be seen as a disadvantage.

Scotvec modules may have had more success in relation to this second, in-service market. Criterion-referencing, the specification of outcomes and competencies, the absence of levels or grading and the flexibility of Scotvec modules meet the demands of this market; modules are versatile units of 'curriculum currency' for planning or negotiating the curriculum of in-service and YTS provision. By contrast the absence of differentiation by formal levels of modules or by grades of pass, the difficulty of deriving an aggregate measure of a student's attainment, and the problems of credibility of assessment discussed earlier, all inhibit the acceptability of modules in the pre-employment market. This may help to account for their apparent lack of success in external, as compared with internal, labour markets. These problems are aggravated by the failure to incude Highers, the reluctance of universities to recognize modules and the tendency for status hierarchies affecting this market to be self-reinforcing. Yet had Highers been included, the Action Plan would still have encountered the same problem if in a different way: of how to respond to the diverse and conflicting demands of the different institutional contexts which the Plan seeks to cover.

Conclusion

The paradoxical theme running through this chapter is that the strategy of the Action Plan, for all its radicalism, can also be seen as a response to impotence; at least its strategy reflected a judgment that major institutional change was either not practicable or not desirable. This does not mean either that the strategy was inappropriate or that it will fail. The data presented here must be interpreted cautiously, based as they are on the experience of the first year group to be affected by the Plan. The success of the Action Plan depends on the knowledge, understanding, and sometimes cooperation of many people. As these develop, so may its success increase. And in the long term its intrinsic logic may even modify the institutional logics which currently constrain it. The Action Plan may help to change those institutions to whose restructuring it was an alternative. In the meantime, the concept of institutional versatility provides a key to the strategy of the Action Plan, and to many of its current strengths and limitations.

ACKNOWLEDGEMENTS

Work on this chapter was supported by the Economic and Social Research Council (grant C00280004), of which the Centre for Educational Sociology (CES) is a Designated Research Centre. Earlier versions of this chapter were presented at the 1987 annual conference of the British Educational Research Association (BERA) held in Manchester and to an internal seminar of the Scottish Vocational Education Council. The author is grateful to participants on both occasions, to colleagues in the CES and to Geoffrey Squires for helpful comments. Responsibility for errors and for interpretations and opinions rests with the author.

Notes

1. Nearly a third of each school year group in Scotland is too young to leave school at the end of the fourth year and must stay on to the Christmas of the fifth year (see appendix 3, and chapters 1 and 9 in this volume for further details of these 'conscripts'). Providing a suitable curriculum for these 'Christmas' or 'winter' leavers has been a major problem for secondary schools.

2. Based on logit analyses, using sex, SCE qualifications, date of leaving school (winter/later) and school modules to predict, respectively, entry to YTS among school leavers, and YTS modules among YTS entrants. The reduction in likelihood-ratio chi-square associated with school modules is 8.87 in the first analysis and 6.06 in the second (d.f. = 1). See chapter 3 in this volume for a more detailed illustration of logit analysis.
3. Likelihood-ratio chi-square = 9.01, d.f. = 1.
4. Likelihood-ratio chi-square = 7.86, d.f. = 1. The effect remains significant (6.29, 1) if the control for current occupation is replaced by a dichotomous variable which measures whether the current (spring 1986) occupation was the same as the YTS occupation in spring 1985: see following section.
5. The balance is due to fewer of those recruited externally ticking 'not sure'. In terms of the four response categories shown in table 8.4, those kept on by YTS sponsors responded in the ratio 30:20:25:25 per cent; those who found jobs elsewhere in the ratio 29:18:48:4 per cent.

REFERENCES

AINLEY, P. (1985) 'The modules are coming', *Times Educational Supplement*, 6 December.

HART, J., ROGER, A., MULVIE, A. AND MUNN, P. (1987) *Managing Modules: Guidance and Choice in Further Education Colleges*, Edinburgh, Scottish Council for Research in Education.

JONATHAN, R. (1987) 'The case for and against modularisation', *Scottish Educational Review*, 19, 2, pp. 86–97.

MCPHERSON, A. (1984a) 'Post-compulsory schooling: The fifth year' in RAFFE, D. (Ed.) *Fourteen to Eighteen: The Changing Pattern of Schooling in Scotland*, Aberdeen, Aberdeen University Press.

MCPHERSON, A. (1984b) 'Post-compulsory schooling: The sixth year' in RAFFE, D. (Ed.) *Fourteen to Eighteen: The Changing Pattern of Schooling in Scotland*, Aberdeen, Aberdeen University Press.

MANSELL, T. *et al.* (1976) *The Container Revolution: A Study of Unit and Modular Schemes*, London, Nuffield Foundation.

ORGANISATION FOR ECONOMIC COOPERATION AND DEVELOPMENT (OECD) (1985) *Education and Training after Basic Schooling*, Paris, OECD.

PIGNATELLI, F. (1987) 'The Technical and Vocational Education Initiative and Scottish educational developments' in TWINING, J., NISBET, S. and MEGARRY, J. (Eds) *World Yearbook of Education 1987: Vocational Education*, London, Kogan Page.

RAFFE, D. (1985) 'The extendable ladder: Scotland's 16+ Action Plan', *Youth and Policy*, 12, spring, pp. 27–33.

RAFFE, D. (1987) 'The context of the Youth Training Scheme: An analysis of its strategy and development', *British Journal of Education and Work*, 1, 1, pp. 1–31.

RAFFE, D. and TOMES, N. (1987) *The Organisation and Content of Studies at the Post-Compulsory Level: Country Study: Scotland*, OECD Educational Monograph, Paris, OECD.

ROBERTS, I. (1987) 'Modular structures: Their strengths and weaknesses', in TWINING, J., NISBET, S. and MEGARRY, J. (Eds) *World Yearbook of Education 1987: Vocational Education*, London, Kogan Page.

SCOTTISH EDUCATION DEPARTMENT (SED) (1979) *16–18s in Scotland: The First Two Years of Post-Compulsory Education*, Edinburgh, SED.

SCOTTISH EDUCATION DEPARTMENT (SED) (1983) *16–18s in Scotland: An Action Plan*, Edinburgh, SED.

SCOTTISH EDUCATION DEPARTMENT (SED) (1986) *Vocational Education and Training: The Scottish Approach*, Conference Report, Edinburgh, SED.

SPENCER, E. (Ed.) (1984) *Modules for All? Discussion Papers on New Proposals for the Education of 16–18s*, Edinburgh, Scottish Council for Research in Education.

SQUIRES, G. (1985) 'Organisation and content of studies' in ORGANISATION FOR ECONOMIC COOPERATION AND DEVELOPMENT (OECD), *Education and Training after Basic Schooling*, Paris, OECD.

SQUIRES, G. (1986) *Modularisation*, Manchester, Consortium for Advanced Continuing Education and Training of the Universities of Manchester and Salford, UMIST and Manchester Polytechnic.

SQUIRES, G. (forthcoming) *Organisation and Content of Studies at the Post-Compulsory Level: General Report* (provisional title), Paris, OECD.

TAYLOR, D., CLARKE, S., FORD, I. and GRAY, E. (1986) *Articulation of the 16+ Development Programme*, Reports Nos 1, 2 and 3, Glasgow, School of Further Education, Jordanhill College.

WATKINS, P. (1987) *Modular Approaches to the Secondary Curriculum*, York, Longman for the School Curriculum Development Committee.

Chapter 9

Changing Certification: Vocationalism and the School Curriculum

Nils Tomes

INTRODUCTION

The 1980s have seen a restructuring of post-compulsory education in Britain as a whole. There has been movement towards the rationalization of educational resources, brought about in part by falling school rolls, and also towards the redesign of diverse and over-complex certification arrangements to make systems which are both more comprehensible and more flexible to policy priorities. Scotland has led the rest of Britain in implementing a new post-compulsory framework and provides interesting insights into the ways in which educational reform can develop. Of course, any new framework is necessarily structured around existing systems. In Scotland, the new non-advanced post-compulsory education policies have to accommodate the current post-compulsory schooling arrangements which have differing goals and priorities. The Scottish fifth year, forming as it does a transitional stage between compulsory schooling and further and higher education, encompasses many of the problems and opportunities of the changing framework, and highlights some of the limitations to development.

This chapter focuses on the experiences of fifth-year pupils in the early years of educational reform. It sets out to look at the position of the new type of certification within the fifth-year curriculum and within the certification portfolio. It also looks at whether uptake of this new form of accreditation is confined to specific client groups. The implications for progression are discussed.

The Scottish Young Peoples Survey provides data for fifth-year pupils over the developmental years of the new educational reforms, and this is used to examine current patterns of certification. There are, naturally, several client groups within the Scottish fifth year, and they are differentially affected by the adoption of a new framework. Here, we look particularly at two groups: pupils who were serving their last term of compulsory schooling and who left school at Christmas in the fifth year, and pupils who stayed on at school voluntarily beyond this point.

THE CHANGING SCOTTISH FIFTH YEAR

Participation in post-compulsory schooling in Scotland has risen, partly due to changing school entrance regulations and partly due to rising youth unemployment. A further factor influencing staying-on behaviour is the change in the characteristics of the pupils' family backgrounds, with more pupils now coming from higher social-class backgrounds and with parents who have higher levels of education. The Scottish fifth year has taken on new characteristics, diversifying from the pattern of delivering SCE qualifications in traditional academic subjects to pupils destined for higher education. It has new needs to meet. At the same time as there is increased demand from pupils for fifth-year education, demographic trends mean that there are fewer pupils overall. Much of the impetus to rationalize post-compulsory education came from the need to plan for a contraction of the sector, to cope with a situation in which individual institutions may no longer have the resources to cope with the diversity of needs of their different client groups.

Scottish post-compulsory schooling differs from that south of the border. In Scotland, secondary schooling begins a year later than in England and Wales, making the fourth year the final compulsory session for most pupils. With the traditional emphasis on providing a general education for as many people as possible for as long as possible, Scottish post-compulsory schooling is organized on a 'one-plus-one-year' basis with the fifth year being a major exit point. Over half of the pupils in fourth year stay on into the fifth year at school. One in five of pupils stays on into the sixth year. One-year certificated courses are available to those who stay on at school, and may qualify them to enter higher education at the end of the first (or second) post-compulsory year. Scottish courses are less specialized with pupils taking certificates in four or five subjects to qualify for higher education.

This contrasts with the framework south of the border where most of the pupils who stay on are committed to a two-year 'A' level course and cannot qualify for entry to higher education until the certification point at the end of the upper sixth. These courses are more specialized, with pupils taking a smaller number of subjects at 'A' level.

One other salient difference is that Scotland does not have a tertiary sector with sixth-form colleges in the way that England does, and the first year of full-time post-compulsory education takes place principally in secondary schools. That being said, in many areas of Scotland, where geography permits, secondary schools have moved into consortium arrangements with colleges of further education and other secondary schools, to give a more flexible institutional framework for the delivery of post-compulsory education. These consortia would have been one rational response to falling school rolls. Their formation was speeded and consolidated by the introduction of the Action Plan, one of several policy initiatives which have been changing the profile of Scottish post-compulsory education.

POLICY INITIATIVES

The Scottish Education Department's Action Plan (SED, 1983) has attempted to rationalize post-compulsory provision, breaking down the boundaries between schools, colleges, training centres and, to some extent, workplaces. The 16–18 sector is an important one as it is in a crucial position between secondary schooling, further and higher education and the world of work. There are fewer statutory constraints upon provision for people in this age group and so this sector is more amenable to policy initiatives.

Developed from a consultative document circulated in 1979, the Scottish Education Department's Action Plan was published in 1983 and has since reformed existing non-advanced further education provision. The unit of non-advanced education or training was no longer to be 'the course'. Provision for students over the age of 16 is now divided into short units, or modules, which can be combined flexibly to provide a nationally certificated programme of appropriate length and content. These modules are accredited through the National Certificate by the Scottish Vocational Education Council (Scotvec), which incorporated both the Scottish Business Education Council and the Scottish Technical Education Council.

Modules are internally assessed and have criterion-referenced assessment based on what the students can do rather than on what they have learned. With the emphasis being on 'outputs' rather than 'inputs', increased flexibility in the delivery of non-advanced further education is made possible, and the barriers between varieties of education and training institutions have been lowered: students can study at several institutions simultaneously, if that is appropriate, or can be accredited through training organizations instead of colleges or schools. The National Certificate framework is discussed more fully in chapter 8 in this volume.

A parallel, but later, initiative in England and Wales was the Review of Vocational Qualifications (MSC and DES, 1986) which pointed to the 'unhelpful divide between so-called academic and so-called vocational qualifications' and the 'many barriers to access to qualifications and inadequate arrangements for progression and transfer of credit', similar to the situation which existed in Scotland before the introduction of the Action Plan. The Review recommended the introduction of a national certificate, the National Vocational Qualification (NVQ), which would be awarded by examining bodies which would in turn be accredited by the newly set up National Council for Vocational Qualifications (NCVQ). This differs from the Scottish arrangements where there is a single validating body. The proposals are to be implemented by 1991 and are designed to allow for full credit transfer and progression through to higher education.

Previously, certification types have been tied to particular institutional sectors. The Action Plan has not only brought about the modularization of all non-advanced further education but, within schools, it has extended the vocational element of the curriculum and provided short-course certification. The mode of delivery is flexible, meaning that fifth-year school pupils can take modules as part of their curriculum in conjunction with other courses. They can be taken by school pupils either in their own school or on a consortium basis in conjunction with other schools and further education colleges. This flexibility means that curriculum diversity can be maintained in a contracting sector without too heavy a burden upon individual institutions. It also means that the links from school to further education have been drawn closer. The Scotvec National Certificate, the means by which the Action Plan modules are accredited, allows for credit transfer. Pupils who take modules whilst they are at school may use the credits gained in the non-advanced further education sector, either through college courses or through off-the-job training. Progression is an inbuilt feature of the Action Plan.

How have modules been used within the fifth-year curriculum? Who takes them and how are the modules perceived? Do they provide a desirable form of certification for all client groups? And do they encourage progression to National Certificate courses at college? Data from the early years of the Action Plan's implementation can begin to provide some of the answers.

SURVEY DATA

This chapter draws on data from two national surveys of people who had been in their fourth year of secondary schooling in 1983/84. The 1985 Scottish Young Peoples Survey contacted these people around nine months after they left fourth year and the 1986 survey followed them up a year later. Appendix 1 gives the technical details of these surveys.

The 1983/84 cohort was the first year group to have National Certificate modules available for study in school. For this reason, with the system in transition, knowledge of modules was not widespread, even amongst those people who were taking them. Questions on modules taken in the fifth year at school were asked in the 1985 survey, and a set of questions which duplicated these were asked again in the 1986 survey, at a time when people were becoming more aware of modules and would have received any certification for the modules that they had completed in fifth year.

STAYING ON INTO THE FIFTH YEAR

Over the past ten years, there has been an increasing trend towards pupils staying on into the fifth year at school. Between session 1976/77 and 1983/84, the proportion leaving school by the end of the fourth year had fallen from 54 per cent to 36 per cent for girls and from 56 per cent to 43 per cent for boys.

With the adoption of common arrangements for entrance to primary schools, in the 1970s, the age profile changed such that pupils were entering school younger than before. The school-leaving arrangements are age-related.[1] The regulations define three school-leaving age (SLA) groups, people in the first two of which are eligible to leave at or by the end of fourth year. Those whose sixteenth birthday falls between the beginning of October and the end of February following their fourth year have to stay on at school until the end of the Christmas term of fifth year. They form the third school-leaving age group (SLA3). Appendix 3 gives further details of these arrangements.

Between 1978 and 1983, the SLA3 group increased in size from 17 per cent of the year group to 27 per cent, and is expected to stabilize at 35 per cent by 1988 (SED, 1985). There is still substantial regional variation in the proportions of fourth-year pupils who are defined as belonging to the SLA3 group. Proportions vary from over a third in Borders, Dumbarton, Dumfries and Galloway and Central, to under a quarter in Tayside, Lothian and Highland.

For the 1983/84 fourth-year cohort, which is reported on in this chapter, the proportion in the SLA3 group was 29 per cent. This means that a large proportion of pupils who started a fifth year at school did so because they were too young to leave at the end of the fourth year. For these 'conscripts', compulsory schooling had not yet ended. Fifty-seven per cent of pupils in the 1983/84 fourth-year cohort stayed on into the fifth year. Just under half of the people who started the fifth year in 1984/85 (46 per cent) were 'conscripted' and 40 per cent of these people subsequently left school at Christmas. This contrasts with pupils in the modal school-leaving age group (SLA2) who formed a similar proportion of fifth-year starters but of whom

93 per cent continued beyond Christmas. Increasingly, the fifth year cannot truly be said to be the first post-compulsory year, which is its more common image, and one which has influenced provision.

The analyses in this chapter relate to all those people in the cohort who started a fifth year at school, regardless of whether they stayed on to complete that year. For some purposes, these people are divided into two subgroups: those who left at the end of the Christmas term of fifth year, who are called *Christmas leavers* here, and those who remained at school after this point, called the *continuers*.

As was outlined above, people in the third SLA group were not permitted to leave school until the end of the Christmas term. The overwhelming majority of Christmas leavers in the survey cohort were from the SLA3 group. The continuers group was, however, composed of pupils from all SLA groups as many conscripts stayed on voluntarily anyway. On leaving fourth year, those people in the 1983/84 fourth-year SLA3 group who were conscripted into the fifth year had a higher qualifications profile than those in the modal SLA2 group. Four per cent more of the conscripts had some 'O' grade qualifications and 1.5 per cent more had 'O' grade passes at A–C. The difference was most noticeable in the band with one to five 'O' grades at A–C where there was a 3 percentage point difference. Pupils in the modal group were more successful in gaining larger numbers of 'O' grade passes.

THE PLACE OF THE NATIONAL CERTIFICATE

The National Certificate was grafted onto an already existing examination system which was centred on the SCE qualifications, the 'O' grade and the Higher. There are costs and benefits in taking modules and it is likely that uptake of modules is concentrated amongst particular client groups.

The SYPS survey data allow us to look at who it was who took modules by examining the attainment profiles, leaving dates and other characteristics of those who did and did not take up the opportunities of the National Certificate. Generally, the uptake of modules in the fifth year seems to be related to the qualifications you already have, whether you are eligible to leave school before Christmas and whether you do in fact leave by Christmas.

A logit analysis with binomial errors took as factors school-leaving age (SLA) group, term of leaving and fourth-year qualifications, and examined the proportion of pupils who reported taking modules. The SLA1 group (first eligible to leave at Christmas in fourth year) was excluded from this analysis as it is a small and, perhaps, atypical group. Two second-order interaction terms were significant: school-leaving age group with term of leaving and fourth-year qualifications with term of leaving. Fourth-year qualification level was significant as a first-order term. Amongst the Christmas leavers, uptake of modules was related to school-leaving age group (here comparing those in the modal SLA2 group with those who were in the SLA3 group) with 21 per cent of those in SLA2 taking modules and 37 per cent of those in SLA3 taking modules. There was no significant relationship of this sort amongst those who continued past Christmas, nor was there a simple direct relationship of SLA group to modules uptake across the whole year group.

Table 9.1: Proportionate uptake of modules within each school-leaving age group

	SLA2	SLA3
Christmas leavers	21%	37%
Continuers	22%	25%

In short, 'conscripted' pupils who left at Christmas (and who may well have identified themselves to the school as intending Christmas leavers, or who were identified by their teachers as such) were much more likely to take modules than those who were not compelled to stay on and who left early (table 9.1). SLA3 pupils who continued past Christmas were not statistically distinguishable from SLA2 pupils in terms of their modules uptake. Pupils from the SLA2 group who subsequently left school early were also indistinguishable from the continuers.

If we look at the qualifications which pupils already held on entering fifth year, we can see two distinct attainment profiles for Christmas leavers and continuers. Of the Christmas leavers, half held no A–C award at 'O' grade and four out of five held two or fewer passes. Of the continuers, three out of five fell into the top attainment band with five or more 'O' grade passes, with an upward skew of attainment.

With rising youth unemployment, more pupils who would not have stayed on at school in more favourable times choose the fifth year as an alternative to taking their chance in the labour market. The survey data show that those who elected to stay on past Christmas were by no means all higher-attainers; nearly one in ten held no fourth-year qualifications. Around a fifth of the continuers could be identified as non-traditional stayers, having two or fewer 'O' grade passes. Figure 9.1 shows the pattern of fourth-year qualifications.

There was a direct relationship between level of fourth-year qualifications and modules uptake across the whole year group, with pupils with two

Christmas leavers: fourth-year qualifications

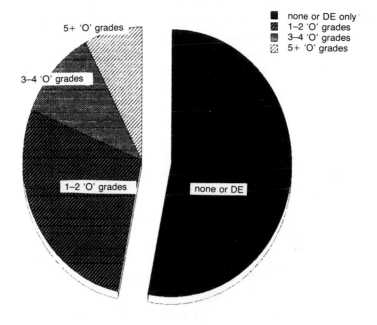

Continuers: fourth-year qualifications

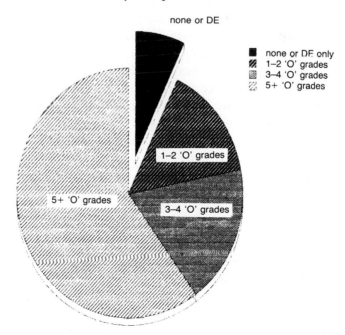

Figure 9.1:

or fewer 'O' grades being more likely to take modules than their better qualified classmates: 33 per cent of those with no fourth-year 'O' grades took modules, compared with 38 per cent of those with one or two 'O' grades, 24 per cent of those with three or four 'O' grades and 19 per cent of those with five or more 'O' grades. Fourth-year qualifications are taken here as an indication of the level of general attainment.

Table 9.2: *Proportionate uptake of modules within each fourth-year qualification band*

	None or DE only	1–2 'O' grades	3–4 'O' grades	5+ 'O' grades
Christmas leavers	31%	46%	27%	26%
Continuers	38%	34%	24%	18%

There was a further relationship between this factor and term of leaving (table 9.2). Among those pupils with one or two fourth-year 'O' grades, 46 per cent of Christmas leavers took modules compared with 34 per cent of the continuers. The relationship was not significant for any of the other fourth-year bandings.

In summary, modules were being taken more often by conscripted pupils who left at Christmas, non-traditional stayers with lower levels of attainment and, particularly, pupils with smaller numbers of fourth-year 'O' grade passes who left at Christmas.

Modules would seem to have been targeted at, or taken up by, conscripted pupils whose commitment to the fifth year may be short-term. It might be expected that, given the longer time to take modules over the course of the fifth year and the fact that modules may be taken as 'taster' courses, pupils who continued past Christmas would be more likely to report having taken a module at some point. This was not the case. Modules were, then, being used as short-duration courses for early leavers and particularly for early leavers with moderate academic records. Amongst continuers, modules uptake was related to the level of previous attainment, with the newer client group of lower-attaining pupils taking modules most frequently.

It is to be remembered that in the years before the Action Plan was introduced, virtually all of the Christmas leavers' fifth-year experience would have been uncertificated. Modules, then, would seem to be making a substantial contribution to increasing the accountability of schooling for the pupils in this group.

Christmas leavers: level of study

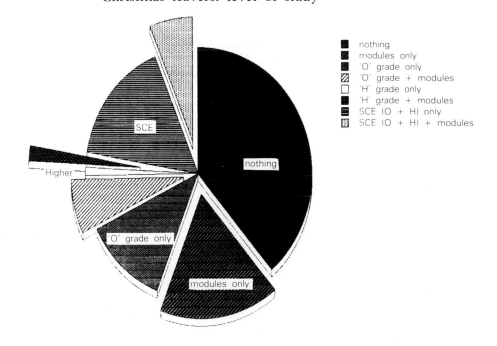

■	nothing
▨	modules only
▦	'O' grade only
▨	'O' grade + modules
☐	'H' grade only
■	'H' grade + modules
≡	SCE (O + H) only
▦	SCE (O + H) + modules

Continuers: level of study

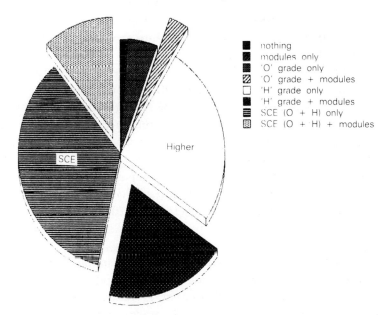

■	nothing
▨	modules only
▦	'O' grade only
▨	'O' grade + modules
☐	'H' grade only
■	'H' grade + modules
≡	SCE (O + H) only
▦	SCE (O + H) + modules

Figure 9.2:

MODULES AND LEVEL OF STUDY IN THE FIFTH YEAR

Most fifth-year pupils were studying for some type of qualification, even those who left at Christmas. Figure 9.2 shows the proportions studying for different levels of qualification, and table 9.3 compares the combination of SCE qualifications studied for by pupils respectively taking, and not taking, modules.

Table 9.3: Level of SCE exam studied in the fifth year (percentages)

	Neither	'O' grade	Higher	'O' grade + Higher	Total
Christmas leavers					
did modules	54	22	5	19	100
didn't	57	18	2	24	101
both	56	19	3	22	100
Continuers					
did modules	1	17	24	59	101
didn't	1	8	33	58	100
both	1	10	31	58	100

A logit analysis showed that there was an interaction between studying for 'O' grades in fifth year and level of fourth-year qualifications in terms of the likelihood of taking modules in fifth year. Here, pupils were grouped according to their fourth-year attainment into those with fewer than two 'O' grades, three to four 'O' grades and five or more 'O' grades. Lower-attaining pupils who were studying for 'O' grades were more likely to be taking modules than those who were not, and middle-attaining pupils (with three or four 'O' grades) were more likely to be taking modules if they were not studying for further 'O' grades. Level of attainment was also significant as a first-order term, with pupils with two or fewer fourth-year 'O' grades being most likely to take modules.

Just over half of the Christmas leavers reported that they were studying neither for 'O' grades nor for Highers, though around a fifth were studying for 'O' grades and the remainder for Highers with, perhaps, some additional 'O' grades. Christmas leavers studying only 'O' grades were more likely to have taken National Certificate modules as well.

Amongst the continuers, who were overwhelmingly studying for some SCE examination, it was again those who were studying only for 'O' grades who were most likely to have started modules. Those who took only Highers were more likely *not* to take modules.

Many of those pupils who subsequently left at Christmas had started on a longer-duration curriculum, with 44 per cent studying for at least one SCE examination, at 'O' grade or at Higher. Most of those studying for examinations did so at the lower level with 41 per cent studying for at least one 'O' grade, and 25 per cent studying for at least one Higher. A quarter of the Christmas leavers reported studying for four or more SCE examinations compared with 92 per cent of the continuers.

Overall, a quarter of fifth-year pupils took modules while at school. One in ten took only modules. These were taken as a principal qualification mainly by Christmas leavers, with a third of these pupils taking National Certificates with them into the labour market.

It would appear that modules formed a larger part of the timetable for those pupils taking fewer traditional school subjects. Uptake of National Certificate modules decreased linearly with the number of subjects studied overall, across the whole year group. The fuller the timetable, the less likely modules were to find a place. This also held true when counting only the number of subjects studied for SCE examinations, with modules uptake decreasing sharply with increasing numbers of SCEs.

Over half of the Christmas leavers had not embarked on SCE courses at either 'O' grade or Higher, compared with 99 per cent of the continuers. These people would seem to have embarked on a non-academic track. The structural differentiation which the existence of an 'academic' and a 'non-academic' track implies forces a dichotomization of pupils into one or the other. Pupils who make the wrong choice at this stage, or who are wrongly placed in one track or another, may find it hard to make good the ground which they have lost.

Christmas leavers also took a greater *number* of modules than did the continuers. Of those Christmas leavers taking modules, a quarter took four or more, a third took two or three and the remainder took a single one. Three-quarters of the continuers who did modules took one or two. However, it was only within the continuers group that there was a significant relationship between the number of modules taken and attainment, with the more highly qualified taking one or two modules and the least qualified taking three or more.

Was the National Certificate forming a central part of the curriculum? Conscripted Christmas leavers in the lower attainment groups, and non-traditional continuers who were studying for additional 'O' grades in the fifth year, were most likely to take modules. It is perhaps no accident that these are the two newest client groups, for whom the traditional academic route through the Higher certificate is not appropriate: the first because of the duration of the courses and the second because of the level of study.

The National Certificate would seem to have been adopted as a solution to providing for the more diverse fifth year. The solution is an immediate one, but there are longer-term issues in adopting this type of certification.

THE POSITION OF HIGHERS

In the earlier plans to bring all 16+ non-advanced education into one framework, the SCE Higher certificate was included as one of the qualifications which would be modularized. The Higher is principally school-based, for those in the 16–18 age group, and is a one-year course taken after 'O' grades in the fifth year. The modularization of the Higher would have meant that an integrated system could have been established in which there was the potential for the free movement of 16–18-year-old students across curricular areas and up through the certification hierarchy. The Higher certificate has, however, a cherished place in the Scottish education system and great value is placed on it as an entrance qualification both by employers and by universities. Its possession is taken to indicate respectable academic attainment and future potential.

Scottish universities are, to date, unwilling to accept the National Certificate as a principal entrance qualification, most particularly because of its means of assessment in which externally examined end tests form a small part (see chapter 3 in this volume). In the face of this opposition, the SCE Higher has been retained as an independent form of certification. It lies outside the National Certificate framework and remains the principal means of direct access to higher education.

The retention of the Higher certificate poses a problem for the provision of an integrated approach to post-compulsory schooling. Those pupils who aspire to a place at university need to acquire this type of certification. This, in effect, has forced the retention of an academic corridor within the post-compulsory sector, with progression to higher education being tied to this particular type of certification. This is, in turn, tied to a particular type of institution. For 16–18-year-olds, this institution is the school. This differentiation of certification tracks has far-reaching effects on the rest of the fifth-year provision.

Typically, at least four Higher passes are required for university entrance, and the acquisition of these fills a sizeable proportion of the fifth-year timetable. Pupils intending to continue their education to a higher level cannot afford to devote much of their time to working for a type of certification which does not allow for this progression, as such time would be spent at the expense of specific-purpose qualifications. The price of diversity may be the failure to achieve the desired Highers passes.

In contrast to this, it can be said that the Higher certificate, by its dominance of the fifth-year curriculum, works against the interests of the newer client groups. Pupils who have not been markedly successful in their fourth-year examinations cannot have their educational needs fully met through following a course that is designed principally for the upper attainment groups. This includes pupils who are staying on because they are too young to leave school and pupils for whom the declining youth labour market does not hold much promise. For many years, the Higher has been the main focus of fifth-year activity. It inevitably has had a downwards influence on the earlier years of secondary schooling, giving it an air of unquestioned legitimacy as it appears to be the obvious culmination of a scholastic career.

This does mean that the Higher, rightly or wrongly, articulates quite closely with third- and fourth-year provision in terms of its overall approach. There are further amendments to the Higher planned to bring it into line with the third- and fourth-year Standard grade reforms which were implemented after the Munn and Dunning Reports of the late 1970s (SED, 1977a and 1977b).

The Higher accredits mostly traditional academic subjects such as English, mathematics, languages, sciences and humanities, and also a handful of vocational subjects such as secretarial studies and woodwork. It is not well placed to deal with the increasing diversity of the curriculum as the emphasis on vocational education in the post-compulsory sector grows.

The use of the National Certificate in schools appreciably broadens the range of subjects on offer, with over 2000 entries in the modules catalogue. The means of delivering modules and the means of assessment do not, however, articulate well with lower secondary schooling although they do allow a close articulation to further education. Pupils are therefore faced with a difficult choice, having to weigh up factors of subject area, certification type, length of course, type of assessment and vocational relevance when deciding on their most beneficial route through the fifth year and on into adult life. It can be a choice with expensive consequences and one which many pupils are not equipped to make at this stage.

CURRICULUM

If modules are fulfilling two different functions, one of certification for the Christmas leavers and one of curriculum diversification for the continuers, we would expect to find different patterns of modules uptake on a subject-by-subject basis.

In fact, there were two particular areas within the modules catalogue where higher-attaining pupils were picking their subjects: computing, and business and administration (which includes typing, information processing, accounting and economics). These two areas cover generic skills which can be transferred to new situations but which are not considered to be academic subjects with the same buying power as, say, history or chemistry and which would not be worth investing an appreciable amount of curriculum time in.

Christmas leavers predominantly took their modules from the 'inter-disciplinary studies' area, which covers such subjects as communication, mathematics, creative subjects, physical education and personal and social development. These come from the core curriculum areas, and it would seem that the National Certificate was being used to provide a more general education for these pupils. Modules from the engineering, built environment and caring sections of the catalogue were also taken more frequently by Christmas leavers than others. This points to the increasing vocational emphasis being focused on the lower-attaining groups who may be entering the labour market sooner than the others. Amongst the Christmas leavers, there seemed to be little association between fourth-year attainment level and the choice of particular subjects, with modules being picked up by people irrespective of their academic ability. The pattern differed for the continuers with modules in almost all subject areas being taken more frequently by the lower-attainers.

EVENTUAL CERTIFICATION FROM FIFTH YEAR

By term of leaving, 99.5 per cent of those who left at Christmas got no SCE awards compared with 11 per cent of those who stayed on. A handful of the Christmas leavers returned to school in the summer term to sit their examinations. Around one in five of those who continued after Christmas could be identified as a 'traditional' fifth-year pupil, having got at least five 'O' grades and then becoming eligible to enter higher education with four or more Higher certificates.

Nine out of ten continuers gained some kind of SCE qualification, with three quarters of these getting at least one Higher. Three in ten of those who took SCE examinations did so in conjunction with modules.

Figure 9.3 shows the types of fifth-year qualifications which pupils in the two leaving groups got as a proportion of each group. The patterns of qualifications differ markedly. The National Certificate was the major source of certification for Christmas leavers, whereas uptake of modules was spread fairly evenly across the qualification categories for the continuers. The numbers of continuers within each of the SCE certification categories differed. Proportionately, modules were taken by almost twice as many pupils who subsequently gained 'O' grades or no SCE qualifications as pupils who took Highers or combined 'O' grades and Highers.

The pattern of certification which emerges is that for the Christmas leavers the National Certificate was the principal, or only, route to accreditation, and for those who continued at school beyond Christmas modules formed a smaller proportion of the overall examination portfolio.

Christmas leavers: fifth-year qualifications

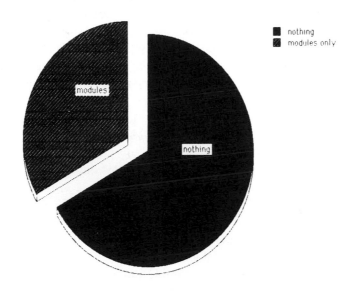

Continuers: fifth-year qualifications

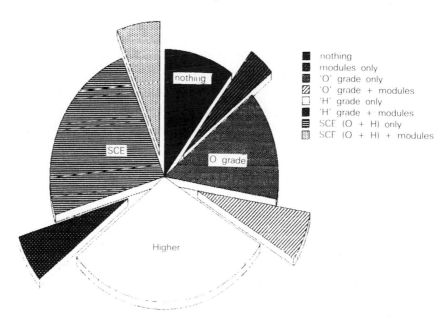

Figure 9.3:

Within the latter group, pupils without Highers were most likely to have Scotvec National Certificate holdings, those being the pupils who formed the newer client groups of post-compulsory schooling.

Apart from those who left at Christmas, National Certificate modules were mostly taken in conjunction with SCE qualifications in the fifth year. Just over half of the people taking modules also gained a Highers pass and a further third got at least one 'O' grade award as their highest qualification.

LONG AND SHORT COURSES

For fifth-year pupils in general, the possible short duration of modular courses has two uses: they can be slotted into gaps in the timetable which could not otherwise be filled in by certificated work of longer duration, such as 'O' grades or Highers, and they can be blocked together to provide a full programme over a short period. The first of these patterns would seem to suit those following a principally SCE programme, whilst the second would seem appropriate to those pupils eligible and intending to leave at the end of the Christmas term of fifth year. It is possible to use modules to form a longer-duration programme but this was not the pattern in Scottish schools in 1984/85, where no pupil reported taking more than seven modules.

Modular courses must be displacing other activities from the curriculum. In the past, there has not always been appropriate certificated provision for the lower-attainers who have to stay on, or who have elected to stay on, into the fifth year. These pupils have often been seen by teachers and administrators as a problem rather than an opportunity. They are so obviously not a part of the traditional academic fifth form that they in some senses have been invisible participants. Schools have often not attempted to provide a coherent course for the Christmas leavers, in any educational sense.

> At the start of fifth year, I was put into a class for Xmas (*sic*) leavers, and the subjects I was given compared to the other four years at ★★★★★ were degrading and insulting. So after three weeks of that I left and never set a foot back into the school.

Modular courses would simply displace non-certificate work for this group.

For the Christmas leaver the National Certificate provides short-course certification. This appreciably adds to the qualification portfolios of the Christmas leavers in that a number of modules can be completed within the first term of the fifth year. Previously, there was little provision for this group of people which would have resulted in certification. 'O' grade and Higher are taken over the span of a year and if the course is not completed will have no pay-off in certification terms.

For the non-traditional continuers, the principal advantage would seem to be in terms of level of study. The SCE qualifications are specifically designed for the upper-attainment range and the National Certificate provides accreditation at a more appropriate level and with a more palatable form of assessment.

For the higher attainers, there is a genuine conflict in that SCE subjects command more of a premium whilst taking up appreciably larger amounts of time than modules, and so the diversity which modular courses bring may be bought at the expense of higher-education-oriented certification. However, most pupils following a largely Highers course will have non-certificate parts to their timetable traditionally taken up with subjects such as arts and crafts and skill-based subjects such as typing, and it is these parts with which the new modular courses will be competing in that additional certification can be provided for a small time-investment each week.

THE CONSUMERS' VERDICT

Asked for their opinion of the National Certificate, pupils generally found their modules interesting, that they developed new skills by doing them, that they formed a coherent and varied course. They were less convinced of the vocational value of modules (though the Christmas leavers were more positive about the employment-related aspects of modules) and did not seem to see them as taster courses for further education. Modules were not thought to be difficult, though pupils did not find them easy either. These views on the apparent ease of modules are likely to be shaped by the different type of assessment used as much as by the subject matter covered.

The means of assessment in the National Certificate differs substantially from that of the traditional externally marked, terminally assessed SCE examination, using instead continuous, internal assessment. This form of assessment is consonant with a more individually-based student-centred approach to learning, as would be appropriate for what is intended to be a certificate which accredits acquired outputs rather than taught inputs. Modules, having provision for remediation and reassessment, can be seen as providing a simpler and more direct route to certification for people who are less likely to acquire an SCE certificate, and filling the certification gap. In the past, other forms of certification, such as CSE Mode 3, have been used for this purpose. This use of the National Certificate can be seen by the pupils themselves:

> I think there should be a CSE or Scotvec certificate for arithmetic. Because if you fail the 'O' grade, you get nothing to say you sat the 'O' grade. This would give people something to show for all their effort.

Being released from the burden of terminal assessment may, for many, make the overall educational experience seem more positive and contribute to the apparent ease of the modules.

That the Christmas leavers were more likely to see their modules as a training for a future job that they wanted to do, and that they felt the modules had helped them to understand the world of work, is understandable in the light of their early departure for the labour market.

NEW CERTIFICATION FOR SHORT COURSES

There was some anxiety over the first years of the Action Plan's implementation that there was not a coherent curriculum strategy for post-compulsory pupils, with the suggestion that topics such as mobile plant vehicle maintenance were not an appropriate focus for schools, and that vocationalism may be taken too far.

The need for further rationalization was officially recognized in a recent SED circular. It focused on the need for short-course certification which the National Certificate had been fulfilling to date but attempted to draw the educational, as distinct from the vocational, subjects back into the fold of SCE certification. Both Scotvec and the Scottish Examination Board, which certificates 'O' grades and Highers, were to provide short-course certification but in the areas most appropriate to their traditional subject disciplines.

> The Secretary of State accepts the case for wider availability of nationally certificated short courses in schools not only in technical subjects but also in other areas of the curriculum. Such courses can fulfil a valuable function in a number of different contexts, in particular by adding balance, variety and flexibility to the curriculum in the form of:
> — extension courses enabling pupils to study a particular aspect of a main subject area in further depth
> — 'taster' courses introducing pupils to a subject for possible later study
> — courses to develop a particular expertise as a possible adjunct to a range of other disciplines (e.g. keyboard skills)
> — as a series of linked but separately identifiable courses covering, e.g. the creative and aesthetic mode (including drama) or classical studies
> — as components of a progression of courses which may be more suitable in certain vocational areas than full two-year or one-year courses, e.g. agriculture, horticulture or nautical studies. (SED, 1987)

Short courses relating to SCE 'academic' subjects would be certificated through the Scottish Examination Board, though schools would still be free to utilize those National Certificate modules which they considered to be compatible with a school curriculum. This should, in effect, increase the articulation of short courses with existing SCE provision whilst maintaining a diversity in schooling which can be delivered either within the resources of a consortium or on an individual school basis. This would, hopefully, reduce some of the negative aspects of structural differentiation for fifth formers and allow a more coherent educational provision. On the other side, it may reduce the proportion of pupils who make use of the credit transfer arrangements of the National Certificate to progress to further education and rebuild the boundaries between schooling and further education which the Action Plan was designed to break down.

PROGRESSION

Over the early years of the Action Plan, when the National Certificate was unrivalled in the provision of short-course certification, there seemed to be a definite impetus for pupils to progress to other further education courses. The experience of National Certificate work at school would seem to materially affect the uptake of further education for some pupils in the Christmas-leaving group.

The survey data for those people who left school by the end of fifth year on their subsequent enrolment on courses show a differential pattern of uptake amongst the school-leaving groups, according to whether the pupils had taken modules at school.

A logit analysis looked at starting full-time modular programmes after school, taking as factors fourth-year attainment, whether the pupil did modules at school and term of leaving (before or after Christmas of fifth year). The analysis was done using data for pupils who left school by the end of fifth year, to eliminate the effects of sixth-year staying. One second-order interaction term was significant, that of attainment with uptake of school modules. Both term of leaving and previous attainment were important as first-order terms.

Pupils who left school at Christmas were significantly less likely than those who continued to have started a full-time modular programme by the next session (6 per cent compared with 15 per cent). Given that these were the pupils who had a heavier investment in the National Certificate, it would suggest that the acquisition of a 'starter' set of modules through school did not encourage pupils to make good this investment.

Table 9.4: *Proportion who started a full-time modular programme after school, by whether took modules at school and fourth-year qualification band*

	None or DE only	1–2 'O' grades	3–4 'O' grades	5+ 'O' grades
Took modules at school	3%	9%	12%	22%
Didn't take at school	5%	12%	17%	9%

Pupils with fourth-year 'O' grade passes were three times as likely subsequently to take a full-time programme of modules than other pupils (12 per cent compared with 4 per cent). Looking at the interaction of this term with the taking of modules at school, it was the higher-attaining pupils who had taken modules at school who were more likely to have subsequently started a full-time modular programme (table 9.4).

Table 9.5: *Proportion who had taken modules at school, by whether started a full-time modular programme after school and fourth-year qualification band*

	None or DE only	1–2 'O' grades	3–4 'O' grades	5+ 'O' grades
Started a full-time programme	24%	32%	22%	34%
Didn't start a full-time programme	34%	39%	30%	15%

It was those pupils whose attainment was in the one to two 'O' grade banding who were most likely to have taken modules at school (table 9.5), but there was no significant relationship with the subsequent uptake of full-time modular programmes. Of those pupils who had gained at least five 'O' grades in fourth year, those who had taken modules at school were significantly more likely to take a programme of modules full-time after school than those who had not sampled modules. These pupils were, perhaps, more vocationally oriented, though it is interesting to note that it is only this group, who would have other avenues open to them through their SCE certification, who made use of the credit transfer of the National Certificate.

The uncertainty of the access which the National Certificate gave to other educational and employment opportunities may be a limit to progression and a reason why pupils were not capitalizing on their investment. As chapter 8 in this volume shows, pupils who took modules at school were more likely to subsequently take modules as part of the Youth

Training Scheme. The progression route for fifth-year pupils does not necessarily lie within the formal education sector. Subsequent uptake of the National Certificate by pupils who took modules at school may take place at a later stage, something on which the current SYPS data is unable to comment.

Some of the progression issues highlighted in Scotland by the National Certificate have their parallel south of the border in the Certificate for Pre-Vocational Education (CPVE). One of the major problems with the adoption of the CPVE by schools, colleges and YTS schemes, identified by the Further Education Unit (FEU, 1987), was that 'planning [for progression] was not generally across all possible progression routes in all establishments' and that '[m]any YTS agents and employers had not heard of the CPVE or were not clear as to its progression value'. The position of the CPVE was made more marginal by the Business and Technician Education Council (BTEC) deciding to extend its first courses to 16-year-old full-time students (FEU, 1986), with these courses having clearer lines of progression to more advanced courses. Thus, the CPVE shares some of the problems of the National Certificate in being accepted as a valued qualification by students, teachers and employers alike when the lines of progression are seen to be limited. Uptake of the CPVE has been principally by pupils who were thought to be not 'good enough' to repeat or take GCSE or 'A' level qualifications. The CPVE was seen as successful in recruiting students only where the students felt it provided a route to a particular vocation, mainly in the areas of business administration and personal services.

THE LIMITS TO CHANGE

Whilst the Scottish fifth has changed its characteristics, it is in a way which has perhaps made the least difference to the traditional Highers-oriented academic sector.

This stage of post-compulsory schooling is trying to fulfil two separate functions: one essentially specialist, preparing higher-attainers for university, and the other essentially general in extending a broad-based education for lower-attainers. This latter is similar, in the demands which it places upon curriculum innovation, to that of ROSLA, the raising of the school-leaving age from 15 to 16, which took place over a decade ago. It is to be remembered that a sizeable proportion of pupils who start the fifth year are doing so as part of their compulsory schooling, and that schools are required to provide a general education for pupils under compulsion.

One in five of all those who started fifth year attained neither SCE nor Scotvec qualifications, and so gained no tangible credit from this school stage. As the most frequently cited reason given by young people for starting a fifth year was to gain qualifications which would improve their job prospects, this ambition would seem not to have been met for a substantial proportion of the year group. A third of those with no SCE qualifications do have the National Certificate accreditation. This would seem to make progression to non-advanced further education more possible, though this was a promise which was not fulfilled at this stage. The National Certificate does not, however, give direct admission to much of the academic corridor.

The potential benefits of the introduction of the National Certificate have not been fully explored, in part due to the lengthy period of industrial action undertaken by school teachers. Utilization of the National Certificate has not been uniform across Scotland, with the percentage of fifth-year pupils identified as taking modules varying from 42 per cent in Dumfries and Galloway and 32 per cent in Fife to 13 per cent in Glasgow.[2] For some regions, the provision of modules on a consortium basis with a local college is not possible due to the unyielding barriers of geography, and school-based provision can be developed only to the limitations of its staffing.

The National Certificate provides an avenue to meaningful courses both for those leaving school part of the way through the fifth year and for those staying on to the end. Modules provide the short-course certification which has been absent from Scottish schooling to date. It is possible that the attractiveness of quick end-certification is displacing conscripts from SCE courses which they might otherwise have embarked upon and completed. Looked at from the other direction, the National Certificate may be providing a solid baseline for participation in continuing or further education.

Progression and articulation are important aspects of any type of certification. SCE courses, in as much as they are widely taken as a representation of general ability, provide progression to both further and higher education. In addition, they are still sought by employers seeking new recruits. The certification corridor which pupils predominantly doing the National Certificate enter is one which allows a coordinated progression to non-advanced further education (NAFE) and through NAFE to advanced education. What it does not easily allow is for a later transfer to the university education corridor although transfer in the other direction is, of course, a possibility. National Certificate credits are not negotiable currency in the academic area. This being said, many of the Christmas leavers do not hold ambitions for an academic career, and the National Certificate is in a position to make a substantial contribution to their certificate holdings. What is, as yet, uncertain is the value of the National Certificate in terms of entry to employment, and chapter 8 of this volume addresses this issue.

In the rest of the UK, CPVE was to have provided certification for non-traditional school stayers, bringing a vocational emphasis into post-compulsory schooling and providing shorter courses than the two-year 'A' level. Under the present arrangements, CPVE is unable to assure progression, either to NAFE or to higher education, as the framework within which it operates is being redesigned in the light of the Review of Vocational Qualifications, and credit transfer arrangements have not been agreed with the examining bodies. Until the NCVQ decides on the position of CPVE within the new framework, it functions as a stand-alone qualification which is taken on its own merits. Registrations for the CPVE have been falling over the past year, with pupils being switched over to taking other qualifications such as the BTEC first award at foundation level which, at least, provides for progression within a vocationally specific area. This trend is expected to continue. The position in the rest of the UK as regards the options available to young people who stay on into the first post-compulsory year is less good than in Scotland, at present, where credit transfer arrangements ensure a measure of progression, and year-long academic-oriented courses at both 'O' grade and Higher have been long established with clear lines of progression.

Currently, there is poor articulation between the National Certificate and other qualifications which school pupils have been or are taking, making it somewhat of an anomaly and increasing, or making more apparent, the structural differentiation for the fifth-year client groups.

It is possible that we will see a sharper decline in the eventual attainment of conscripted pupils as the Action Plan develops and provision for fifth-year pupils becomes more differentiated. Pupils who may be considering leaving at Christmas will have the option of short courses with quick end-certification and may not embark on the longer SCE courses in the ways in which they did in previous years. Conscript pupils may stop attempting to attain, at least in terms of academic-oriented qualifications. As yet, however, it is too early to assess the longer-term effects of the introduction of the National Certificate.

So far, modules have a unique place in the school curriculum in terms of their duration, their criterion-referenced assessment and their coverage of topic areas not necessarily covered by more traditional forms of certification. They have been valuable in extending a curriculum that has been too firmly oriented to the needs of Highers pupils, providing some diversity.

The SED has identified the need to extend short-course certification to pupils within compulsory schooling, the value of such courses having been tested out through the first round of TVEI schemes which provided National Certificate modules for scheme pupils in the third and fourth years. The certification of subjects related to the traditional school curriculum through the use of Standard grade may have the effect of bringing all of compulsory education, including that for the fifth-year conscripts, under a single certification head. It may also reinforce the divide between the post-compulsory sectors. The use of Standard grade to certificate 'courses to develop a particular expertise as a possible adjunct to a range of other disciplines (e.g. keyboard skills)' should bring most of the Higher candidates who were taking the National Certificate back into the SCE fold.

At the moment, pupils whose ambitions are focused on advanced or further education cannot allow displacement of their SCE curriculum, as too heavy an investment of time in the National Certificate would preclude their gaining qualifications for direct entry to university. The provision of additional SEB-certificated short-courses should rationalize some of the anomalies in the certification of Highers pupils, although the universities' acceptance of Standard grade short-course accreditation is as yet unclear as certificates will be ungraded and the assessments largely internal, as with the National Certificate.

The National Certificate, with its credit transfer, can of course provide progression through to the college sector, and it is possible that a change to Standard grade certification may make this progression more difficult. Other SCE qualifications can, however, be traded in both the university and college sectors and are the accreditation which allows choice. The National Certificate cannot, at present, be directly traded up.

This chapter has looked at the emerging pattern of fifth-year provision over what is a developmental period. The certification framework is, however, still in transition, and the experience from the first years provides an early insight into the directions in which provision is changing, and the consumers' responses to those changes. The full potential of the change has not yet been realized or exploited.

NOTES

1. 'Pupils who reach the age of 16 on or between 1 March and 30 September can leave school on 31 May. There are three school-leaving age groups (SLA), each of which is defined by the pupil's date of birth. The first two allow pupils to leave school at, or before, the end of their fourth year of secondary schooling. Pupils who reach the age of 16 on or between 1 October and the end of February can leave school at the end of the winter term. These arrangements were laid down by the Education (Scotland) Act 1976 and are now embodied in the Education (Scotland) Act 1980' (SED, 1985).

2. 'The launch of the authority's post-16 initiative coincided with the start of what proved to be a long drawn out and intensively fought campaign of industrial action by teachers in schools. This action has certainly impeded progress with

the post-compulsory strategy across the region' (Strathclyde Regional Council, 1987).

REFERENCES

FURTHER EDUCATION UNIT (1986) *CPVE: More Confusion*, Stanmore, Department of Education and Science.

FURTHER EDUCATION UNIT (1987) *Progression from CPVE*, Stanmore, Department of Education and Science.

MANPOWER SERVICES COMMISSION and DEPARTMENT OF EDUCATION AND SCIENCE (1986) *Review of Vocational Qualifications in England and Wales: A Report by the Working Group April 1986*, London, HMSO.

SCOTTISH EDUCATION DEPARTMENT (SED) (1977a) *The Structure of the Curriculum in the Third and Fourth Years of the Scottish Secondary School* (Munn Report), Edinburgh, HMSO.

SCOTTISH EDUCATION DEPARTMENT (SED) (1977b) *Assessment for All: Report of the Committee to Review Assesment in the Third and Fourth Years of Secondary Education in Scotland* (Dunning Report), Edinburgh, HMSO.

SCOTTISH EDUCATION DEPARTMENT (SED) (1983) *16–18s in Scotland: An Action Plan*, Edinburgh, SED.

SCOTTISH EDUCATION DEPARTMENT (SED) (1985) *School Leavers: Statistical Bulletin no. 5/E2/1985*, Edinburgh, SED.

SCOTTISH EDUCATION DEPARTMENT (SED) (1987) *Use of Nationally Certificated Short Courses in Schools*, Circular no. 1157, Edinburgh, SED.

STRATHCLYDE REGIONAL COUNCIL DEPARTMENT OF EDUCATION (1987) *Post-compulsory Education: Position Relating to Secondary Schools, 1986–87*, Report by Director, March.

Chapter 10:

The View from the Hutch: Educational Guinea Pigs Speak about TVEI

Colin Bell and Cathy Howieson

INTRODUCTION

The MSC's Technical and Vocational Education Initiative (TVEI) was introduced in stages in Scotland starting with five projects in 1984, a year after England and Wales. These were located in Borders, Dumfries and Galloway, Fife, Renfrew and Glasgow. A single project (in Lothian) began in 1985 and another (in Tayside) in 1986. By 1987 there were projects in all mainland regions in Scotland, and in all divisions of Strathclyde Region. So at the spring 1987 sweep of the Scottish Young Peoples Survey (SYPS) TVEI was in its third year of operation in Scotland. This sweep covered a 10 per cent sample of a year group (the previous session's fourth year) from all Scottish secondary schools; this included the first cohort to start TVEI (in third year) in the first five Scottish projects. The sample was boosted to cover the other 90 per cent of the year group from the nineteen TVEI schools involved in the five first-round projects. These extra sample members received a specially designed TVEI questionnaire. Responses were received from 2532 out of the 3307 young people who comprised the entire year group from the nineteen schools (minus the 10 per cent in the main survey). This is equivalent to a response rate of 78 per cent of presumed contacts and 76 per cent of the original target sample. (The difference between the figures is made up by those returned undelivered by the Post Office.) The equivalent response rates from the main survey, based on the year group, were 81 per cent and 79 per cent respectively.

This chapter presents an initial analysis of the TVEI questionnaire returns that is largely qualitative, although our first analyses of the quantitative data tend to back up the main points of our arguments. We only present material here from TVEI pupils and disregard at this stage the important data from non-TVEI pupils in TVEI schools. If still in school the pupils would have been in their fifth year. Some would therefore be in their third TVEI year but others were 'in-fill', that is, they had taken the places of those who had left school after the end of fourth year or even at Christmas of the fifth year. This is a complex situation made even more so by the fact that projects vary in their policies over in-fill (from doing no in-fill, through partial in-fill to complete in-fill) and have changed their policies over time. This is simplified in this chapter as we present material from young people if they have *ever* been on TVEI. Subsequent analysis will have to take these complexities into account.

TVEI projects are based on consortia of three, four, five or six schools and colleges. Pupils variously chose to be in, were chosen or were picked at random for the first cohort. The consequences for the pupils for this style of educational innovation will be one of the main themes of this chapter. Nearly one-third of the year group in the TVEI schools was in the first TVEI cohort, although the exact proportion varies from project to project and school to school. These were self-consciously pilot projects from which educational authorities were meant to learn. The national extension of TVEI to all schools and all regions was announced in the summer of 1986 in the White Paper *Working Together — Education and Training* (Cmnd 9823). This was actually before we were appointed as Scottish evaluators of the pilot projects.

TVEI's ambition is to give 14–18-year-old boys and girls of all abilities a more relevant and practical preparation for adult and working life. Within the broad criteria set for TVEI by the Manpower Services Commission (MSC), projects have taken different approaches; some have a greater technological slant than others which perhaps pay more attention to personal and social development. It is also the case that the aims and emphasis of TVEI have changed and been reinterpreted over time. TVEI programmes consist of a core that is common to all TVEI pupils and options. Together core and options vary from about 30 to 60 per cent of Scottish TVEI pupils' timetables. In Scotland the core usually includes information technology, personal and social development, careers and work experience which have been introduced or enhanced by TVEI. Work experience and a residential experience usually form part of a TVEI programme, in some cases as part of the core. Options include subjects chosen by students to meet their needs, such as business studies, computing, catering, textiles, control technology, pneumatics and caring. Many established curriculum subjects have also been enhanced through TVEI funding which has been used to add to existing subjects by providing resources, adding to the curriculum or helping to change teaching methods. English, maths, music, art, geography, Latin and home economics are all examples of subjects that have been enhanced. Few subjects have not been enhanced in at least some TVEI schools in Scotland. As well as an attempt to introduce technology across the curriculum, there have been equally important changes in the modes of teaching, emphasizing a problem-solving approach, experiential learning and more negotiated, individualized study.

This chapter analyzes some of the pupils' reactions to TVEI expressed in the back-page comments — comments written open-endedly on the back pages of the questionnaires. It is therefore more specific than the following chapter. Our main aim is not only to consider TVEI in itself, but also to use pupils' reactions to TVEI — an example of a radical educational reform which encompasses much current thinking on education — to illustrate

(a) pupils' comments on several trends in education embodied in TVEI, namely different teaching and learning methods and attempts to make the curriculum more relevant and more vocational; and

(b) aspects of the implementation and management of an educational reform.

Before considering this, we will outline the approach we used.

THE QUESTIONNAIRE

The TVEI questionnaire was split into two versions with different prompts inviting respondents' open-ended comments on the back page. The first version (T1) reads:

> We would like to know more about TVEI at your school.
>
> What do you think about TVEI? Would you recommend TVEI to other people like yourself? Do you think TVEI helps young people to know more about industry and work? Does it help them to find out about jobs? And does it help them to get jobs?
>
> Even if you haven't been on TVEI, we'd like to hear what you think.

The second version (T2) reads:

> We would like to know more about TVEI at your school.
>
> What do you think about TVEI? Would you recommend TVEI to other people like yourself? Is TVEI different from other lessons at your school? In what ways? Should other subjects at school be more like TVEI?

Even if you haven't been on TVEI we'd like to hear what you think.

We have read carefully their responses and were in danger of being deafened and confused by the cacophony of 'shouts of joy and cries of pain' (see chapter 11 in this volume). However, as will be shown, it has proved possible to draw out and analyze the impact of and reaction to this significant innovation in education from the pupils' perspectives.

Table 10.1: Percentage making back-page comments: TVEI takers

	Boys	Girls	All	N
On TVEI in S3/4 only	50	68	57	429
On TVEI in S3/4 and in S5	59	76	67	246
On TVEI in S5 only (in-fill)	62	68	66	113
All TVEI takers	54	71	62	788

Note: Participation on TVEI based on self-reports.

As can be seen in table 10.1 the gender differences in responses to the back-page prompts are striking. Whereas overall 62 per cent of all those who took TVEI made comments (compared to 51 per cent of those in TVEI schools who did not take it), 71 per cent of girls compared to 54 per cent of boys made a comment.

After reading all the back-page comments, we decided that they could be classified on a five-point scale:

++	+	=	−	− −
5	4	3	2	1
Very favourable	Favourable	Balanced and mixed	Hostile	Very hostile

We found that not all that much was gained by maintaining the distinction between 5 and 4 and between 2 and 1, especially because of the problematic nature of intercoder subjectivity.

As table 10.2 shows, 48 per cent of the first Scottish cohort made comments that could be classified as favourable or very favourable and an additional 26 per cent made comments that we judged to be mixed. Only 26 per cent were judged to have made negative comments — not at all bad for the first cohort of a hastily implemented educational innovation bedevilled by an industrial dispute. The table also shows that these overall figures obscure considerable inter-project differences, reflecting the considerable variations in the style and manner of delivery of TVEI across the five projects. However we do not intend to explore these variations in this chapter.

Table 10.2:   *The first cohort's judgment on TVEI: TVEI takers (coding of back-page comments from TVEI questionnaire: percentages)*

Project	Hostile and very hostile	Balanced and mixed	Favourable and very favourable
A	36	27	36
B	49	29	21
C	21	25	54
D	11	24	64
E	12	20	67
Overall	26	26	48
n = 486			

Note: This table is based on those who made comments and who had *ever* been on TVEI in S3, S4 or S5.

Often we quote a single sentence taken out of the context of the often lengthy comment (many were a page and several ran to two sides of small cramped handwriting). We do this in order to pursue the analytic purpose of this chapter: to systematize the consumers' views of an educational reform. The pupils, of course, were less concerned about this and so, in what follows, occasional damage is done to the coherence (and at times also the inconsistencies) of the pupils' views. As a counter to our more analytic approach, we will start with three whole back-page comments to illustrate their richness and our difficulties in selecting 'bits and pieces':

> It was a pilot TVEI scheme. About eighty people from [names the school] were chosen to go on the course. At first many people saw TVEI as a skive but after a while people thought it was interesting. I personally thought TVEI was worthwhile because it gave a wide range of industrial visits so one could actually see what was going on. It also taught a whole range of new skills, e.g. soldering, acid etching, cable forming. TVEI is a very recommendable course to follow. The classes are very different from the usual lessons in school not in the unusual subjects taught but in the attitude of teachers. For once one is allowed to give over their own ideas and by doing this methods of work can be improved. Other subjects at school should be taught in the same way, continual assessment, with no dread of a big exam at the end of it all. If this method was brought into practice then I'm sure the standard of work would be higher and that not as many people will fail exams due to pressure and of course exam nerves.

We judged this back-page comment as 'favourable'

A back-page comment we judged as 'balanced and mixed':

I enjoyed TVEI because it allowed me to get work placements which helped me to decide what kind of jobs to do. TVEI also showed me how to apply for jobs and what kind of jobs were available to me. Some of the modules I liked, e.g. Introduction to Computers because most jobs now have computers involved in them so I can say I have worked with computers. I did not enjoy the recording and reviewing because I found it boring as I was writing the same thing every week. I would recommend TVEI to other people because the people involved are trying to change TVEI at the places in the course we found boring and did not like. TVEI was different from other lessons because it had a more relaxed atmosphere and you were allowed to say freely what you thought of the work you were doing. The teachers did not treat you like children but like equal adults.

And the following we judged as 'hostile':

TVEI is an extremely boring, dull and tedious subject. The work is too easy for the more intellectual of us (ie an IQ over 1). It assumes that you want to take the subject. The tutors give you very little help (except for a few exceptions). There is no option to get off the subject although the vast majority of the people there asked wanted to get out. Money is flagrantly wasted, e.g. the computer situation at X School where pupils don't get the use of them, the amount of folders used, the wasting of resources. TVEI never listen to pupils complaints. COURSES ARE REPETITIVE, e.g. the course in fifth year is the same as third and fourth year. The course does not relate to careers, social development or mental development. Also because of TVEI I am missing out in Music, RE, Social and Health, Art Appreciation and triple PE. Work placements are extremely dull, e.g. I got placed in Y microelectronics, not what I was wanting. I would discourage anyone from taking TVEI. I woud certainly not say that any other school subjects should be like this as in other subjects. We would be totally thick. WHY DON'T TVEI SCRAP THE COURSES THEY HAVE STARTED AND TRY TO FIND WORK WHICH INTERESTS PUPILS, e.g. photography, computers, constructional electronics, PE, office practice etc. Also better tutor/student cooperation should be enforced. I have nothing but complaints on the present courses. We are guinea pigs who have rebellion in our hearts because of the vast mismanagement of our lives by the tutors and organisers. TVEI HAS BEEN A TOTAL WASTE OF TIME. The money spent on TVEI should have been spent on better supplies for the school. Higher pay for teachers.

PAYING PUPILS TO STAY ON AT SCHOOL. Keeping a better NHS and Higher Education, 2 million pounds could give much more happiness than it has given. Other lessons at school are totally different. 1) more mentally taxing 2) better organized 3) pupils can achieve more 4) more specialized 5) less money spent on them 6) more practical 7) higher standards 8) better teachers 9) less resources 10) more prospects 11) harder exams 12) better courses 13) more vigorous 14) greater chance in the outside world.

These three back-page comments came not only from the same project but from the same school!

'YOU WERE SOMEONE NOT SOMETHING': CHANGES IN TEACHING AND LEARNING METHODS

Much current rhetoric in education is concerned about developing negoti-ated, individualized learning as well as developing group-work skills. There is talk about enabling pupils to work at their own pace and giving them responsibility for their own learning. TVEI is about encouraging such moves in pedagogic style — away from didactic to more informal practical methods, including to 'sites other than schools' beyond the classroom. How did the pupils see this? As we shall see 'own pace/own time' can be viewed as wonderfully enabling but also as the teachers 'skiving' and an indication that TVEI pupils are second-class citizens.
At its simplest:

It was different to other subjects because you didn't slog over a book all day.

To the more complex response:

I think that TVEI is an excellent course, because it gives you independence to do things on your own and also it allows you to go places where you otherwise would not have went [names an English industrial town and factory where work experience placement was]...

The respondent continues discussing modules and certification and mentions the advantages of going to the Tech.
Across a large number of comments are some remarks on how they were treated within TVEI — which show the pupils' appreciation at being treated like adults (one of the key terms) as in:

The teachers and adults made you feel like adults the way they treated you. I think other classes should be like TVEI because you get classed as a group and not an individual.

But this should be balanced with the rarer:

It is different and they treat you like babies.

TVEI has made strenuous efforts to move away from traditional examination towards more continuous assessment sometimes using the new forms of certification. This is realized and usually appreciated by the pupils:

There isn't an exam at the end of it, you get tested all the way through the year so your not worried about sitting the exam at the end.

and:

In TVEI you are competing more against yourself than others.

and:

I liked the idea of being tested on something after each topic or learning outcomes.

Associated with this move towards less traditional forms of assessment there has been a parallel move toward profiling and filling in logs. This is not always appreciated by the pupils:

Although some parts of the course seem irrelevant and useless (filling in lots of sheets) the overall course is very worthwhile.

and:

We spent eight weeks filling in pathetically useless information.

and:

...endless reams of simply useless booklets and sheets which you simply had to read over, fill in 'discuss' etc concerning either trivial or simply unnecessary matters.

That this is also associated with the pilot nature of the projects is recognized:

Everyone in TVEI is obliged to make regular reports on recording and review sheets. In every report I looked at TVEI was criticized most strongly. The administration at TVEI claimed that a pilot scheme always has difficulties in the first year.

There is also a feeling of considerable engagement from many of the comments — that the 'new pedagogy' is closely related to the organization of courses:

You take part in everything and don't just watch. You are treated more like an adult. You take part in organising the course, if there is something you think should be altered you can tell the teachers and they will alter it whereas in normal subjects you must do what the teachers tell you to, more subjects should be like TVEI as it would be more interesting because you get to play a bigger part in lessons.

and:

I think TVEI is a good idea and would recommend it to anyone who wants to do a course that allows more freedom than ordinary classes. TVEI lets you make decisions on your own and placed responsibility on you.

Of course pupils' reactions are not necessarily all in this same direction — one person's 'freedom' is another person's tedium:

TVEI in my school was a time for being relaxed and bored.

But also:

TVEI...gave me something to look forward to when I did go to school. TVEI is different as it wasn't boring you werent (*sic*) sitting writing during lessons all the time and teachers treated you with more respect than with other subjects in English, Maths etc you were just another face and name that teachers were getting paid to learn. With TVEI you felt as if you were something different. You werent (*sic*) just a face, another name or number you were someone not something.

The pupils also appreciate the small class sizes (which of course allowed a more pupil-centred approach) and simply:

The way of teaching was better and because of smaller classes a better teacher/pupil relationship is formed.

and:

There is a very pleasant atmosphere which helps you do the work more efficiently.

as well as:

It gives you the chance to think for yourself and do your own work rather than some teacher looking over your shoulder.

Others drew our attention to 'more relaxed business-like manner' at the TVEI Centre where 'the usually uncomfortable school uniform was not required'.

'A GOOD LOOK AT THE OUTSIDE WORLD': MOVES TO VOCATIONAL RELEVANCE

A recurring theme in recent educational debate and one voiced especially by politicians and industrialists is the alleged failure of British schooling to offer 'a relevant education' which prepares pupils for 'the real world'. Leaving aside issues about the definition of terms such as 'the real world', the basic argument is that much of the curriculum is outdated, too theoretical and academic, irrelevant to the needs of modern society and in particular to the needs of industry and 'the world of work'. It is still alleged that such an education also fosters an anti-industrial spirit in pupils so that they (especially the more able) are reluctant to consider a career in industry. It is therefore argued that education should develop links with industry and the curriculum be redesigned to be more practical and 'relevant' to 'real life' problems and issues. Underlying all of this is the belief that Britain has failed to value vocational education (especially compared to its industrial competitors) which is seen as a low-status area. TVEI represents one of the most comprehensive attempts to modify traditional secondary education and move it in a more vocational direction.

How have pupils reacted to TVEI efforts to remodel the curriculum? In the back-page comments, pupils frequently remark on the more practical nature and usefulness of TVEI courses compared with other school subjects:

> TVEI is different from other lessons because there are more practical lessons involved in the courses and the courses are based upon technology.

> Other subjects should be more like TVEI in that TVEI is practical and not all theory which is very beneficial.

TVEI is frequently seen as a better preparation for life after school.

> TVEI gives you a good look at the outside world, whereas history and geography doesn't show you what you yourself are up against.

And yet a certain conservatism exists within this positive attitude to the TVEI courses — a feeling that not all subjects should be interfered with in the pursuit of 'relevance':

> Only sciences and Craft and Design should be made more like TVEI and have more technology in the courses.

Despite making positive comments on TVEI:

> TVEI gives young people something to enjoy at school instead of everyday maths and English etc.

This ex-TVEI student goes on to say that:

> Other subjects should be more like TVEI but others should be left as English and maths, arithmetic and science subjects, if you take them and change them it isn't school anymore, it is just like a technical college. School is where you learn it that way.

Other express a similarly ambivalent attitude:

> TVEI was totally different from other courses as it was a pleasure to get out of something like maths... some of the subjects should be like TVEI but things like maths and English should be kept the same.

The idea of learning about 'the world of work' through work experience, industrial visits, setting up mini-companies and so on seems to find favour with most pupils. Of course anything such as work experience which takes pupils out of school is very likely to be popular but pupils' comments demonstrate that it was also a worthwhile experience whether as a way of learning about industry, finding out more about possible areas of work for the future or testing out career ideas more specifically:

> It [TVEI] gives you a better look at life by taking you to the industries which most people end up in. Work experience was good. I went into the industry which I hope finally to end up doing. I learned how to work with people who you don't really like and people older than me.

> The work placements were an excellent idea. Rather than just talking about industry and what it was like we went out on work placements.

> I loved the work placement I learnt more about work and what I wanted to do when I leave and what was expected of me in my job in one week of placements than I have ever learnt in school. It was very scary going all by myself because I have never done anything like this before but it was worthwhile.

> Through work experience you can get an insight into the job you possibly want to do when you leave school. On the other hand you may realise that it is not the job for you.

Few objected to the principle of going on work experience. Complaints generally related to the suitability of the placement:

> Work experience is a good way of finding out about jobs but at our school we got placed anywhere available even if the place was of no interest to us.

A small minority were more negative:

It helps a little but not enough about industry and work.

and:

TVEI... has helped me in no way to learn anything I never knew before about industry and jobs.

Apart from work experience other efforts to offer a more 'relevant' education were commented on:

TVEI organised a residential trip to X [a large industrial town] which included industrial visits, interview techniques and careers work. This was very worthwhile.

and:

TVEI helps you find out about jobs and how to go about asking questions about work.

Preparation for interviews was seen as helpful:

The interview techniques we learned would be a good help [in getting a job]. I know these helped me get my part-time job because I was totally prepared as we had been shown to be.

In the light of the current emphasis on self-employment it is interesting to see this feature in the back-page comments. It seems that TVEI made some impact in highlighting the idea of self-employment to pupils:

It would be the best idea anybody of my age could do if they took TVEI... they would know how to run their own business one day.

TVEI will teach you more about what you can do after school... then you could start up your own business, you could manage the work coming and going out of your factory.

and:

There is no way TVEI could possibly get you a job. The only job it would help you with would be the self-employment. We talked quite a lot about self-employment.

A few commented on whether TVEI offered more or better careers guidance than that normally available:

TVEI does teach you about jobs [more] than you would learn from your careers officer.

and ironically:

> TVEI was a good thing but we missed careers periods at school
> which I thought were valuable in finding out about interview
> techniques and what jobs were available.

Did pupils think that following a vocational course like TVEI woud help
them get a job? The bulk of responses were rather cautious and most seemed
to judge this question on the basis of a very direct link between TVEI and
job finding:

> It really does help people to find out about jobs but it doesn't really
> help them to get jobs.

A frequent comment:

> The work experience did give a valuable insight into working life
> but I personally do not think that being on TVEI will improve job
> prospects, not unless a full time job was offered after the placement.

As one youngster succinctly put it:

> It doesn't really have a lot to do with job creating.

At most:

> If you are lucky you might get a job out of it when you leave school.

> The more experience we get the better prospects for us of getting a
> job in the future.

The back-page comments show that the majority of the TVEI pupils
who made comments, did enjoy and appreciate the vocational emphasis of
TVEI. However, this is only half the picture. Their comments also illustrate
that while TVEI courses are frequently seen as enjoyable and useful, overall
they are still less valued than traditional education because of problems about
the status of vocational education, its perceived client group and its value in
the market places of employment and further and higher education. There
are frequent comments that TVEI is geared to less academic pupils:

> I think TVEI is alright for those pupils who are not all that good with
> academic subjects but better with their hands and common sense.

More frequently similar views are expressed in a less egalitarian manner:

> TVEI... seemed to be a "drop-outs" subject...

> TVEI is a very good idea for children who are not likely to get that
> many 'O' Grades due to incapability.

Some pupils, while recognizing the image TVEI has acquired for some,
do try to refute it:

> My friends still tell me that TVEI is for the less intelligent people but I don't think so. I would recommend it to anyone.

and:

> TVEI in my school is regarded as a subject which is for pupils who are not bright enough to study for Highers. This is wrong. It is a good system to widen the knowledge of the pupils.

A common view is that TVEI is geared to factory work and manufacturing industry; this adds to the problem TVEI has with its image:

> TVEI seems to assume that when everybody leaves school they will be working in factories.

A pupil's description of one TVEI project's residential experience highlights an emphasis, at least in that instance, on manufacturing industry:

> We went away on a trip to X [a large industrial town], we went to a [brewery] b [food factory] and c [engineering factory] and we learned how factories were run, about production lines.

In addition, TVEI is sometimes seen as being about low-level work in industry:

> I felt it was aimed at pupils who wanted a job on the factory floor though I wanted to go and see things about management and so on.

The widespread perception of TVEI as a low-status subject is reinforced in some cases by timetabling difficulties in combining TVEI with 'O' grade subjects and Highers — this exacerbates tendencies to see TVEI as geared to the non-academic. When it comes to a choice between TVEI and another 'O' grade or Higher TVEI seldom wins:

> To take TVEI the pupils must drop 2 subjects at 'O' levels. In return they get experience and certificates. Many say the certificates are not as important as the 'O' Levels.

> My time [on TVEI] would have been better spend (*sic*) taking another 3 or 4 'O' Grades.

> TVEI... is a total waste of time, in that, for a few certificates I had to sacrifice several 'O' Grades... I would not recommend TVEI to anyone wanting to sit examinations.

The support for traditional certification is very strong — if for no other reason than its perceived market value in employment and further and higher education:

The chances of getting a job because of TVEI-based education are almost non-existent. The local companies are more interested in traditional exam results.

The basic idea [of TVEI] is good unfortunately exam results and 'O' Levels are more important to employers than job experience and skills. Today the person who drops exams and takes TVEI is at a disadvantage against other pupils.

...it takes up the time of 2 'O' Grades therefore lessening their chances to go to university.

and:

I wouldn't recommend it to anyone...thinking of going to college in the future.

Although some TVEI courses offer certification through Scotvec National Certificates these have yet to prove their value.

The main disadvantage of TVEI is that certificates for the SCOT-VEC modules do not seem to have such a high standing as traditional 'O' and Higher Grades.

There are only a few dissenting voices:

TVEI provides an alternative method of education in that they prepare and train you for topics which will be useful practically and theoretically in a job. Whereas in school the people learn little practical skills of the job he or she wants to do. Hence students who take TVEI will be more prepared academically and practical than a school leaver therefore an employer will take on the student who has more scope into the job but may not necessarily have more academic awards.

Although an essentially instrumental view of the value of education coupled with an association of TVEI with the less academic pupils emerge from the comments, at the same time there are frequent remarks that TVEI is worthwhile because it deals with new technology — seen as important in the future for everyone:

TVEI is a good idea...in the world of today even the slightest experience with new technology is beneficial.

Computers have a lot to do with TVEI which will be involved in industry in the future. People won't get jobs in the future if they know nothing about computers.

Businesses are installing more and more new technology and it is good to have an insight into these things.

TVEI is a good scheme which offers young people the chance to learn all about computers, electronics and other courses which would help you in the future.

The association of new technology, a desirable and high-status area, with TVEI seems to temper the traditional attitudes to vocational courses as low ranking. Perhaps new technology will be the critical factor in changing attitudes to vocational education. At the same time, the stranglehold of traditional certification is crucial. Until employers and further and higher education change their attitudes to and use of certification then the value of alternative courses and alternative certification will be questioned by pupils whatever their merits.

'ON A WING AND A PRAYER': THE IMPLEMENTATION AND MANAGEMENT OF AN EDUCATIONAL INNOVATION

TVEI is, of course, a deliberate 'educational innovation' introduced through pilot projects in selected schools and with selected cohorts of pupils within them. It was also introduced at great speed and should stand as a constant reminder to industrialists, employers and the Government of the rate at which education can react if stimulated in the correct way. Proposals were prepared in February for submission in March, with August as the official starting date. This was very tight timing at best but in Scotland it was made even tighter because some schools start their new timetable in June, not August. We see clearly the impact on the pupils of the speed of implementation.

The comments on (dis)organization are particularly related to the early days:

It was usually always disorganised. We were sent anywhere. ONCE WE SPENT A DOUBLE PERIOD IN A *BOOK CUPBOARD*. I would never recommend TVEI to anyone unless they have really pulled their socks up.

and again:

When TVEI started out at my school I was amongst the first batch of pupils to go on it. It was not very well organised. It had been put together so quickly. Things are better now though I prefer TVEI to the rest of my subjects because you are assessed as you go along and it makes you think about a career move.

Despite these difficulties pupils could still be very much in favour:

TVEI is a good course and should be continued. I just hope that the disorganisation experienced at my school isn't the same throughout Scotland. It seems that everything we do or the chance we get of going somewhere is on a wing and a prayer.

– even excited:

When I started TVEI it was the first year it was ever taught so it was a little hectic but I would recommend it. You learn a lot about life outside school.

TVEI had to be 'sold' to potential entrants at the end of second year. Where pupils comment on this it is to complain about a degree of 'overselling' as in:

I think that TVEI is a very good course to run although I don't think it was as good as everybody was making it sound at the start.

and:

It was blown up to be great.

and:

We were not given what we were promised...it was different from other subjects as there was no real organisation.

and:

When TVEI came out it promised wonderfull (*sic*) things, only half of which we got.

and, at even greater length:

A delightful little personally addressed book was sent to all the impressionable youngsters, not expected to achieve good exam results at the end of third year. It claimed that TVEI would be a good course for us and went on to describe all the new vocational and technological courses we would be offered...we..embarked on this course full of expectation and received nothing but the courses already offered but at a lower level.

But more typical would be:

I found that TVEI was not what it was cracked up to be, but saying that I found the courses interesting and varied.

and the delightful:

TVEI wasn't all roses for us but it should get better in the future.

Pupils fully recognize the efforts put into TVEI:

I admire the TVEI Tutors for their honesty — they are learning with us — and they really do listen...on the whole TVEI is trying very hard, they make mistakes but the tutors admit it.

One consequence of the TVEI model of delivery, based as it was on selection, was a feeling that it was divisive. The issue of selection, an ever-sensitive issue in Scottish education, was most strongly felt by pupils:

TVEI is enjoyable but everybody should be given the opportunity to attend it, not the chosen few.

At the time of the pilot projects TVEI would not have been widely known to pupils outside the original schools. From a rare example of a pupil who moved away and yet retained a TVEI place:

The TVEI scheme should be made more readily available to other schools in Scotland as many people that I know would have liked to have had a chance to do it.

Pupils have their views on how this educational experiment could have been differently organized:

Perhaps a better idea of implementing TVEI would be to allow many more pupils the benefit of it by sending a certain number say for a week, and then repeating the process with different pupils so that everyone had a chance.

That the projects were pilots allowed pupils to be in the position of being able to say:

I feel that TVEI is a good idea but due to the amount of experimentation that surrounded the course I failed to get anything out of it other than 2 module certificates (1 of which I still have not received).

If there is a phrase that encapsulates this point of view it is 'guinea pigs' — it came up a lot and often in a not unsympathetic way:

TVEI was new when I started the course and we were like guinea pigs but now the teachers are more organised and it is a great deal better, if I was asked by someone going into third year about TVEI I would definately (*sic*) recommend it.

and we were told that:

Other classes shouldn't be like TVEI because they are more sure of what they have got to do and the TVEI are still learning from the pupils.

There are many aspects of the management of TVEI that are simply not evident to pupils taking part. Several issues do, however, come through. One is the notion of equity — that any new course should be available to everyone. Perhaps if a new course or programme is to be piloted, then at least all pupils in a pilot school should be offered the chance to participate. Although the speed of implementation caused difficulties such a tight deadline is not necessarily totally or even mainly negative — it did make new programmes happen and sometimes created a feeling between teachers and pupils of working together to develop a new and exciting project. Strict deadlines can be creative but can also lead to disorganization and stress for everyone concerned. We can also see from TVEI the dangers of over-selling any reform: publicizing and explaining new courses is vital, but overly optimistic representations of what is on offer can be counter-productive.

CONCLUSION

Although we are cautious about generalizing on the basis of the back-page comments, nevertheless the insights from pupils' comments can illuminate youngsters' reactions to new experiences in their schooling and help further our understanding of their attitudes and responses to educational reform. We have also, it should be pointed out, much more supporting evidence based on our extensive fieldwork in the projects and on preliminary analysis of the quantitative data from the survey.

Many of the pupils believe that TVEI changed teaching and learning methods and these changes seem to be appreciated by the pupils. Pupils appear both to enjoy learning in this way and also to see it as increasing their motivation and attainment, including in examinations. Profiling is the major exception: this seems to be a matter partly of pupils not appreciating the purposes and use of profiles and partly of the unimaginative way they appear to have been used. We are not necessarily questioning the concept of profiling but the TVEI experience suggests that more attention should be given to how profiles are applied in practice.

From the TVEI pupils' back-page comments, it would seem that while many of them appreciated the efforts of TVEI to be more vocationally relevant and practical, the issues of the low status of vocational education and the emphasis on traditional certification are continuing problems. A novel element in this is new technology which perhaps could be the means of breaking down traditional attitudes to vocational education.

We would like to return here to the model of educational innovation that TVEI represents. Crucial aspects of delivery, for instance, were also a function of the experimental nature of TVEI. The issue more generally is what will happen in the extension of TVEI to all schools and education authorities? The positive point to make is that issues of organization and selection will be resolved and so it would appear likely that extension should face few of the problems of the pilot. But then again are the perceived changes in teaching and learning methods, the so-called new pedagogy, based on the small class sizes made possible with extra TVEI resources that just will not be available under the extension of TVEI?

This model of innovation has consequences that have not always been helpful to the wider educational ambitions of TVEI. The need to identify an experimental group of TVEI pupils within each school, on the basis of a timetabled TVEI core and options from which all TVEI pupils must choose, meant that many pupils had to choose between TVEI and one or more traditionally certificated subjects. This put off many parents and deterred many academic pupils from taking TVEI, and often reinforced its low-status image.

The model of innovation of TVEI also created political problems in that it was seen as a threat to the comprehensive principle, and as elitist and divisive. Not only was this an aspect of TVEI which received considerable attention in the educational press and elsewhere but it was also one that concerned pupils taking part in TVEI. These perceptions deflected from the content of the innovation. Unless there are strong methodological or educational reasons for innovating in this way, with hindsight we would argue for introducing innovation across whole year groups in whole schools.

And yet these were meant as pilots from which lessons were to be learned. We think that one of the hardest lessons to learn is how to maintain flexibility and innovatory activity under the extension of TVEI. Pilots very easily become set in tablets of stone. We feel that there is a danger too of some teachers reverting to more traditional didactic approaches — especially in the face of the spectre of national testing. Pilot projects were surely never meant to be blue-prints but places to try out new ideas — and disregard those that did not work. Some of those who had these ideas tried out on them have had their say in this chapter.

ACKNOWLEDGEMENTS

The Scottish Young Peoples Surveys are conducted by the Centre for Educational Sociology (CES) in conjunction with the Scottish Education Department (SED). The CES acknowledges the financial support of the

Economic and Social Research Council, the SED, the Manpower Services Commission (MSC), the Industry Department for Scotland and the Department of Employment. The Scottish Evaluation of TVEI was conducted jointly by the CES and the Department of Education of the University of Edinburgh and was funded by the MSC. We would like to acknowledge and thank Cathy Presland and Carola Flockhart for their help in transcribing and coding the back-page comments; and Shona Adie for taking the manuscript through many revisions. The MSC's TVEI Unit in London made some helpful suggestions and prevented us from making some errors. Our colleagues, David Raffe and Kenneth King, improved those earlier versions. The opinions expressed in this chapter are our own, and do not necessarily reflect the views of the bodies or individuals mentioned above.

Chapter 11

Shouts of Joy and Cries of Pain: Investigating Young People's Comments on Leaving School and Entering the Labour Market
Geoffrey Walford

My life has been great since I left school. I have a job as an apprentice hairdresser and it's a job that I am happy with and have always wanted to be. I have now worked for the firm for three years and enjoy it very much. (Apprentice hairdresser, six 'O' grades, C3).

Life has been hell since I left in the fourth year. I have found it difficult to find a FULL TIME JOB because all they are offering is YTS Jobs. I don't feel as if I've had enough help. (Unemployed, no 'O' grades, C3)

Since I left school I have found life very enjoyable, since I've had the money to go out more often. I never had much difficulty finding a job since a job was virtually waiting for me. (Electrical engineering apprentice, seven 'O' grades, C3)

Life for me has been boring and depressing at times with not being able to find a job. The thing I found difficult about looking for a job is once you have tried every place you can think of, for the particular job you want and don't succeed, what do you do next? (Unemployed, six 'O' grades, C3)

Most of the other chapters in this book deal with quantitative data drawn from the Scottish Young Peoples Surveys of 1985 and 1986. They exploit the fact that these data have been derived from questions asked of a representative sample of young people, and the authors are able to make generalizations from these replies to describe various aspects of the lives of the population of Scottish people who were then leaving school and entering the labour market.

This chapter, and the one by Bell and Howieson, are different. They deal with qualitative rather than quantitative data, which means that simple generalizations cannot be made about the whole population but, instead, they allow some of the young people who took part in those surveys to voice their own individual views about their experiences.

The source of the data for this chapter is the written replies which young people who were part of the survey sample in 1985 made to an open-ended invitation to tell more about themselves. Successive questionnaires in the Scottish School Leavers Survey series and the Scottish Young Peoples Survey series have ended with a blank page headed with a number of questions intended to persuade the respondents to write freely about themselves, their schools, their present work or unemployment, reactions to the questionnaire and so on. For obvious reasons, these written replies have become known as back-page comments, and have been widely used over the years both as a source of substantive data, as a means of checking the quality of data obtained in the main quantitative part of the questionnaire and as a way of improving future questionnaire design. In particular, two books have been published which reproduce many of the comments collected in earlier surveys (Gow and McPherson, 1980; Hughes, 1984). This chapter first describes the nature and status of the qualitative data obtained from the 1985 survey. This is followed by a discussion of the special challenges and opportunities offered by the data and an outline of some of the uses to which it can be put. Finally, the chapter considers the specific substantive contribution that the data can make in terms of the reactions from young people to their situation on leaving school and entering the labour market.

QUALITATIVE DATA FROM A POSTAL SURVEY

As appendix 1 to this book makes clear, there were several versions of the questionnaires used in the 1985 survey, such that respondents did not all receive an identical questionnaire. Altogether, there were four different questionnaire types used which varied according to the age and examination experiences of the respondents, and six different versions for each of the four types so that a larger number of different questions could be asked. However, the position is much simpler in terms of the prompts given on the back pages to encourage the open-ended replies, for there were only four different versions in total. Approximately a quarter of the respondents received each of the four versions.

All four of the comments given at the head of this chapter, for example, were directly prompted by the following:

(Version 3)

Would you like to tell us more about yourself, in your own words?

What has life been like since you left the fourth year? What things have you found difficult about looking for a job or a place at college? Do you feel that you've had enough help? Do you think you've made the right decision about leaving school?

Have you thought about going on the Youth Training Scheme? Do you think this scheme is worthwhile? Does it help young people to find jobs? Does it help them in other ways? Is it better or worse than staying on at school or going to college?

We will read very carefully what you write here.

At the bottom of the page are the words 'There is more room on the back of this page'.

It can be seen that this particular prompt from version 3 is, in fact, ten separate questions. As a further example, the prompt for version 4 is slightly shorter, but still has seven separate questions.

(Version 4)

Would you like to tell us more about yourself, in your own words?

What do you think is important about your time at school that we haven't already asked you about? Which other things have been important, since you left the fourth year?

Have you enjoyed filling in this questionnaire? Which bits were easy to fill in, and which bits were hard? Should it be shorter or longer? Should we ask about different things?

We will read very carefully what you write here.

Obviously, the purpose of such multiple question probes is to indicate the very different type of response that is anticipated at this point in the questionnaire. Most of the preceding questions are closed-option type, while the back-page prompts try to encourage a much wider response. The majority of respondents clearly recognized the change in desired response, for only a very few tried to answer the questions one by one with short replies. The vast majority of the respondents did treat the final pages very differently from the way they treated the rest of the questionnaire. However, for a large number of the respondents this different treatment resulted in them simply leaving the whole of these pages blank. It must be assumed that these respondents treated these pages as being rather more 'optional' than the rest of the questions, and, for whatever reasons, decided not to complete the pages, yet still return the questionnaire.

For the whole of the 1985 survey 54 per cent of those who returned questionnaires made some sort of back-page comment. For this particular detailed study of these comments only a sample of the whole number of questionnaires was examined. This sample was a random selection of 500 of the questionnaires returned by those who had left school having sat 'O' grade, 'O' level, CSE or another such examination, but not Highers or 'A' level (C type questionnaires), and 288 of the questionnaires returned by those who had left school having sat Highers or 'A' level (D type questionnaires). Thus the data for this chapter come from a sample of approximately 14 per cent of the returned C type questionnaires and 8 per cent of the D type questionnaires. Fifty-two per cent of the sample respondents to C type questionnaires had made written back-page comments and 58 per cent of those who answered D type questionnaires had made such comments.

A simple numerical count of the number of comments, however, is somewhat misleading, for the length and 'quality' of comments varied considerably. While one respondent wrote a four-page 800-word essay on her life and future aspirations, others were far more reticent. One certificate student, for example, wrote the single word:

Pointless! (Full-time labourer, two 'O' grades, C3)

leaving it ambiguous as to whether it was his life which he felt had been pointless since leaving fourth year or merely that he felt it was pointless to write about himself on the questionnaire. Other respondents, though still sparing with words, made their meaning very clear.

I object to being harassed by unsolicited mail. (Full-time Royal Navy, four 'O' grades, C2)

wrote one certificate person, while a fellow 'O' grade leaver was able to compress a wealth of information and feeling into few words with the comment,

I will be 17 in June, and have been unemployed since last June with no prospects for a job. (Unemployed, one 'O' grade, C2)

These last three comments clarify one further and most important aspect of the nature of this data source. Respondents not only choose how much they wish to write, but they also choose which question to answer. The probes are so lengthy, and contain so many different individual questions, that respondents can pick the topic area of their choice. Indeed, some of the back-page comments have little connection with the actual questions posed beyond responding to the first one which asks, 'Would you like to tell us about yourself, in your own words?'

In order to further understand the potential and limitations of these back-page comments as a data source it is worth considering the reasons why young people might choose to make such open-ended responses. Clearly there can be a great diversity of reasons for giving a written response, but each must be influenced by the way in which individuals interpret the questionnaires and the purposes of the researchers. This interpretation may vary widely, for the information that the respondent has about the survey is limited to what he or she receives along with the questionnaire. For example, one of the items included in the questionnaire package is a letter from a female doctor which attempts to encourage response. In the letter they are told that the results of the survey 'should help those who plan education and training to understand what it is that young people do, and what they want' and that it is their own views that matter and that they will be treated in strict confidence. The name used in the letter is the real name of the survey organizer, and some of the back-page comments are addressed personally to her. Undoubtedly, some of the respondents may have a medical doctor more in mind than a social scientist, but we do not know the extent to which this might influence the desire to respond.

What distinguishes the half who do make a reply from those who do not, is that they have interpreted making a comment as a meaningful activity for them. In some cases this may be simply a case of 'doing what needs to be done', where the back pages are treated as an integral part of the questionnaire and to be completed as a 'duty'. The fact that many of the comments are of a sufficient length to just fill one page, without going on to the second, lends some support to this interpretation. One page might be viewed as having written 'enough'. In other cases comments appear to have been written because the respondent had nothing better to do. A few of the replies explicitly thanked the researcher for sending the questionnaire as it gave the respondent 'something to do'. In many other cases, however, it is clear that the comments were given because the young people simply had something which they wanted to say. They interpreted the questionnaire as one of the very rare opportunities that they might have for commenting on their schooling and the position that they found themselves in as they entered the workforce. Several of the replies specifically thanked the researcher for being interested in the experiences of young people, and emphasized that they were more than prepared to help further if necessary. They wanted to tell someone of their experiences and feelings, perhaps in the hope of changing things for the better in the future. In short, many of the replies were shouts of joy from young people whose lives were currently exciting and fulfilling, while others were cries of pain from teenagers facing a world of unpleasantness and uncertainty.

What is clear is that, while there is no way of knowing why about half of those who returned the questionnaire did not make any back-page comments, it is unreasonable to assume that they would have written 'somewhat similar' comments to those who did respond. It is much more reasonable to assume that those who did respond were distinctly different from those who did not, for they had something to say, had interpreted the questionnaire as a chance to say it, and to an older person who might have some influence and who was prepared to listen.

Thus, the open-ended comments gathered from these back pages of the questionnaire cannot be regarded as representative in any simple way. Those who replied were a self-selected group. The questions that they decided to reply to and the ways in which they responded to those questions were again also individual choices. The resulting data thus present an interesting challenge to those who wish to use them for social research. What is important is that, rather than attempting to use these replies in a pseudo-quantitative way to assess the proportions of young people giving each type of comment (and by implication generalizing to the wider population), the data ought to be used in ways which recognize and exploit the unique strengths and possibilities of this particular data source. The next section attempts to indicate these strengths and proposes ways of using the data to further our understanding of the ways in which young people view the process of leaving school and entering the labour market.

VALIDITY AND RELIABILITY OF THE DATA

One of the respondents to the 1985 survey voiced the problem of the validity and reliability of these back-page comments as data sources very succinctly with his own comment:

> I don't think this part of your booklet is any use. Why? Because people are just going to exagerate (*sic*) what they do in life or how they succeed in life. There are a lot of bullshitters on this planet. (Full-time clothing cutter, six 'O' grades, C1)

Most readers would no doubt argue that he is himself exaggerating the extent of the problem, but this acknowledgement just substantiates his point. The problem is the old one of, 'How do you know if the informant is telling the truth?' and, as Dean and Whyte (1958) suggest in their now classic paper, the important thing is to consider the data in the context in which they were collected and in the light of the use to which it is desired to put the data.

Simple 'exaggeration' of the facts, or deliberate lying are, in practice, likely to be rather unimportant in these back-page comments. Gow and McPherson (1980) have argued quite persuasively that there is every reason to believe that most of the comments can be taken to be honest and trustworthy at this level. There is little reason to deliberately deceive. However, the problem of reliability and validity is deeper than this.

Dean and Whyte (1958) were concerned with data gathered through interviews, where there is the chance to probe answers and to assess non-verbal as well as verbal responses, but their discussion can also be applied to written open-ended responses of the type considered here. They argue that statements can range from the purely subjective to the almost completely objective, with most falling somewhere in between. It is necessary to try to distinguish between the subjective and objective components, but for both it is important to recognize that 'the informant's statement represents merely the perception of the informant, filtered and modified by his [or her] cognitive and emotional reactions and reported through his [or her] personal verbal usages'.

In an ethnographic study the researcher is able to observe activities as well as ask questions. Further, questions can be asked of many participants, individual respondents can be re-questioned, particular responses probed, documentary evidence assessed and a general process of triangulation built up. None of this is possible in the case of these open-ended comments and the only limited degree of triangulation that can be achieved is with the closed-format responses of the earlier part of the questionnaire.

Thus the uncomfortable fact is that distortions clearly can occur in the open-ended replies that cannot be detected by any process of triangulation. At the 'objective' end of the spectrum there can be distortion for several reasons. The respondent may simply not have observed the detail of what happened or cannot recall what it was that he or she did actually observe. The perceptions of events themselves are selective, being part of a process of interpretation such that, for example, once a YTS trainee perceives that he or she is being given only low-level work, new work demands may be perceived as being low-level simply because the trainee is being asked to do them. The YTS manager may interpret the new work in a totally different way. Informants will also often try to protect themselves against acknow-ledging their own failings and weaknesses. It is only the very rare young person who, when dismissed from a job, is emotionally secure enough to be able to acknowledge that the employer may have been in the right. None of these are necessarily deliberate distortions, but they can be the result of the individual's perception processes.

The problems with answers which are more 'subjective' are even greater. The back-page comments are the direct result of the particular prompt questions that appear at the top of the first of the blank pages in the questionnaire, but the respondents' replies are clearly not only influenced by these. The pages come at the end of a questionnaire which has dealt with school, educational qualifications, YTS, employment and so on, so that there is likely to have been a 'response set' built up throughout the questionnaire which influences the nature and status of the open-ended comments. Completing the questionnaire may remind the respondent and reinforce the assumption about the desirability of employment that is generally held in society. Thus, people who are unemployed may, by the time they reach this stage in the questionnaire, be feeling far more depressed about their lack of a job than they might be usually. In the same way, completion of the questionnaire by those in a dull but secure job may well cause them to draw comparisons with the unemployed, and thus respond more positively to their job than they might otherwise have done.

There are particular problems where the informant is asked to give subjective comments on feelings or attitudes about the past, as where, for example, the young people who responded to these questionnaires were asked to comment on how difficult it was for them to find work, or their feelings about work experience in schools. As Dean and Whyte (1958) argue, there is a widespread tendency to modify recollections of the past in such a way that they fit more comfortably into our current perceptions. Hypothetical questions about what respondents might be doing in five or ten years' time are also liable to be misleading.

The responses on the back pages of the questionnaire will also be highly situationally specific. The views that are given will be influenced by the way in which the purposes of the research are interpreted by the respondent. Again, this is not necessarily deliberate deception, but merely part of the process of interaction where we modify our beliefs and understandings to be more in accord with those of people with whom we are communicating. The questionnaire 'must be seen as just one of many situations in which an informant may reveal subjective data in different ways' (Dean and Whyte, 1958).

Thus the back-page responses will be a mixture of comments on the respondent's current emotional state, opinions, attitudes, values, hypothetical reactions, and the actual tendencies of the informant to behave or feel. These will differ, one with another, and may well be contradictory. Further, there is little reason to suspect that informants will necessarily have well-thought-out attitudes and values on the subject of the questionnaire. Indeed, it is not uncommon for respondents to thank the researcher for sending the questionnaire because completing it helped them to think about their lives and futures.

To summarize, the researcher has to be very careful about the uses to which these data can be put. If the intention was, say, to gauge the extent of satisfaction with YTS or employment, then these back pages could only be used with the greatest of difficulty. Not only is their reliability and validity suspect in absolute terms, but they are derived from a non-representative sample. But, as the next section indicates, this does not mean that these comments are worthless for research.

USES OF BACK-PAGE COMMENTS

The major ways in which back-page comments from these postal questionnaires can be used may be described under five somewhat overlapping categories. These are:

1 cross-checking with replies to closed questions;
2 improving questionnaire design;
3 encouraging high response rates;
4 illustrating;
5 generating grounded theory.

The bulk of this chapter concentrates on the last of these uses, so the first four will be only briefly outlined.

Cross-checking with Replies to Closed Questions

Back-page comments are read very carefully at the time of the coding of the questionnaires in order to gain extra information about qualifications, YTS experience, precise nature of work and so on. This information is used to supplement that obtained from the preceding closed questions and to act as a simple test for the reliability of the data through self-consistency. The open-ended comments frequently enable coders to clarify earlier information given, and to identify cases where there may be ambiguities.

Improving Questionnaire Design

The second use is closely linked to the first, for where ambiguities are revealed through back-page comments this can point to the possible need to review questions in future questionnaires. It is not unusual for respondents to write about the specific problems that they had in completing parts of the questionnaire. For example, one certificate student wrote:

> I'm sorry but I don't understand the first question on page 6. I'm sitting six modules and I have already passed three. (YTS gardener, one 'O' grade, C3)

Another young person claimed:

Your questionnaire at some points was incredibly confusing, for example the part about college. There were a few questions that did not have answers that applied to me at all. (YTS bricklayer and joiner, one 'O' grade, C4)

Such comments can alert the researchers to what might be common problems. This does not necessarily mean that changes can be automatically made. It is known, for example, that the questionnaires are not easy to complete for those who have studied English rather than Scottish qualifications, and for those who have studied in further education rather than schools, but to allow for every eventuality would make the questionnaires more complicated for the majority. The back-page comments also allow the young people to write about aspects of their lives which the questionnaire itself has not covered, which can lead to the recognition that it might be worthwhile asking questions about these other topic areas.

Encouraging High Response Rates

The third of the uses of these back-page comments is rather different in nature, and might be regarded as more instrumental. It is felt that giving young people the chance to write about themselves, and about the areas of their lives that the questionnaire has not asked about, encourages more of them to reply. If this is correct, the back-page comments are useful whether or not anyone actually read them! There is, however, a longer-term aspect to this use of the comments to encourage response, for it is not uncommon for respondents to ask specific questions about YTS, work, social services and so on, and to seek the advice of the researchers. All of these enquirers are responded to individually, not, of course, by actually giving advice, but by pointing the young person towards an appropriate advice agency, often by enclosing a copy of *Young Scot* (1986). This is done not only because it is felt that the survey should give something in return to young people for their time in completing the questionnaires, but because it enhances the reputation of the survey and similar research in the eyes of the respondents, teachers, careers officers and others involved with the survey. It is particularly important where the survey may wish to contact the young person again, as in the cohort study.

Illustrating

In academic articles and reports based on the survey data the back-page comments are quite commonly used as examples where a particular point of

view is stated or experience discussed. There is no pretence that the
quotations selected for inclusion in the report are representative of the views
of young people, but are merely illustrations included for their intrinsic
interest or because they state a particular view well. They might, for
example, illustrate some of the positive and negative views about YTS that
are held by some of these young people. Good examples of this type of use
of the data can be found in chapter 10 of Gray *et al.* (1983), which discusses
pupils' experiences of selection, or the chapter of Burnhill (1984) which
describes young people's reflections on staying or leaving. However, it has to
be admitted that in the latter example there are occasional lapses into spurious
generalizations from the illustrative data. But this is a lapse which is
unfortunately very common in the use of qualitative data in educational
research, and an error which I know myself to have committed in some of
my earlier work.

Generating Grounded Theory

The fifth main way in which these open-ended responses may be used is
based upon treating the data in a way similar to that of historical data or data
from documents obtained from searching in a library.

In dealing with any historical data it is important to remember that all of
it was written for a specific purpose, and from a particular point of view.
The historian of education might well make use of school histories and
government reports, party political manifestos and newspaper reports, HMI
reports and academic articles. S/he may use autobiographies, published
diaries, speeches, sermons and personal documents. All of these data sources
have their own biases which result from the particular purpose that the writer
had in mind. Historical sources are usually not representative in any simple
way, both because of selectivity in what has survived, and because those who
wrote usually did so simply because they had something to say. The essence
of the idea of using these back-page comments as a source of generating
grounded theory is that they should be treated as another form of 'historical
document'. The important difference and strength of them as a data source is
that they were produced by a wide range of young people most of whom
would otherwise have been unlikely to have left personal documents on their
experiences of school and entering the labour market.

The term 'grounded theory' comes from the work of Glaser and Strauss
(1965, 1967) which has been very influential in the construction of theory of
ethnographic work. Their basic belief is that the discovery of theory from
data — which they call grounded theory — is a major task for sociology.
They do not deny the need for the eventual testing of theory, but believe that

there was at that time an over-emphasis on quantitative testing of hypotheses and a neglect of the process of discovery of the concepts and hypotheses that are relevant for each particular research area. Woods (1986), explains the process in the following way:

> The main emphasis is on discovery rather than testing of theory, but analysis is sequential — it is both guided by and guides data collection. Categories and their properties are noted and 'saturated'. Concepts emerge from the field, are checked and re-checked against further data, compared with other material, strengthened or perhaps re-formulated. (p.147).

While not without their critics (see, for example, Brown, 1973; Trend, 1978), the ideas of Glaser and Strauss have been widely acknowledged in research based on fieldwork. There has been far less emphasis on a neglected chapter in the major book (Glaser and Strauss, 1967, chapter 7) which argues for the increased use of libraries as a data source. They argue that there are some striking similarities between fieldwork and library research:

> When someone stands in the library stacks, he is, metaphorically, surrounded by voices begging to be heard. Every book, every magazine article, represents at least one person who is equivalent to the anthropologist's informant or the sociologist's interviewee. In these publications, people converse, announce positions, argue with a range of eloquence, and describe events or scenes in a way entirely comparable to what is seen or heard during fieldwork. (pp.163).

It can be argued that, not only are there some striking similarities between fieldwork and library research, but there are also major similarities between being in a library and being faced with a data stack of back-page comments. If back-page comments can be treated in a comparable way to historical personal documents, then theory can be generated from them in the same way as from historical documents by following a process of systematic analysis. This analysis consists of drawing from the comments the categories, concepts and meanings that the writers display in their writings. By doing so, hypotheses can be drawn which may then structure further research, or be tested using additional data sources. In using the back-page comments in this way there is a similar need to take into consideration the source of the data and any resulting possible biases. Shouts of joy and cries of pain must be used for what they say about the authors' interpretations of their own circumstances and the purposes of the survey, rather than any absolute statements of fact.

It would be foolish to push too far the analogy between fieldwork, library research and research based on these open-ended comments. There are clearly major differences between them, and there are restrictions on what it is possible to do in terms of developing grounded theory from these back-page comments. Turner (1981) sets out Glaser and Strauss' ideas in terms of a nine-stage recursive process, by which fieldwork is used to generate theory in a rigorous way. It is unlikely that such simple data as open-ended responses collected through a postal survey could form an adequate data source for all of these stages. The latter stages would usually require further data to be specially collected. The term 'grounded theory' is thus not rigidly used in this chapter, but indicates only that the data can be used in a somewhat similar way to that proposed by Glaser and Strauss. It will be shown that the back-page comments are more than adequate for the early stages of the process outlined by Turner where labelled categories are developed which fit the data closely, examples of each category are accumulated, definitions of each category abstracted, and these definitions then used as a guide for further research and as a stimulus for theoretical reflection. In the end, such data can be only used for the generation of theory and not the testing of research hypotheses of any but the most simple kind.

Although they do not use the term 'grounded theory', a recent article by Raffe and Smith (1987) includes a section which comes very close to grounded theory, where they discuss young people's attitudes to YTS. They use data from the 1984 and 1985 Scottish Young Peoples Surveys to explore attitudes to YTS. To do this exploration they use an impressive array of statistical data from the two surveys and exploit the fact that it is possible to generalize from these data to the wider population of Scottish young people. The substantive findings in this paper thus rest on the quantitative data, yet in the discussion, the analysis is supplemented with work which uses back-page comments to draw out various themes. One of the themes which they discuss, for example, deals with the nature of the negative views held by many young people of YTS and of its use by government or employers. They discover four overlapping strands in the ways that some of these young people interpret YTS as being exploitative, relating to the YTS trainees being substitute workers for permanent employees, the allowance not being an adequate reward for their labour, the allowance not being adequate when compared with external criteria, and that YTS led too infrequently, or too unpredictably, to a job.

These ideas, which are drawn directly from the data, could be easily reformulated into hypotheses and form the basis of further work. This might be further searching of the back-page comments to seek for alternative interpretations and conflicting cases, or it might lead to searching other existing data stocks, or serve as the basis for a completely new research study to determine the extent of each of these interpretations within the wider population of young people.

GROUNDED THEORY ON LEAVING SCHOOL AND ENTERING THE LABOUR MARKET

The final section gives some indications of the ways that the back-page comments can be used to draw out ideas about how some young people interpret their lives. No claim is made that these ideas are particularly sophisticated or even original, it is merely hoped to show that these comments can act as a fertile source for the generation of concepts and hypotheses.

Challenging Assumptions

An interesting example is the following 'shout of joy':

> I am pleased I could help you with some questions but as you may have read, I am married now and have a beautiful 4 month baby. I am sorry I couldn't help you more. Yours faithfully, [Signed] Mrs. A. Person.

What is clear from this comment is that this young woman, at the time of completing the questionnaire, had a very different view of what was important in her world than the view implicit in the questions asked by the researchers. Although it comes as no surprise to find that some of the young people in the survey are married and/or have children, comments like this serve to emphasize the restricted framework in which most of the discussion about young people and the labour market takes place. There are usually hidden assumptions within most research work in the area that unemployment is necessarily an undesirable thing from the point of view of the young person, and that teenage pregnancy is almost a disaster for young women. Without doubt, both of these assumptions are often correct, but a quote like this one should act as a challenge to researchers' assumptions and generate new questions. What proportion of young women wish to have children as quickly as they can? How is pregnancy related to unemployment?

Obviously the back-page comments cannot begin to answer these complex statistical and cultural questions, but they can give further information on the variety of different interpretations. Comments like the following can alert the researcher to the variety of relationships that may exist between employment, unemployment and childbearing:

> I am 16-and-a-half and had to leave the YTS becuase (*sic*) I am pregnant. I am looking forward to having a baby and staying at home to be a mother. ('doing something else', no 'O' grades, C5)

While the comments from the two young women above view parenthood favourably, those from two other young women give a somewhat different emphasis:

> I am unemployed and awaiting the birth of my baby. I think once the baby is born I may look for a part-time job as the Supplementary Benefit I get a week is difficult to live off of. I would have returned the booklet earlier but I was staying at a different address as my ex-fiance and I got a house of our own. I hope my answers will be of help to you in your survey. (Unemployed, four 'O' grades, C3).

> Its important to do well at school and to stickin if i had no played trant all the time I think my resualts would be better, but I hope to sit my 706 Sitting giles at college for Basic cookery If I get in allso if I have someone who agrees to look after the baby, then again I Might be Married and wont have to work my husband will be. (Unemployed with 4-week-old baby girl, one 'O' grade, C1)

The ideas embedded in these questions cannot be followed up using the questionnaire data, for no explicit questions were asked about childbirth at all. Comments like these also do not necessarily mean that such questions ought to have been asked, for every questionnaire must have limits on its subject area and the total number of questions that can be asked. What such questions do, however, is to alert the researcher to very different frames of meaning which might otherwise be overlooked, and suggest many and varied hypotheses for related new research.

Investigating Key Words

One of the aspects involved in grounded theory in fieldwork is the 'tracking down' of the meanings of key words that researchers notice other people are constantly using. Glaser and Strauss (1967, p. 166) use the now classic example from Becker *et al.*'s *Boys in White* (1961) of which Strauss was a co-author. This particular study is concerned with the education and training of doctors, and the key word used by physicians about some of their patients was 'crock'. The process of trying to understand the meanings that these physicians held about patients when they used this term led the authors to uncover important medical perspectives. In library research the reader may also be struck by the use of certain key words. Strauss (1961), for example, analyzes the ways in which writers of popular literature on American cities frequently claim that their particular cities are peculiarly 'American' or perhaps the 'most American'. The search for key words can be just as fruitful in the generation of grounded theory from open-ended back-page comments.

Let us look at the following comments:

> I don't think that I'll regret leaving school, as I have landed very lucky in getting a full-time job. I started in [shop] on the YTS on 3 September 1984 until August 1985 but after five and-a-half months they took me off the course and kept me on full-time. I like my job very much and have been very lucky to be where I am after only leaving school ten months ago. (Full-time shop assistant, three 'O' grades, C1).

> I regard myself as being very lucky to have a full-time job, which I enjoy. (Full-time junior accounting assistant, seven 'O' grades, C1)

> Since last October I have been very lucky I'm looking after mentally handicapped children, It was'nt (*sic*) really difficult to decide what to do but it did require some thought. (YTS, no 'O' grades, C2)

> When I left school in May I was very lucky and very pleased to get a job so soon. I really did not know what I wanted to do when I left school. I would have done anything. I was lucky getting a cadetship — now I am starting my nurse training. (Full-time cadet nurse, six 'O' grades, C1)

> I made the right decision on leaving school when I did, and count myself lucky to have been able to get a job which I enjoy. (Full-time apprentice engineer, five 'O' grades, C3)

In each of these comments the writers use the term 'lucky' — they consider themselves lucky to have been able to get a full-time job, lucky to get a job so soon, and lucky to be able to get a job that they enjoy. Such use of the word was frequent in the comments, and came from people from a wide geographical area. What do these young people mean by this word? Does it imply that they feel they have very little control over their entry into the labour market, and that there is little that they can do to enhance their 'chance' of finding an appropriate job? Does it signal a dependent view of the world and, perhaps, the expectation that others will make the decisions for them?

   One of the general procedures open to ethnographers is that of checking accounts with different groups of participants. With these back-page comments the degree of triangulation possible is necessarily very limited, but it is possible to discover whether the same sorts of concepts are used by groups of young people with different educational experiences. All of the comments above were made by young people who left school after taking some 'O' grades but not having taken Highers. Do some of those who took Highers use a similar vocabulary to describe the process of gaining employment?

Here are some examples:

I have been one of the few lucky people who have had very little difficulty in finding a job. (Full-time job, seven 'O' grades, two Highers, D3)

I started writing to places around February last year and I was very lucky to get a job by May. I do not think YTS Schemes are worthwhile (although I have not done one) because you do hard work for very little money and at the end of the six months you go back on the dole again. You are very lucky to be kept on. (Full-time bank clerk, seven 'O' grades, four Highers, D3)

I must admit that I was quite lucky with my job as I got it straight away (not too many disappointments). (Full-time audio typist, seven 'O' grades, one Higher, D3)

I was very lucky. I had a full-time job as soon as I left school after 6th year. (Full-time student nurse, nine 'O' grades, three Highers, D3)

These are just a few of a large number of similar comments discovered in the small sample of comments analyzed for this chapter. It can be clearly seen that the idea of 'luck' is held by some of those with good Highers qualifications as well as those with only 'O' grades.

The word is not only used in the context of directly considering jobs, of course.

I would say that I did learn quite a bit at school but work and holding certificates are two different things. Actual work is completely different to any kind of experience you have in school, although I was lucky because our school gives two weeks work experience to every pupil in the fourth year which is an advantage to determine what sort of job you may be looking for. (Full-time sales clerk, four 'O' grades, C1)

Here, the young person feels 'lucky' in the school attended. There are also indications that some of the young people themselves recognize the implications of their use of the word 'lucky'. The following quote is an example:

I feel that I have been very lucky in finding a job, but it was also through perseverence in continuing to write to folk about three times to show keeness. (Full-time junior bank clerk, six 'O' grades, C3)

This particular young person makes it clear that, while there were elements in her job seeking that she perceived to be outside her control, there were also ways in which she believed she could try to influence the process. Now, some readers might argue that the use of the word 'lucky' is simply part of the everyday speech of young people and adults, and all that is being done here is to exaggerate the importance of a colloquialism. Such a claim underestimates the power of speech to influence our ways of thinking and the ways in which popular speech patterns might reveal much about the ways in which many of us may collectively view our worlds. Others may argue that the way the term 'lucky' is used in these comments is related to the degree of modesty that respondents may have in responding to the questionnaire. No doubt there is some truth in this, but what the use of this particular word does is to highlight the need for further research. Potential hypotheses flow rapidly: How widespread is the use of such expressions seemingly indicating lack of control, and perhaps lack of initiative? What meanings do users have in mind when they use such expressions? Are similar expressions used in other cultures? Might there be some connection between these views of the world and the collective decline of the industrial British culture (Wiener, 1981)?

Investigating Cliches

In everyday communication colloquialisms, catch phrases and simple repetitions are frequent and an integral part of discourse. Such comments should not be ignored. Just because such phrases are commonplace, and often expressed in the form of rather tired cliches, does not mean that they should be overlooked. They may well be used simply because they express a degree of consensus of meaning about the facts, and may act as a convenient indicator of such consensus.

Take the following two examples:

When May 1984 came I was glad because I thought school was a bore. I did not study a lot for my 'O' Grades because really I think they are a waste of time, they do not help you to find a job (it's not what you know, it's *who* you know). Once I left school I thought it was great, then you miss all of your pals, you miss all of the laughs. but the worst thing is that you put on weight will (*sic*) all the sandwiches, you get unfit because you are too tired to exercise after a hard day's work. (YTS joiner, eight 'O' grades, C4)

Now that I have left school I am writing away for Apprenticeships I have now found out that you need Qualifications to help you on your way but in this day and age it's not what you know it's who you know. (Full-time job, two 'O' grades, C0)

The second comment is confused, but both give a lead into a different area of investigation, for they both suggest that contacts might be an important factor in gaining jobs for some people. Thus, in contrast to those young people who viewed the processs of obtaining a job as a matter of luck, these two respondents indicated that they thought there were clear ways of obtaining a head start. With this idea in mind, the comments from other young people in the survey can be checked to see whether backing for this idea can be found.

In practice, a search through the small sample of comments used for this chapter revealed several cases where young people talked about the role of contacts in gaining them jobs. For example:

> Yes I did find it difficult to decide what I wanted to do when I finished fourth year because I either wanted to go (*sic*) a secretarial course or do a catering course in college. My Aunt helped me to make up my mind because she had just opened a hotel and offered me a full time job after I have done two years at college. (Full-time education, two 'O' grades, C2)

> I am enjoying this course very much a (*sic*) gaining a lot of experience and learning many new techniques. My course is due to finish in August of this year when I think I will work in my mother's salon. (Full-time fee-paying hairdressing course, two 'O' grades, C2)

Such comments were far from unusual, as were comments which indicated that the young person was entering the same occupational area as his or her parents, which leads to the suspicion that contacts may actually have been used to obtain the job. Such comments give no indication of the extent of such activity, of course, but once again suggest new areas of research.

Another good example of what might be gained through the investigation of cliches can be seen through the way some young people describe their Youth Training Schemes. Raffe and Smith (1987) have already discussed the way in which respondents use the terms 'cheap labour' and 'slave labour' in their back-page comments. The term 'cheap labour' is one which is used as one of the alternatives in one of the fixed-response questions. Thus, those young people who replied to this question may well have been influenced by it. The term 'slave labour', on the other hand, is not used in the questionnaire at all, yet it is frequently used in open-ended comments. It is probably best regarded as another example of a cliche to be investigated. It would seem that it is a very commonly used phrase to describe YTS, both by those who have taken part in the schemes and those who have not. What meanings do these young people give to the phrase? What aspects of slavery do they draw an analogy with? Is it again an indication of the lack of power that young people feel in confronting the labour market?

Discovering Links with Macro-sociological Variables

Much of sociology is concerned with the investigation of inequality and the ways in which various inequalities may be related to a range of sociological variables. Within the sociology of education social class, for example, has been a major topic of interest, and this has been joined more recently by questions about gender and race. These back-page comments can be analyzed for the insights which they may give on the associations between variables found from the statistical data, in particular, they may refine ideas about social class and gender inequalities. Interestingly, none of the sample of replies used for this study gave any comments which linked with ethnic groups or racism.

These open-ended comments can also highlight the need for researchers to investigate further major variables. The following accounts give an example of this:

> In December I started a thirteen-week Manpower Services Commission Job. This was with the [local] Regional Council. This finishes in March. Around this area there is not much work to be found and qualifications don't really matter, however in some cases your age does. Usually I am too old. I am only 19 years old. (Unemployed, nine 'O' grades, three Highers, D3)

> I feel that being unemployed is a complete let-down and being 17 years of age doesn't help because when you look in the papers or job centre for a job it says that they are looking for someone over the age of 18 or someone who has experience. I don't see how us young ones can get any experience at all if we are not even considered for jobs. (Unemployed, six 'O' grades, one Higher, D3)

> What is difficult about finding a job or place in college was that if you are only 16 or 17 at the time the employer doesnt (*sic*) want to know because you are too young. If you are 18 and above you are too old for a job. (Full-time catering course, five 'O' grades, one Higher, D3)

> I feel the attitude of teachers in school towards the outside is misplaced. To try to disuade many people from leaving school and attempt to receive full-time employment seems somewhat foolish, in my opinion. "Stay on and get some qualifications so you can have a better chance." This statement used by many teachers seems logical enough, but is it? If you stay on to sixth year you pass the age of eligibility to become an apprentice. This lessons (*sic*) the scope that is offered. Therefore, it seems futile to do this. (Full-time apprentice electrician, six 'O' grades, C3)

These comments must be interpreted in the context of the respondents' present state of employment or unemployment, but they do indicate the existence of a further major variable which has received less attention than it deserves in the literature on young people and the labour market. None of these young people actually uses the word, but the problem they refer to here is simply ageism in the labour market.

Ageism is so deeply embedded in the British education system that most sociologists of education have failed to notice it as a potential area of inequality. Those who have been concerned with the transition from work have often largely left unquestioned the age-related criteria that employers and trainers set for young people, which often have little real connection with the person's ability to do the job. There is no reason for supposing that all those under 17 would automatically be unable to act as a receptionist, for example, any more than there are reasons for supposing that the job could only be done by women. There are, of course, a few researchers who have begun to take this area seriously (for example, Ashton, Maguire and Garland (1982), Raffe (1984b) and Payne (1987)) but these 'cries of pain' from young people show some of the unnecessary problems that they face in their search for work, and demand that more researchers document the extent of such barriers to equality, and formulate ways of overcoming them. How many employers can show good reason for their age-related employment policies? Does the use of such criteria actually lead to employers not obtaining the most appropriate person for the job? How widespread is the feeling of injustice against these policies amongst young people?

Once again, a search of back-page comments from young people can be made to assess the potential variability of their interpretation, but the main use of the comments must be that they can lead to the generation of new theories and new hypotheses for research.

CONCLUSION

This article has looked at some of the possible uses of the qualitative data collected by the Scottish Young Peoples Survey in response to an open-ended invitation to write about themselves. The nature and status of these comments was discussed, and it was argued that such comments cannot be treated as representative of the wider population in any simple way, neither could many aspects of their validity or reliability be checked. However, in spite of these limitations, the comments can still be a valuable source for research. Five possible categories of use were outlined, concentrating particularly on the idea of generating grounded theory from the data. The essence of the last idea is that the written responses may be used in a way similar to that of historical data or documents obtained from searching a library, to uncover new theories, concepts and hypotheses.

The comments are a particularly good source for this activity in the area of the youth labour market as they are derived from young people with a complete range of educational experiences, and from a wide geographical spread. Further, while respondents may reply because they have something specific that they want to say, it is unlikely that many of these young people would have left any documents about their views and experiences of schooling and entering the labour market if it had not been for the survey.

As a data source for grounded theory the back-page comments also have their limitations. For example, all of the comments are brief, and written in the context of replying to a questionnaire. While some searches for alternative interpretations and conflicting cases can be made, the scope for comparison is limited. It is much more likely that hypotheses and theories generated will have to form the basis for further searches of other data stocks or further fieldwork or survey research.

Nevertheless, it has been shown that these comments can act as a fertile source for challenging assumptions, investigating key words and cliches and discovering links with macro-sociological variables. They also have the intrinsic and non-negligible value of often being insightful and interesting 'shouts of joy' and 'cries of pain' from some Scottish young people as they face leaving school and entering the labour market.

REFERENCES

ASHTON, D., MAGUIRE, M. and GARLAND, V. (1982) *Youth in the Labour Market*, London, Department of Employment.

BECKER, H., GEER, B., HUGHES, E. and STRAUSS, A. (1961) *Boys in White*, Chicago, IL, Chicago University Press.

BROWN, G.W. (1973) 'Some thoughts on grounded theory', *Sociology*, 7, pp. 1–16.

BURNHILL, P. (1984) 'Young people's reflections on staying or leaving' in RAFFE, D. (Ed). *Fourteen to Eighteen*, Aberdeen, Aberdeen University Press.

DEAN, J.P. and WHYTE, W.F. (1958) 'How do you know if the informant is telling the truth?' *Human Organization*, 17, pp. 34–8 reprinted in BYNNER, J. and STRIBLEY, K.M. (Eds) (1979) *Social Research: Principles and Procedures*, London, Longman.

GLASER, B.G. and STRAUSS, A.L. (1965) *Awareness of Dying*, Chicago, IL, Aldine Publishing.

GLASER, B.G. and STRAUSS A.L. (1967) *The Discovery of Grounded Theory*, New York, Aldine Publishing.

GOW, L. and McPHERSON, A. (Eds) (1980) *Tell Them From Me,* Aberdeen, Aberdeen University Press.

GRAY, J., McPHERSON, A.F. and RAFFE, D. (1983) *Reconstructions of Secondary Education: Theory, Myth and Practice since the War*, Henley, Routledge and Kegan Paul.

HUGHES, J.M. (Ed.) (1984) *The Best Years? Reflections of School Leavers in the 1980s*, Aberdeen, Aberdeen University Press.

PAYNE, J. (1987) 'Does unemployment run in families? Some findings from the General Household Survey', *Sociology*, 21, 2, pp. 199–214.

RAFFE, D. (Ed.) (1984a) *Fourteen to Eighteen: The Changing Pattern of Schooling in Scotland*, Aberdeen, Aberdeen University Press.

RAFFE, D. (1984b) 'School attainment and the labour market' in RAFFE, D. (Ed.) *Fourteen to Eighteen. The Changing Pattern of Schooling in Scotland*, Aberdeen, Aberdeen University Press.

RAFFE, D. and SMITH, P. (1987) 'Young people's attitudes to YTS: The first two years', *British Educational Research Journal*, 13, 3, pp. 241–60.

STRAUSS, A. (1961) *Images of the American City*, New York, Free Press.

TREND, M.G. (1978) 'On the reconciliation of qualitative and quantitative analysis: A case study', *Human Organization*, 37, pp. 345–54.

TURNER, B.A. (1981) 'Some practical aspects of qualitative data analysis: One way of organising the cognitive processes associated with the generation of grounded theory', *Quality and Qauntity*, 15, pp. 225–47.

WIENER, M.J. (1981) *English Culture and the Decline of the Industrial Spirit 1850–1980*, Cambridge, Cambridge University Press.

WOODS, P. (1986) *Inside Schools, Ethnography in Educational Research*, London, Routledge and Kegan Paul.

Young Scot '86 (1986) Edinburgh, The Scottish Community Education Council.

Scottish Surveys since 1977
Nils Tomes

THE SURVEY SERIES

The Centre for Educational Sociology (CES), at the University of Edinburgh, carries out the Scottish Young Peoples Survey in conjunction with the Scottish Education Department (SED). The surveys contact national samples of young people from across Scotland.

There are two components to the series, one cross-sectional and the other longitudinal. The cross-sectional surveys, originally called the Scottish School Leavers Survey, contact pupils who leave school in any one session, whether from third, fourth, fifth or sixth year. The longitudinal surveys contact a school-year-group cohort of young people who were in the fourth year of secondary schooling in a particular session.

The design of the two series overlaps such that young people who leave school at the end of their fourth year figure in both the cross-sectional and the longitudinal components, though because the questionnaire content of the two components also overlaps they are not asked to make any additional questionnaire returns.

Each survey has been timed to contact the young people around nine months after the session in which they left school, or in which they were in fourth year. Questionnaires are despatched to their home addresses in March.

The Scottish School Leavers Survey has been carried out biennially since 1977 with qualified school leavers' surveys stretching back to 1971. Since 1985, when a school year group was first surveyed in addition to the school leaver group (following a smaller-scale pilot survey in 1984), the Scottish School Leavers Survey has been subsumed within the Scottish Young Peoples Survey series.

The surveys are multi-purpose, covering educational experiences, attainment, labour-market history, training, course enrolments and family background. In order to make the questionnaires seem more pertinent and to keep their length down, different questionnaire types are targeted on sub-populations. Each type asks for the same core information but then additional topics are included as appropriate. In addition, within each of the questionnaire types, more peripheral items may be divided into one of several versions which are despatched to equivalent random sub-groups within each targeted group. This extends the possible topic coverage.

As the survey series has developed and as each has been designed to meet specific research needs, so the design of the samples and of the survey questionnaires has varied. Whilst the sample design for each biennial survey has differed slightly, each sampling frame has been constructed with the purpose of collecting nationally representative data. The sampling differences are compensated for by statistical means and this is discussed later in the paragraph on *Weighting*.

The response rates quoted for each of the surveys are calculated on the most conservative basis, taking valid responses as a percentage of the original target sample. Those people for whom there was no up-to-date contact address and who consequently could not receive their questionnaire have been retained in the denominator as it gives a better indication of coverage and the representativeness of the resulting data.

THE SCOTTISH SCHOOL LEAVERS SURVEY

The Scottish School Leavers Survey is a regular biennial series of national surveys which contact young people from across Scotland. The surveys have taken a variety of different forms, developing out of the SED's own surveys of pupils qualified to enter higher education to become surveys which contact a cross-section of leavers of all attainment levels. The 1977 survey was the first to contact a comprehensive sample, and this sample definition has been retained for subsequent contacts.

The sampling fractions and means of sampling have varied from survey to survey.

The 1977 survey had a sampling fraction of around 0.40 and contacted young people who left school by the end of the 1975/76 session.

As part of the programme of collaborative research, which aimed to decentralize all stages of the research process, the sample definition was extended to include leavers from across the attainment range. As the objectives of this programme could not be met fully through the SED's own sampling exercise, the sampling frame was constructed from two sources.

For a sampling fraction of 0.20 of qualified leavers, names, addresses and sample details were collected through the SED's own survey of SCE-qualified leavers, from sample members who had given their consent for their details to be forwarded to the CES. This sample covered leavers from all schools in Scotland, including maintained, grant-aided and independent.

For a further fraction of 0.25 of qualified leavers and including unqualified leavers who had attempted SCE 'O' grades and Highers, a sampling frame covering maintained schools was constructed through the regional authorities. Relatively late in the process of constructing a sampling frame, it was decided to include non-certificate leavers who had never attempted any SCE examination. As it was too late to collect this extra sample from all authorities in Scotland, only four regions and one island area were covered for this sub group. These areas were Fife, Lothian, Shetland, Strathclyde and Tayside. For the analyses reported in chapters 3 and 4 of this book, the additional sample from Shetland has been excluded.

Overall, for qualified leavers with at least one Higher or 'O' grade award (at A to E) the target sampling fraction was 0.50 in Grampian maintained schools, 0.40 in all other maintained schools and 0.20 in independent and grant-aided schools.

For pupils who attemped 'O' grades but did not gain any award the comparable fractions, sampling only maintained schools, were 0.35 for Grampian and 0.25 for all other regions.

The remainder of the sampling frame covered pupils who left school without having attempted any SCE examination and the sampling fractions for this population were 0.40 for Fife, Lothian, Strathclyde and Tayside. The sample therefore had one element missing. Non-certificate leavers from the other Scottish regions were not covered, meaning that trends analyses including 1977 data are based on leavers from the four Scottish regions. These four regions do, however, account for around three-quarters of the national population.

The completeness of the sampling frames varied with the source of the sampling details. The sample passed on by the SED after their own survey of qualified leavers and after allowing respondents to contract out of the CES survey was 61 per cent complete. Contracting-out was more common amongst the less qualified. The equivalent qualified group sampled through the regional authorities was 82 per cent complete. For non-certificate pupils sampled through the regional authorities the sample was 53 per cent complete. Across the whole achieved sampling frame, the response to the questionnaires was 82 per cent, this being 93 per cent of the SED sample and 78 per cent of the regional sample. This corresponds to an achieved sample coverage of 57 per cent for the SED qualified leavers, 66 per cent for the regional qualified leavers and 39 per cent of the regional non-certificate leavers. Further details of coverage in this and later surveys can be found in Burnhill, McPherson, Raffe and Tomes (1987).

The 1979 survey covered young people who left school in the 1977/78 session and had a smaller sampling fraction, being based on 0.10 of qualified leavers and 0.20 of non-certificate leavers. Qualified leavers, having at least one Higher or 'O' grade award (at A to E), were sampled from all schools in Scotland, including the grant-aided and independent schools. The non-certificate leavers were sampled from all maintained schools in Scotland, covering pupils with no SCE awards or with 'O' grade D or E bands only. There was thus an overlap between the latter two groups.

To compensate for undersampling, a given number (rather than a given proportion) of non-certificate pupils were selected from the sampling frame. No amendment was made to the qualified samples, who were selected proportionately from those people who had not contracted out after the SED's own survey. The effective sampling fraction of the non-certificate leavers was more than twice that of the qualified leavers. Across all the people in the achieved sampling frame, response was 78 per cent, this being 93 per cent of the qualified leavers and 78 per cent of the non-qualified leavers.

The 1981 survey contacted people who left school in the 1979/80 session. Like the 1977 survey, this was also a collaborative research venture with a large sampling fraction of 0.37.

The whole sampling frame was constructed by the SED on this, and subsequent, occasions. In this year, the SED did not carry out its own survey of qualified school leavers having decided to collect its intelligence through the Scottish School Leavers Surveys and a sampling frame was specially constructed with all Scottish schools providing details of pupils eligible to leave school who had odd-numbered birthdates, giving 51 per cent of the population. This return was checked against the SED's Qualified School Leaver return which was made the following autumn, to exclude those pupils who had decided to stay on at school.

Non-certificate pupils did not appear on the QSL return and so those who stayed on were excluded from the sample on the basis of information from their returned questionnaires. Overall, the estimated sampling-frame deficiency was 4 per cent, a considerable improvement on earlier surveys. Pupils were asked if they wanted to contract out at the sampling-frame construction stage and one in ten of the qualified leavers and one in five of the unqualified leavers did so. Overall, 12 per cent opted out.

The sample was drawn from the collected 51 per cent population sample and was proportionately stratified by sex, region and anticipated qualification level, and was systematically selected. The response to the questionnaires was 91 per cent for the qualified and 82 per cent for the non-certificate; allowing for sampling-frame deficiencies and opting out this gave coverage of around 72 per cent of the intended target sample.

The 1983 survey was a smaller survey with a sampling fraction of 0.10. This was the first survey for which the contracting-out procedure was dropped, reducing this source of attrition. The sampling frame covered all secondary schools in Scotland, both maintained and independent, with the sampling fraction being augmented to 0.25 for the Western Isles, Orkney and Shetland. The design was for a proportionately-stratified, systematically-selected, replicated sample.

Sample details were collected for all pupils with odd-numbered birthdates, giving a fraction of 51 per cent of the school leaving population, and the survey sample was drawn from this group. There were twelve stratification cells, defined by sex, anticipated qualification level on leaving school and term of leaving which were ordered by school and by geographical area, from which cases were systematically selected.

Response to this survey was 81 per cent overall. This could be further broken down into response rates of 74 per cent of the non-certificate or non-presenters, 79 per cent for those with 'O' grade qualifications and 86 per cent for those with Highers qualifications.

The 1985 and 1987 surveys also covered 0.10 samples of school leavers from the 1983/84 and 1985/86 sessions respectively. These surveys were, however, subsumed within the larger design of the Scottish Young Peoples Surveys and are described in this context below.

THE SCOTTISH YOUNG PEOPLES SURVEY

With the introduction of the SED's *Action Plan* which reorganized non-advanced education for people over 16 years old, the introduction of the MSC's Youth Training Scheme, the rise in youth unemployment and the diversification of post-compulsory routes, a cohort approach seemed the best way of monitoring these developments.

Following a pilot survey in 1984, the survey series was redesigned to include a year-group cohort which was the basis of a longitudinal series. The longitudinal cohort study samples people who were in the fourth year at school in the previous academic year. The cross-sectional leaver study samples pupils who left school from any stage in that same year. The samples of the two survey studies overlap, with cohort members who left school in fourth year standing in both samples. The series is, then, of mixed design having both cross-sectional and longitudinal elements. The Scottish School Leavers Surveys have been subsumed within the Scottish Young Peoples Surveys.

The 1985 surveys contacted the two overlapping groups in the spring of 1985. The longitudinal cycle consisted of three sweeps of the school-year-group cohort, the first (in spring 1985) in conjunction with the cross-sectional leavers survey, the second one year later (in March 1986) and the third sweep two-and-a-half years after the initial contact (in October 1987).

The two design elements, the cross-section and the longitudinal, are complementary. The three longitudinal sweeps cover, over a three-year period, the same year-group range of young people as are contacted by the single cross-sectional sweep of school leavers. The sample is quasi-random, with sample members being selected by day of birth.

The cohort groups are defined by attendance during a particular school session at a maintained or independent secondary school in Scotland. Qualified and non-certificate pupils are sampled alike. The sampling fraction is 0.10 for the initial surveys in spring 1985.

The overall response rate to the 1985 surveys was 80 per cent across all levels. Response rates differed according to qualification level: for cohort members who stayed on at school the response rate was 84 per cent, for Highers qualified leavers it was 83 per cent, for 'O' grade qualified leavers it was 75 per cent and for non-certificate leavers it was 67 per cent.

The 1986 survey followed up the year-group cohort, targeting the main questionnaire types according to the destination reported at the time of the first survey. Eighty-one per cent of the cohort had responded to the first sweep questionnaires. In addition, a specially shortened questionnaire was sent to those people from whom no response had been received during the first sweep. Around 4 per cent of the cohort were non-contactable at the end of the first sweep, and efforts were made to trace these people throughout the first-sweep cycle and before the second sweep.

Overall, 71 per cent of the original target sample responded to the 1986 survey, with 82 per cent of the first-sweep responders replying to the second sweep. This gave a longitudinal response rate across the two sweeps of 65 per cent of the 1985 target sample. The analyses in this book report on data from this longitudinal component. Response rates again varied across each of the target groups: those who were at school at the time of the previous survey had an 88 per cent response rate, those who were on the Youth Training Scheme a rate of 79 per cent and the others, who received a non-specific questionnaire type, a rate of 76 per cent. Thirty-six per cent of those who had not responded to the first-sweep survey returned their second-sweep questionnaire.

The third sweep of the 1983/84 cohort is in progress at the time of writing.

The 1987 survey cycle was started in spring 1987. The first sweep had a 0.10 sampling fraction of those who were in the fourth year in session 1985/

86 and a 0.10 sampling fraction of those who left school during that session. The definition of the two study groups is the same as for the 1985 survey cycle, outlined earlier. Whereas in the 1985 survey cycle and previous school leaver surveys the questionnaires were targeted by highest level of leaving qualification, in the 1987 survey cycle they were targeted by stage of leaving.

The overall response rate to the spring 1987 sweep was 78 per cent. Response rates differed according to stage of leaving: for the cohort members who stayed on at school the response rate was 86 per cent, for sixth-year leavers it was 79 per cent, for fifth-year leavers it was 73 per cent and for third- and fourth-year leavers it was 70 per cent.

TVEI National Evaluation

The Centre for Educational Sociology and the Department of Education at the University of Edinburgh conducted part of the national evaluation of the Technical and Vocational Education Initiative (TVEI) in Scotland, focusing on education–industry links. One element of this evaluation was a survey of young people who had been in the first third-year intake to TVEI schemes, along with non-TVEI pupils from the same schools (see chapter 10 in this volume). This group is equivalent to the session 1985/86 fourth-year cohort, surveyed in the 1987 first sweep. The cohort sample was augmented to 100 per cent for those nineteen schools involved in the first phrase of TVEI in Scotland.

A specific questionnaire was designed for the 90 per cent of pupils not covered by the national Scottish Young Peoples Survey, with many items in common with the main survey questionnaires. This provided a framework for the evaluation of TVEI, allowing comparisons not only between TVEI pupils and non-TVEI pupils in the same schools but also between TVEI schools and other schools in Scotland. The existence of comparable Scottish Young Peoples Surveys in previous years also allows a comparison of pupils of TVEI schools with pupils in the same schools before they joined the Initiative. Overall response to the TVEI questionnaires was 76 per cent of the target sample.

WEIGHTING

With each of the surveys differing slightly in its sample design and with differing rates of coverage and non-response, statistical procedures are required to compensate for these differences in order to be able to make statements about the national population and to compare data from each survey. The data from each survey are weighted in a manner appropriate to the sample design, weighting by gender and level of attainment to population figures provided by the SED and the Scottish Examination Board, varying the algorithm where stratification or random sampling were used. For the second sweep of the 1983/84 cohort, surveyed in 1986, the data were additionally weighted by the time of leaving school. All analyses in this book are produced using weighted data, with the exception of chapters 10 and 11 which use open-ended comments written by respondents on the back pages of their questionnaires.

THE SCOTTISH EDUCATION DATA ARCHIVE

The data from the Scottish Young Peoples Surveys are held in the Scottish Education Data Archive (SEDA) by the CES and these data are available for secondary analysis by outside users, subject to the CES code of practice which maintains confidentiality for both individuals and schools.

REFERENCE

BURNHILL, P., MCPHERSON, A., RAFFE, D. and TOMES, N. (1987) 'Constructing a public account of an education system' in WALFORD, G. (Ed.) *Doing Sociology of Education*, Lewes, Falmer Press.

Appendix 2:

Survey Data-Sets Used in Each Chapter

Chapter	Authors	Surveys	Coverage
1	Raffe and Courtenay	SYPS: 1985 and 1986 sweeps of 1983/84 S4 cohort England and Wales Youth Cohort Study: 1985 and 1986 sweeps of cohort 1	Scotland: young people in S4 (fourth year of secondary school) in 1983/84 E&W: young people (from maintained schools) eligible to leave school in 1984 (aged 16 on 31 August)
2	Raffe	Various (review chapter)	
3	Burnhill, Garner and McPherson	1977, 1979, 1981, 1983, 1985 and 1987 leavers surveys	Young people who left school in 1975/76, 1977/78, 1979/80, 1981/82, 1983/84 or 1985/86 (restricted to Fife, Lothian, Strathclyde and Tayside)
4	Shelly	1977 and 1983 leavers surveys	Young people who left school in 1975/76 or 1981/82 (restricted to leavers from education-authority schools in Fife, Lothian, Strathclyde and Tayside who entered the labour market)

5	Furlong	1985 and 1986 sweeps of 1983/84 S4 cohort	Young people in S4 in 1983/84
6	Garner, Main and Raffe	1981 leavers survey	Young people who left school in 1979/80 (restricted to Aberdeen, Dundee, Edinburgh and Glasgow)
7	Main and Shelly '	1985 and 1986 sweeps of 1983/84 S4 cohort	Young people in S4 in 1983/84 (restricted to fourth-year leavers who entered the labour market)
8	Raffe	1985 and 1986 sweeps of 1983/84 S4 cohort	Young people in S4 in 1983/84
9	Tomes	1985 and 1986 sweeps of 1983/84 S4 cohort	Young people in S4 in 1983/84 (restricted to those who started fifth year)
10	Bell and Howieson	1987 sweep of 1985/86 S4 cohort: TVEI questionnaire	Young people in S4 in 1985/86 in schools participating in first five Scottish TVEI projects (1984 starts) (restricted to those who took TVEI)
11	Walford	1985 leavers survey	Young people who left school in 1985/86 (restricted to those who had attempted SCEs or equivalents)

Note. The analyses used in chapter 3 (and table 2.1 in chapter 2) use a time-series data-set. Surveys whose sample fractions exceeded 10 per cent are represented in this data-set by random subsamples. Chapter 4 also uses a subset of the 1977 data. Some analyses in other chapters use data on random subsamples who received questionnaire versions containing the relevant questions.

Glossary

'A' level see GCE.

Action Plan often referred to as 16–18s Action Plan or 16+ Action Plan – SED document proposing an integrated modular structure for all non-advanced vocational education in Scotland. Published in January 1983, implemented from 1984 (see National Certificate; Scotvec; and chapters 8 and 9 in this volume).

Advanced education see Higher education.

BTEC Business and Technician Education Council – English-based body awarding vocational certificates.

CES Centre for Educational Sociology, University of Edinburgh.

CGLI City and Guilds of London Institute – English-based body awarding vocational certificates.

Christmas leavers see SLA3.

CI Central Institution – college administered by the Scottish Office, offering mainly advanced and degree-level courses. Nearest Scottish equivalent to polytechnics in England and Wales.

College of Education College offering degree and other higher education courses, mostly for intending teachers.

Conscripts Scottish fifth-year pupils who are below the statutory leaving age: members of SLA3 (see below).

CPVE Certificate of Pre-Vocational Education: qualification awarded for a one-year course, introduced in England and Wales in 1985, for students aged 16 or over. Based on a core-plus-vocational-options model, the course aims to straddle the education/training divide and attract young people unwilling (or unable) to continue 'academic' GCE studies but who have not yet decided on a specific occupation.

CSE Certificate of Secondary Education – subject-based English and Welsh qualification designed for pupils between the 40th and 80th percentiles of the ability range, normally first taken at 16. Together with 'O' level (see GCE below) it is being replaced by GCSE (General Certificate of Secondary Education).

CSYS Certificate of Sixth Year Studies – Scottish qualification gained after a one-year course in sixth year, mainly for pupils who have passed a Higher in the subject.

DES Department of Education and Science – department of UK central government whose responsibilities include all sectors of education in England and Wales and the universities in Scotland.

FE Further education – usually refers to post-school courses or programmes provided full- or part-time in colleges of further education (including technical colleges). The term is sometimes used to refer only to vocational non-advanced courses.

GCE General Certificate of Education – subject-based qualifications awarded in England and Wales, to school pupils and others. 'A' (Advanced) levels are typically first attempted at 18 and are the main qualification for university entrance. The 'O' (Ordinary) level, typically first attempted at 16, is being replaced by the GCSE (General Certificate of Secondary Education).

GCSE General Certificate of Secondary Education – subject-based qualification, typically first attempted at 16, replacing 'O' levels and CSE in England and Wales.

Higher Higher grade of the SCE-subject-based qualification normally first attempted at 17, following a one-year course in fifth year. The main qualification for university entrance in Scotland and the nearest equivalent (but not very close) to the English or Welsh 'A' level (see chapters 1 and 3 in this volume).

Higher education Defined by STEAC (see below) 'to embrace all courses at degree or equivalent level and above, including postgraduate research, courses leading to initial teaching qualifications, and other advanced courses which are provided in central institutions, colleges of education and local authority further education colleges. By advanced courses, we mean courses in the non-university sector in which the standard of instruction exceeds that required for the Scottish Certificate of Education (SCE) Higher grade, the General Certificate of Education (GCE) Advanced (A) level, the Ordinary National Diploma, and the Ordinary National Certificate, or equivalent.' Chapter 3 in this volume follows this definition.

JCP Job Creation Programme – MSC (British-wide) programme of job creation for the unemployed, introduced in 1975. Covered all ages but the young were a priority group. Replaced by YOP in 1978.

JTS Job Training Scheme – MSC (British-wide) scheme offering work experience with training for adults who have been unemployed for at least six months; 18–25-year-olds are given priority.

MSC Manpower Services Commission – British agency established in 1974, responsible for training and (until 1987) employment services on behalf of the government. Now renamed the Training Commission.

NAFE Non-advanced further education – see FE, and see Higher education for a definition of 'advanced'.

National Certificate Title of certificate awarded by Scotvec in respect of the modules introduced following the Action Plan.

NVQ National Vocational Qualification – 'umbrella' qualification which forms the basis for the rationalization of vocational qualifications by the NCVQ (see below).

NCVQ National Council for Vocational Qualifications – body set up following the Review of Vocational Qualifications in 1986 to accredit existing and new vocational qualifications in England and Wales, and to rationalize the vocational education and training system in terms of four 'levels'.

New Training Initiative Long-term programme to reform training in Britain, launched by MSC in 1981.

'O' grade Ordinary grade of the SCE – subject-based qualification normally first attempted at 16 at the end of fourth year, following a two-year course. Closest Scottish equivalent to English and Welsh 'O' levels; being phased out in favour of Standard grade.

'O' level see GCE.

Public-sector higher education Non-university higher education.

ROSLA Raising of the school-leaving age, from 15 to 16 years, in 1973. (Pupils who could otherwise have left in 1973 had to stay on until 1974).

RSA Royal Society of Arts – English-based body awarding vocational certificates.

SCE Scottish Certificate of Education – see Higher, 'O' grade and Standard grade.

Scottish Office Department of UK central government responsible for several areas of policy in Scotland, including education (see SED).

Scotvec Scottish Vocational Education Council – established in March 1985 from the merger of the Scottish Business Education Council and the Scottish Technical Education Council. Awards National Certificates for the modules introduced following the Action Plan.

SEB Scottish Examination board – awards the SCE and the CSYS.

SED Scottish Education Department – department of Scottish Office responsible for all education in Scotland except universities.

SEDA Scottish Education Data Archive – see appendix 1.

SLA1 School-leaving age group 1 – Scottish pupils whose sixteenth birthdays fall in or before the February of their fourth secondary year. Eligible to leave at Christmas of fourth year (or, in a very few cases, earlier). Now a small minority (fewer than one in seven) of each year group.

SLA2 School-leaving age group 2 – Scottish pupils whose sixteenth birthdays fall during the period from March of their fourth secondary year to the following September (inclusive). Eligible to leave on 31 May. Comprise a majority of each school year group.

SLA3 School-leaving age group 3 – Scottish pupils whose sixteenth birthdays fall after the September following their fourth secondary year. Too young to leave from fourth year (the 'normal' final compulsory year), most become eligible to leave school in the December of fifth year (see chapters 1, 8 and 9 in this volume). Those who leave then (or are expected to leave then) are termed 'Christmas' or 'winter' leavers.

SSLS Scottish School Leavers Survey – see appendix 1.

Standard grade Subject-based SCE qualification normally first attempted at 16 at the end of fourth year, following a two-year course. Taken at one of three levels (Credit, General and Foundation). Progressively replacing 'O' grade (the first certificates were awarded in 1986); the nearest Scottish equivalent to English and Welsh GCSE (General Certificate of Secondary Education).

STEAC Scottish Tertiary Education Advisory Council – appointed in 1984 to review the future strategy for higher education in Scotland. Reported in December 1985.

SUCE Scottish Universities Council on Entrance – body representative of the eight Scottish universities, coordinates policy on admissions.

SYPS Scottish Young Peoples Survey – see appendix 1.

TVEI Technical and Vocational Education Initiative – MSC initiative, first introduced on a pilot basis in England and Wales in 1983 and in Scotland in 1984, to explore ways of enhancing the technical and vocational education of 14–18-year-olds (see chapter 10 in this volume).

WEP Work Experience Programme – MSC (British-wide) scheme introduced in 1976 to provide work experience for unemployed 16–18-year-olds. Replaced by YOP in 1978.

Winter leavers see conscripts.

YOP Youth Opportunities Programme – MSC (British-wide) programme introduced in 1978 to provide work experience or work preparation courses for unemployed 16–18-year-olds. Replaced by YTS in 1983.

YTS Youth Training Scheme – MSC (British-wide) scheme offering integrated work experience and training to 16- and 17-year-old school leavers. Introduced as one-year scheme in 1983, extended to two years in 1986.

Notes on Contributors

COLIN BELL is Professor of Sociology at the University of Edinburgh. He wrote his chapter whilst he was Research Fellow jointly in the Centre for Educational Sociology and the Department of Education at the University of Edinburgh. He has previously worked at University College, Swansea and the Universities of Essex, New South Wales, Aston, Wisconsin-Madison, La Trobe and Leicester. His publications include *Middle Class Families*; with Howard Newby, *Community Studies, The Sociology of Community, Doing Sociological Research* and *Property, Paternalism and Power*; with Sol Encel, *Inside the Whale*; with Lorna McKee, *Fathers Childbirth and Work*; and with Helen Roberts, *Social Researching*.

PETER BURNHILL was SED Research Fellow at the Centre for Educational Sociology (1979–84). He was responsible for the design and operational direction of the Scottish School Leavers Survey and contributed to its redesign into a cohort survey. He is now manager of the University of Edinburgh's Data Library and Coordinator of the ESRC-designated Regional Research Laboratory for Scotland. He has published both on education and on survey methods.

GILL COURTENAY is a Research Director at Social and Community Planning Research. She has carried out research on a wide range of social policy issues particularly those related to youth employment and training. Her most recent publication is a report on the England and Wales Youth Cohort Study.

ANDY FURLONG has worked as a Research Fellow at the Centre for Educational Sociology since 1986. After graduating in sociology at the University of Leicester, he was attached to the Labour Market Studies Group at Leicester where he completed a PhD on the effects of youth unemployment on the transition from school.

CATHERINE GARNER studied geography at the University of Edinburgh. She is currently a Research Fellow at the Centre for Educational Sociology and has undertaken work on higher education, the youth labour market and the effects of urban deprivation on educational attainment.

CATHY HOWIESON was, at the time of writing her chapter, a Research Fellow working on the Scottish national evaluation of TVEI, based in the Centre for Educational Sociology and the Department of Education at the University of Edinburgh. She has been involved in youth unemployment and vocational education and training since 1977 in a variety of capacities – as trainer, counsellor and researcher. She also has an interest in women's employment and training issues and is Scottish Coordinator of the European Commission's Women's Employment Network. Publications include *Assessing Changes – Recent Developments in Education and Training* and *Scope for Skills – Vocational Preparation in YOP*.

ANDREW McPHERSON is Reader in Sociology and Co-Director of the Centre for Educational Sociology, of which he has been a member since its inception in 1972. He works on the history, sociology and politics of post-primary education and has co-authored four books in this area: *The Scottish Sixth* (NFER, 1976); *Tell Them From Me* (Aberdeen University Press, 1980); *Reconstructions of Secondary Education* (Routledge and Kegan Paul, 1983); and *Governing Education* (Edinburgh University Press, 1988). He is the author, with Doug Willms, of recent evaluations of Catholic schooling in Scotland, and of the long-term impact of comprehensive reorganization. His current interests include educational and social change, and the demand for higher education.

BRIAN G.M. MAIN studied at the Universities of St Andrews and California (Berkeley). In 1976 he returned to Scotland to become a Lecturer in Economics at Edinburgh and subsequently Reader. He is now Professor of Economics at St Andrews. He has conducted research into a wide range of labour-market and other economic issues, including women's employment and earnings, the incidence and duration of unemployment spells, and the youth labour market and youth training.

DAVID RAFFE is Reader in Education and Co-Director of the Centre for Educational Sociology, where he has worked since 1975. His publications include *Reconstructions of Secondary Education* (with John Gray and Andrew McPherson, 1983), *Fourteen to Eighteen* (1984), and an OECD monograph on Scottish post-compulsory education and training (with Nils Tomes, 1987). His current research interests include secondary and further education, the youth labour market and education and training initiatives for the 14–18 age group.

MICHAEL A. SHELLY is an economist working for Unilever. Previously he was a PhD student and Research Associate at the University of Edinburgh. He remains a member of the Centre for Educational Sociology.

NILS TOMES is a Research Fellow at the Centre for Educational Sociology. Her work has been in the area of educational research, covering multi-ethnic schooling, curriculum option choice, the acquisition of literacy skills, transitions from school certification and also survey methods.

GEOFFREY WALFORD is a Lecturer in Sociology and Education Management in the Strategic Management and Policies Studies Division, Aston University. Following two degrees in physics he taught in schools in Kent, Oxfordshire and Buckinghamshire, then took a two-year MPhil in sociology at the University of Oxford. From 1976 to 1978 he was SSRC Fellow at St John's College, Oxford, He was appointed to a university lectureship at Aston in January 1979 and moved to his current position within the Management Centre in April 1983. During 1986 he was a Visiting Research Fellow at the Centre for Educational Sociology, financed by the ESRC Survey Link Scheme. He is author of *Life in Public Schools* (Methuen, 1986) and *Restructuring Universities: Politics and Power in the Management of Change* (Croom Helm, 1987), co-author of *Teachers into Industry* (AEEM, 1983), and editor of *British Public Schools: Policy and Practice* (Falmer Press, 1984), *Schooling in Turmoil* (Croom Helm, 1985) and *Doing Sociology of Education* (Falmer Press, 1987).

Index